"This exemplary book goes far beyon(tations about language, to reconceptua embodied in spoken and signed words, bols, danced, painted ... and always cc plinary authors are academics, pedagog various practitioners who give us new their own language in their unique learning ecologies and share what this actually looks like in their lifeworlds".

Nicola Yelland, *Professor of Early Childhood Studies, University of Melbourne, Australia*

"If 'it takes a village to raise a child,' this book powerfully shows that it is not only the people in the village, but the land, objects, and the whole host of non-human beings there who shape this development. The book demonstrates that language and cognition are embodied, shaped by an ecology of expansive social and material resources. How children draw from all the resources in their environment to think and talk in creative, spontaneous, and unorthodox ways suggests a complex language development. Judging their communication as deficient stems from our limited ideological assumptions. This book educates scholars to expand their perspectives by listening to the more-than-human communication 'out of the mouth of babes and infants'!"

Suresh Canagarajah, *Evan Pugh University Professor, Pennsylvania State University*

LANGUAGE, PLACE, AND THE BODY IN CHILDHOOD LITERACIES

Challenging dominant views of early childhood language development and knowledge, this thought-provoking volume illuminates the importance of place, the body, and movement in opening space for young children's improvisatory, creative, playful language practices.

Bringing together a rich collection of contemporary research and diverse perspectives, this book centres on the premise that 'where' talk happens – be it spoken, mimed, signed, or assisted through one or more communication tools – is not a neutral backdrop or controllable variable. Rather, it is deeply entangled in the emergence of language from bodies, in how these vocalisations make their way into the world, what they might feel like and set into motion, and how they are received, heard, and listened to by other humans and by non-humans. Chapter authors introduce theories about language, body, and place, while also providing examples of what this work may look like in practice.

This book is key reading for those who work with young children and families, including teachers, pre-service teachers studying child development, speech and language therapists, support workers, and those in the arts, cultural, and environmental sectors. It is also highly relevant to researchers, literacy education scholars, and anyone who endeavours to think more expansively and critically about language and literacy in early childhood contexts.

Khawla Badwan is a Reader in TESOL and Applied Linguistics at Manchester Metropolitan University, UK.

Ruth Churchill Dower is a PhD scholar at Manchester Metropolitan University, UK, exploring young children's nonlingual ways of being through experiments in movement.

Warda Farah is a social entrepreneur, speech and language therapist, writer, and consultant.

Rosie Flewitt is a Professor of Early Childhood Communication at Manchester Metropolitan University, UK.

Abigail Hackett is a Professor of Childhood and Education at Sheffield Hallam University.

Rachel Holmes is a Professor in the Education and Social Research Institute of Manchester Metropolitan University, UK.

Christina MacRae is a visiting research fellow at Manchester Metropolitan University.

Vishnu KK Nair is a lecturer in the School of Psychology and Clinical Language Sciences at the University of Reading.

David Ben Shannon is a lecturer in the School of Education at the University of Sheffield.

Expanding Literacies in Education

Series Editors
Jennifer Rowsell, Carmen Medina, and Kate Pahl
Founding Editors
Jennifer Rowsell and Cynthia Lewis

Playful Methods
Engaging the Unexpected in Literacy Research
Carmen Liliana Medina, Mia Perry, and Karen Wohlwend

Literacy and Identity Through Streaming Media
Kids, Teens, and Representation on Netflix
Damiana Gibbons Pyles

Pluriversal Literacies for Sustainable Futures
When Words Are Not Enough
Mia Perry

Language, Place, and the Body in Childhood Literacies
Theory, Practice and Social Justice
Edited by Khawla Badwan, Ruth Churchill Dower, Warda Farah, Rosie Flewitt, Abigail Hackett, Rachel Holmes, Christina MacRae, Vishnu Nair, and David Ben Shannon

Literacies in the Platform Society
Histories, Pedagogies, and Possibilities
Edited by T. Philip Nichols and Antero Garcia

For more information about this series, please visit: https://www.routledge.com/Expanding-Literacies-in-Education/book-series/ELIE

LANGUAGE, PLACE, AND THE BODY IN CHILDHOOD LITERACIES

Theory, Practice and Social Justice

Edited by
Khawla Badwan, Ruth Churchill Dower,
Warda Farah, Rosie Flewitt, Abigail Hackett,
Rachel Holmes, Christina MacRae,
Vishnu KK Nair, and David Ben Shannon

Routledge
Taylor & Francis Group

NEW YORK AND LONDON

Designed cover image: Lo Tierney

First published 2026
by Routledge
605 Third Avenue, New York, NY 10158

and by Routledge
4 Park Square, Milton Park, Abingdon, Oxon, OX14 4RN

Routledge is an imprint of the Taylor & Francis Group, an informa business

© 2026 selection and editorial matter, Khawla Badwan, Ruth Churchill Dower, Warda Farah, Rosie Flewitt, Abigail Hackett, Rachel Holmes, Christina MacRae, Vishnu Nair, and David Ben Shannon; individual chapters, the contributors

The right of Khawla Badwan, Ruth Churchill Dower, Warda Farah, Rosie Flewitt, Abigail Hackett, Rachel Holmes, Christina MacRae, Vishnu Nair, and David Ben Shannon to be identified as the authors of the editorial material, and of the authors for their individual chapters, has been asserted in accordance with sections 77 and 78 of the Copyright, Designs and Patents Act 1988.

All rights reserved. No part of this book may be reprinted or reproduced or utilised in any form or by any electronic, mechanical, or other means, now known or hereafter invented, including photocopying and recording, or in any information storage or retrieval system, without permission in writing from the publishers.

Trademark notice: Product or corporate names may be trademarks or registered trademarks, and are used only for identification and explanation without intent to infringe.

ISBN: 978-1-032-67791-0 (hbk)
ISBN: 978-1-032-62075-6 (pbk)
ISBN: 978-1-032-67792-7 (ebk)

DOI: 10.4324/9781032677927

Typeset in Sabon
by codeMantra

CONTENTS

About the editors   *xiii*
List of contributors   *xvii*
Foreword   *xxiii*

SECTION I
Introduction   1

1   Language, place, and the body in childhood: theory, practice, and social justice. Introduction   3
Khawla Badwan, Ruth Churchill Dower, Warda Farah, Rosie Flewitt, Rachel Holmes, Abigail Hackett, Christina MacRae, Vishnu KK Nair, and David Ben Shannon

SECTION II
Language as bodily and material   17

2a   Language as bodily and material   19
Rosie Flewitt, Rachel Holmes, and Christina MacRae

2b Making time for unruliness in the special education classroom: resisting the narrowing of neurotypicality in England 31
Yvonne Williams and David Ben Shannon

2c Letting things become what they want to become: uncertainty, improvisation, and resisting the tyranny of talk 45
Charlotte Arculus

2d Facilitating expressive language through body movement: clinical implications 59
Maya Leela

2e Speech Bubbles: how play, joy, and storytelling open up expansive possibilities for language 70
Adam Power-Annand with Abigail Hackett

2f Coming together: roundtable discussion on language as bodily and material 80
Charlotte Arculus, Rachel Holmes, Maya Leela, Christina MacRae, Adam Power-Annand, David Ben Shannon, and Yvonne Williams

SECTION III
Place and language 93

3a Place and language 95
David Ben Shannon, Vishnu KK Nair, and Warda Farah

3b Researching language and place: what is the evidence base? 104
Abigail Hackett and David Ben Shannon

3c Rituals, vocalisations, and creating comfortable spaces: a spatialised view of young children's language in museums 119
Abigail Hackett, Christina MacRae, David Ben Shannon, Robert Chester, Lucy Cooke, Esther Hallberg, Georgina Simmons, Laura Smith-Higgins, and Sally Toon

3d Spaces of Reprieve: an emancipatory practice centring Black and Brown children labelled with communication difficulties 131
Warda Farah and Vishnu KK Nair

3e The entanglement between signed language, embodiment, and place 143
Leala Holcomb

3f Coming together: roundtable discussion on place and language 150
Warda Farah, Abigail Hackett, Leala Holcomb, Vishnu KK Nair, and David Ben Shannon

SECTION IV
Language beyond meaning **157**

4a Language beyond meaning 159
Khawla Badwan, Ruth Churchill Dower, and Abigail Hackett

4b Beyond 'deficit' or 'lack': enjoying the richness of language and meaning-making in a complex early childhood classroom 168
Willow Spencer, Jess Clarke, and David Ben Shannon

4c How might body-listening open up space for body-languaging? 181
Ruth Churchill Dower

4d Who chooses my words? 197
Andrea Lee

4e Listening body 211
Louise Klarnett

4f Coming together: roundtable discussion on language beyond meaning 227
Ruth Churchill Dower, Abigail Hackett, Andrea Lee, and David Ben Shannon

SECTION V
Rights of the Talker 235

5   The Rights of the Talker. A manifesto for chattering, whispering, translanguaging, not-speaking, non-verbalising, screeching, signing, clicking, twirling, stimming, assistive technology-ing, jumping, shouting, grasping, gasping, dancing, drawing, repeating, refusing, gesturing, glancing, smirking, eye-rolling, whistling......   237
Abigail Hackett, Khawla Badwan, Ruth Churchill Dower, Ester Ehiyazaryan-White, Warda Farah, Rosie Flewitt, Karen Grainger, Rachel Holmes, Christina MacRae, Vishnu KK Nair, and David Ben Shannon

Index   *251*

ABOUT THE EDITORS

Khawla Badwan is a reader in TESOL and Applied Linguistics at Manchester Metropolitan University, UK. Her research interests include language education, language and sustainability, social justice, mobility, identity, place, and intercultural communication. Her most recent publication is *Language in a Globalised World: Social Justice Perspectives on Mobility and Contact* (2021). She is editor (with Shoba Arun, Hadjer Taibi, and Farwa Batool) of *Global Migration and Diversity of Educational Experiences in the Global South and North: A Child-Centred Approach* (Routledge, forthcoming).

Ruth Churchill Dower is a PhD scholar at Manchester Metropolitan University, UK, exploring young children's nonlingual ways of being through experiments in movement. Ruth is interested in the sensory environments, pedagogies, and relations that facilitate young children's embodied ideas. Her book *Creativity and the Arts in Early Childhood* explores the origins, impacts, and conditions for creative potential to thrive and how different artforms can be nurtured in early childhood practices. Ruth is the founder of Earlyarts, an online training hub for early childhood and arts professionals. She is also a musician, storyteller, mountain-lover, and former teacher.

Warda Farah is a social entrepreneur, Independent scholar, speech and language therapist, writer, and consultant. Warda's work sits at the intersection of race, language, and disability. Her approach is guided by her own experiences as a neurodivergent Black woman and it subverts the traditional medical model of speech and language therapy by centring language as a multimodal emancipatory tool that resists standard language ideologies imposed on minorities. This lived experience infuses her approach with depth and authenticity, resonating powerfully in the academic realm and beyond.

Rosie Flewitt is Emeritus Professor of Early Childhood Communication at Manchester Metropolitan University, UK. Her many years of ethnographic research reflect a commitment to inclusion and diversity and to understanding how young children communicate through multiple modes such as gaze, gesture, movement, and drawing as well as through spoken and written language(s), in their homes, in early childhood education settings, in non-formal learning environments, and in the wider community.

Abigail Hackett is a Professor of Childhood and Education at Sheffield Hallam University. Her work is mostly ethnographic, working in communities with families and children to understand how language and literacy practices are intertwined with place. She is interested in bridging theory with practice, particularly in highlighting ways of knowing that come from lived and professional experience of being with young children, a perspective which is often undervalued in dominant discourses.

Rachel Holmes is a Professor in the Education and Social Research Institute of Manchester Metropolitan University, UK. She co-leads ESRI's Children and Childhood Research Group and has co-authored numerous studies of early childhood education. Her research focuses on processes of marginalisation in school, with a methodological interest in interdisciplinary work, particularly methodologies of artistic research in educational contexts.

Christina MacRae is a research fellow at Manchester Metropolitan University. She is a former nursery school teacher and her research interests focus on early childhood. She uses ethnographic methods, as she is interested in the ways young children's senses, feelings, and movement are entangled with their emergent literacy practices. Her research has also explored young children's learning through the arts, as well as in museums and galleries.

Vishnu KK Nair is a lecturer in the School of Psychology and Clinical Language Sciences at the University of Reading. He identifies as a cisgendered, non-disabled, South Asian gay man. He trained as a speech and language therapist and has worked in universities across four different countries: India, Australia, the USA, and the UK. His current research utilises critical methodologies and post-colonial frameworks in understanding the intersection between bilingualism, race, and disability. He is committed to decentring the English language, with an emphasis on research and clinical practice that is rooted in racial, linguistic, and disability justice.

David Ben Shannon is a lecturer in the School of Education at the University of Sheffield. He is a former primary and special education teacher. His research explores neurodiversity, sound, and literacy in special and early childhood education. His recent publications include the monograph *Research Mobilities in Primary Literacy Education* and articles in *International Journal of Qualitative Studies in Education*, *Canadian Journal of Disability Studies*, and *Angelaki: Journal of the Theoretical Humanities*.

CONTRIBUTORS

Charlotte Arculus is a UK-based improvisor, an animateur, an academic, an audio-visual artist, an electro-acoustic compos(t)er, and a maker of emergent environments. She has been a freelance, socially engaged arts practitioner for four decades and is a founder member of Magic Acorns. Improvisation, relationality, and emergence are at the heart of Charlotte's creative processes and are common factors across the diverse projects she works on. She brings practice and theory of improvisation and wildness to the heart of what it means to be *present*. In her doctoral research, Charlotte worked with two-year-olds to explore the extra-linguistic dimensions of young children's engagements with the world. That project involved innovative data creation technologies including 360° film, toddler-driven cameras, and sound study.

Robert Chester has worked in the museum sector in the UK for over 20 years. He has a background in Archaeology and, as a fully qualified teacher, he worked in mainstream schools for nearly ten years before specialising in Museum Education. At Sewerby Hall and Gardens, he has taken a hands-on role in the development and delivery of the successful school workshop programme. A believer in lifelong learning, his educational activities are not confined to children, and he is currently working on ways to make the collections at Sewerby Hall and Gardens more accessible to neurodiverse and blind visitors.

Lucy Cooke is the under-5s learning coordinator for East Riding Museums in Yorkshire, England. Her practice enables young children to engage with heritage spaces, through the use of open-ended resources and thematic interpretation. Lucy has a BA (Hons) in English Literature and a Postgraduate Certificate in Education (PGCE) specialising in the lower primary age range, as well as experience in nurseries, playwork, and teaching. She is interested in heritage, learning, well-being, and literacy.

Jess Clarke taught in primary schools in the UK for over ten years. She is a former early years leader and has also supported other early years settings as a specialist leader in Education. She is particularly interested in supporting children who speak English as an Additional Language and in developing their communication skills.

Ester Ehiyazaryan-White is a senior lecturer in Childhood and Education at Sheffield Hallam University, UK. Her research focuses on exploring multilingual children's and families' early literacy practices in home, school, and community contexts. She works with a group of researchers at Sheffield Hallam University's Language and Literacies in Education Research Group on understanding children's early language and education from a non-deficit and strength-based perspective. She has also been involved in classroom-based intervention research focused on children's literacies. Ester is currently undertaking an Early Careers Research and Innovation Fellowship. For this project, she is working co-constructively with teachers in primary schools to explore ways to encourage translanguaging in the classroom.

Karen Grainger is an Emeritus fellow in Linguistics and English Language at Sheffield Hallam University (SHU), UK. She taught on the Communication Studies and English Language degree courses at SHU. She has researched on a wide variety of issues relating to language use and interaction in institutional, intercultural, and electronic contexts. She has published in the areas of the pragmatics of politeness, the sociolinguistics of healthcare, the negotiation of meaning in intercultural settings, and the debate around 'deprived' children's language skills. She was the editor-in-chief of the *Journal of Politeness Research* from 2010 to 2020. She is currently working on the Early Years Communication project with colleagues at Sheffield Hallam University.

Esther Hallberg is the Access and Inclusion Manager for Hull Museums and Ferens Art Gallery, in Yorkshire, England. Originally coming from a more general background in museum and heritage education, Esther developed a specialism in creating bespoke spaces and sessions for very young children as the under 5s project developer at Hull Museums from

2015 to 2018, project-managing the creation of the Explore Art gallery for under-5s which was highly commended at the 2018 Museums + Heritage Awards. In recent years, Esther has followed a personal and professional passion and increasingly focused on access and inclusion within museums.

Leala Holcomb is a Research Assistant Professor at the University of Tennessee, USA. Leala is a former teacher of the deaf. Leala's research interests include signed literacy, writing instruction, and translanguaging pedagogy in deaf education. Leala enjoys providing professional development and consultations to teachers of the deaf nationally and internationally.

Louise Klarnett is a biodynamic craniosacral therapist. Over the last 24 years, Louise has developed an extensive dance and movement practice working with people at all stages of life, from young babies to 90-plus year-olds. She frequently works with those facing challenging circumstances, including health issues (such as cancer or brain injury), trauma, economic deprivation, special educational needs, and profound and multiple learning disabilities. Her work takes place in healthcare, community, and education settings as well as more traditional arts and cultural environments. She leads Continuing Professional Development (CPD) training for numerous organisations as well as workshops at conferences and events. Louise has collaborated on films and begun to write about her work.

Andrea Lee graduated from University College London in 2000 with a Master's degree in Speech and Language Therapy and Pathology. Her clinical specialism is working with children and adults who use communication aids and she is now the Augmentative and Alternative Communication (AAC) clinical lead of the Barnsley Assistive Technology Service. She has completed a pre-doctoral research fellowship and is currently applying for doctoral programmes. Her research focuses on the challenges of symbol vocabularies and the impact of vocabulary options on children with communication needs. Andrea is the author of the *Supporting Adults and Children using AAC* coursebook and accredited training programme published by Elklan Ltd. She is also a trustee of Bliss Communication UK and Blissymbolics Communication International.

Maya Leela is a speech language pathologist and cognitive scientist based in Thiruvananthapuram, Kerala, India. With a PhD from the Universitat Autònoma de Barcelona, her research focuses on early language acquisition and the complexities of communication in children. In her extensive experience as a practising speech therapist, Maya has worked with diverse populations and she emphasises the importance of early intervention. Her commitment to understanding how children communicate through various modalities – such as speech, gesture, and non-verbal cues – guides her therapeutic practices. In both her research and practice, Maya is dedicated to enhancing communication skills in young learners through innovative and inclusive approaches.

Adam Power-Annand is the CEO of Speech Bubbles. He trained in Community Theatre and developed his craft by working as an actor in Theatre-in-Education and leading youth theatres. Since 2009, he has been nurturing the Speech Bubbles programme which uses drama to support young children's communication development.

Georgina Simmons is a learning and development assistant at North Lincolnshire Museum in England. Before beginning work at the museum, she was a Key Stage 1 primary school teacher for nine years and taught English to speakers of other languages. Georgina is committed to creating an environment where people can connect to the museum, its collection, and their local heritage. She works as part of the team that delivers Museum Minis sessions to under-5s, which aims to create a welcoming and engaging space for the museum's youngest visitors and their families.

Laura Smith-Higgins is the arts and heritage learning and engagement manager at North Lincolnshire Council, with previous roles in community archaeology and the heritage sector in the UK. Since childhood, Laura has been passionate about world history and visiting museums and went on to study for a BA (Hons) in Archaeology. Laura's current role is to develop and manage learning and engagement programmes across arts and heritage, building partnerships in the local community and across the education and creative sectors. In 2023, Laura won a Marsh Award for Excellence in Visual Arts Engagement.

Willow Spencer is an early years lead and teacher. She has spent her career teaching in multicultural inner-city primary schools in both the North and South of England. She is passionate about inclusive education and diversity issues within schools.

Sally Toon has worked in the heritage sector for eight years in educational roles and is currently the families and under-5s officer at Hull Museums and Ferens Art Gallery where she oversees a varied and popular programme of artist-led and in-house family activities across five museum sites. Sally has developed the Hull Museums under-5s programme over the past couple of years through regular partnership and artist sessions. Currently, she oversees an innovative programme called Treebabies, focused on paternal mental health.

Yvonne Williams is a Special Educational Needs and Disability (SEND) teacher at a multicultural primary school in an economically deprived area of Leeds, UK. She holds a Master's degree in Early Years and Childhood Studies with a special focus on autism and behaviour. Her instinctive understanding of children's behaviour allows her to adapt her teaching methods in ways that lead to positive outcomes.

FOREWORD

As I sit and contemplate how this book came together, I think about the ways in which we, the authors, all found each other – the ways in which we felt safe enough to go outside the realms of our academic silos and not only think together but also be together. We came together with differing perspectives, experiences, and practices, but at the core we all held a desire to ignite the love and deep care we have for children and the passion for our work with them. This book needed *to be* and we recognised its importance: we knew that it could no longer be contained in our collective imagination, that it had to be brought into physical existence.

When we think of the way language unfolds, we know that it cannot be a solitary act. It is a deeply embodied, communal, and situated practice. It is the deliberate gesture of a child waving, the screams that fill the bustling playground, the joyful insistence or quiet murmur of invented words shared amongst children. In all its forms – spoken, signed, sung, whispered, danced, and painted – language pulses with life, shaped by the individual. All of this happens in *spaces* – spaces that are physical, metaphysical, imagined, and co-constructed. These spaces are not mere backdrops but are active contributors to the emergence of language, influencing its ebbs, flows, rhythms, and possibilities.

This book is a reminder that language is never disembodied, never neutral, and never separate from power-laden geographies or human and more-than-human relationships. It is a reminder that as educators and practitioners we have been taught to view children's language development through the narrow lens of curriculum standards and developmental milestones. This lens has been influenced by colonialism and frameworks of human exceptionalism, which position language as a tool for assimilation and control, particularly for those from Black, Brown, and marginalised backgrounds.

We want to draw attention to the idea that difference is not deficit. To view it as such leaves no room for the joyful, improvisational, and intentional practice of childhood communication.

Whilst many theories attempt to box, measure, and diagnose children's language, children's language practices seem to resist the confines we have built. Children's voices and bodies weave new possibilities for meaning, creating vocabularies that defy the narrow expectations of 'appropriate' development. Through the lens of spatial and more-than-human theories, this book invites us to listen anew to these acts of defiance. It offers tools to help us resist dominant discourses that prioritise linguistic standardisation over justice, conformity over creativity, and individual achievement over collective flourishing.

Importantly, this book reminds us that language, with all its beauty, is also a site of struggle. The policies and practices shaping early childhood literacy often reduce language to an apolitical, disembodied construct. These frameworks undermine the cultural and bodily dimensions of language that are so central to the lives of children in diverse communities and the wider world.

The work presented here is a call to action. We hope educators are able to shift their gaze towards the body, place, and movement in young children's language practices. We celebrate the creativity and ingenuity of children whose communicative acts are often misunderstood or undervalued within our educational systems. We hope this book sparks imagination and curiosity and unleashes new pedagogical possibilities. Let us reimagine the very purpose of early years education: not as a site of compliance but as a space for play, liberation, and justice.

As you engage with the theories and practices in this volume, consider the urgent need to dismantle the colonial legacies that continue to shape our classrooms and communities. Let this work inspire you to move beyond the narrow confines of policy and curriculum, to listen more deeply, and to view the embodied, situated experiences of children as central and as the starting point for building more equitable and joyful futures. Language, place, and the body are entangled in ways that are as complex as they are beautiful. To honour these connections is not merely an intellectual exercise – it is a moral imperative. I believe this book binds us as thinkers, friends, and community. Hopefully it will encourage more heartfelt, joyful conversations and actions that help soothe, heal, and honour ourselves and the children who are our future.

Warda Farah
Language Waves

SECTION I
Introduction

1
LANGUAGE, PLACE, AND THE BODY IN CHILDHOOD

Theory, practice, and social justice. Introduction

Khawla Badwan, Ruth Churchill Dower, Warda Farah, Rosie Flewitt, Rachel Holmes, Abigail Hackett, Christina MacRae, Vishnu KK Nair, and David Ben Shannon

Introduction

Children's language always happens *somewhere*. Playful voices float on the air from the playground or bounce off the walls of a classroom. Chatter in a quiet space causes adults to jump and tut, or an interjection at a moment of reverence during a quiet religious ceremony causes chuckles. A favourite British Sign Language or Makaton sign is repeated gleefully out of context, or invented words are whispered and sung to a special cuddly toy in a corner of the home. The premise of this book is that *where* language happens – be it spoken, signed, danced, or assisted through one or more communication tools – is not a neutral backdrop or controllable variable in *how* language happens but is deeply entangled in the emergence of words and signs from the body. Place and space and the context of the body are integral to how these vocalisations make their way into the world, what they might feel like and set into motion, and how they are received, heard, and listened to, whether by humans or non-human beings.

Whilst there are many books for educators and researchers about young children's language, few account well for the role of body and place. This is surprising because anyone who spends time with children will likely have noticed one or more of the following:

- Often children can happily chat in one place yet remain silent in another (often less familiar) one.
- When a child feels they are the only 'different' one in the room, it impacts their willingness to communicate.

- Body movement is important to children's vocalising, singing, chanting, shouting, signing, picture exchange, and storying.
- Children might use different modes for communicating and different kinds of talk depending on context and location.
- Children often transcend the boundaries imposed by named languages and modalities, allowing fluidity, complexity, and creativity in their everyday linguistic practices.
- Children interact with objects around them, bring them to life in unexpected ways, and develop imaginative languaging practices with/through these objects.
- Children can read the room and feel when it is appropriate to use languages they associate with 'home'.
- So much of what comes out of children's mouths is difficult to recognise as words but instead is a mix of musical babbling, creative vocalisations, and experimentations with what the voice can do (often occurring alongside moving and playing).

Internationally, an emerging body of interdisciplinary research is helping us to make sense of why children's language – including their talk, their vocalisations, their singing, their embodied expressions, and their other forms of multimodal meaning-making – seems so entangled with place and body. The aim of this book is both to introduce educators, parents, carers, and families to some of these theories (which are not usually the most dominant ones in current policy and curriculum) and to provide case studies of how practitioners and researchers are working with place, the body, and movement to open up space for children's improvisatory, creative, playful language practices.

> **WHAT DO WE MEAN BY 'TALK' AND 'LANGUAGE'?**
>
> It is important to our definitions of 'talk' and 'language' that we do not limit these concepts to what is 'spoken'. Of course, lots of children don't use spoken language, instead speaking British Sign Language, or making use of communication tools such as Makaton signing, picture exchange, or assistive communication devices. Moreover, lots of children communicate using non-words, nonsense words, words (seemingly) out of context, or wordless vocalisations. This is important for all children. However, it is particularly important in our practices with children labelled as having a speech and language difference. Such children might use words that seem out of context – naming cars, quoting famous YouTubers, or repeating words or phrases verbatim – in ways that are deeply meaningful for them and those

closest to them but unclear to those unfamiliar with their communication practices. Others might not use words at all, and they communicate using a rich range of movement, gestures, vocalisations, and utterances. In this book, we take a broad stance as to what we mean when we say 'talk' and 'language', to encompass all those strategies mentioned here, and more.

MORE-THAN-HUMAN?

This book describes children's language as 'more-than-human'. The idea of the more-than-human is an invitation to shift our focus from the role of humans (teachers, parents, the children themselves) to consider what else might be involved in the vocalising, moving, connecting, playing, experimenting, and meaning-making that make up children's language. In other words, the more-than-human is an invitation to consider how non-human, *tangible* 'things' such as craft materials, food, the weather, sounds in the environment, animals, and sticks and stones can be significant in shaping the ways that children use language. Place is a particularly important tangible influence on children's languaging. It plays a fundamental role in constraining or encouraging different kinds of activities and, so, different kinds of language. With the notion of the more-than-human, we also extend the invitation to consider *intangible* things, such as a feeling, a good (or bad) mood, an atmosphere, trust, power, oppression, and relationships. Even the human body itself, made up as it is of many non-human elements, involves the more-than-human! Therefore, the term more-than-human is a deliberately open one, inviting us to consider language beyond an individual child or child/adult dyad and instead to look around and ask *what else?* It might not be possible to pin down and account for everything, but to acknowledge that these more-than-human things are worthy of our consideration is a very good starting point.

Children's language, place, and the body: a summary of the research

Children use different kinds of communication, in quite different ways, depending on place, context, and bodily sensation. Pinning down exactly what these differences are is difficult for researchers because:

- These differences are particular; there are few generalisable rules.
- Many techniques of analysis from linguistics and developmental psychology have in the past tended to prefer 'data' collected in quiet

environments, but this is not compatible with understanding how children communicate in busy, noisy environments, such as early education settings.
- Experimental methods have been developed to collect naturalistic data from children whilst they play, explore, and get on with their day. These are valuable but none are perfect (no methodology ever is!).
- Overall, despite a small but growing body of work with young children growing up in ethnic and linguistic minority communities, early childhood research in the UK continues to be dominated by 'typically developing', white participants, often from middle-class, able-bodied families. This skews the findings and shapes our understanding of 'normal' in racist, classist, and ableist ways.

Of course, there are exceptions to these trends. Previous studies have involved large-cohort data sets, with children wearing continuous recording devices (Maybin, 2012; Tizzard & Hughes, 1984; Wells, 2009): by definition, these projects cannot confine their data collection to quiet environments. More recently, long-term ethnographic research has also been vital for our understanding of young children's language practices in context (Flewitt, 2005; Hackett et al., 2021). Researchers have also begun experimenting with continuous audio-recording of children's talk in everyday contexts, using a range of new technologies (Dean, 2021; Richardson & Murray, 2017). Each of these studies offers us glimpses of the complexity of young children's language use, revealing how language is only one of many forms of communication and how it is deeply entangled with power, relationships, place, and the body.

Plurilingual children are affected in quite particular ways by the entanglement of place, context, and language, given the largely monolingual framing of many English educational contexts (García et al., 2021; Viruru, 2001). Historically, many children were banned from speaking home languages in school settings (Anzaldúa, 1987; Saavedra & Esquierdo, 2020). Anzaldúa (1987) viscerally recalls the punishment, rejection, and other negative consequences she experienced for speaking Spanish in school in the United States. Children are still receiving the same message, both directly and indirectly, that minority home languages and dialects are not welcome in classroom spaces, where standard English is the preferred or only accepted medium (Badwan, 2021). Scholars interested in bilingual and translanguaging practices have employed careful ethnographic, qualitative, and action research approaches to gain insights into how children use space to find opportunities to resist school-based language restrictions, seeking out private spaces where they can use their home languages and create a sense of belonging through language use (Björk-Willén,

2016; Fashanu et al., 2020). Moreover, anti-racist scholars have illustrated the significant harm that uncritical approaches to language education can cause to students of colour (Baker-Bell, 2020; Garcia et al., 2021) while, at the same time, children find opportunities to resist that harm (Frieson, 2021).

Language in the more-than-human world and joining in with place

Often in literature about early language, there is an emphasis on the role of adults in talking to young children and scaffolding activities through talk. In our research, we have noticed that children are not always focused on adults and nor do they necessarily wait for cues from them. Instead, a particular object, the feeling of a space, or the opportunity to run in a particular kind of circle around a place, drives children's energy, creativity, and communication. Children's language is often bound up in their energy and movement. The risk with paying too much attention to the role of adults in prompting children's talk is that we might under-value the vital energies that children invest in their communication through other modes and the close attention they often pay to their peers. Indeed, for some children who do not verbalise (for physical, emotional, or other reasons), communicating through movements or gestures becomes even more important. And yet these modes are deemed less 'appropriate' than talking, thereby positioning the child as already 'not good enough' (Burman, 2012; Murris, 2016).

In this book, we set out how different theories connected with the idea of the more-than-human offer expansive insights into how language is always entangled with bodies, objects, and places in a world where place is always political. Below, we outline the parameters of these theories and pose provocative questions for readers to consider how understanding talk as more-than-human might resonate with their own experience.

Language as bodily and material

Bodies jiggle and spin; arms and hands stretch and sweep. Breath must be thrust through throats and vocal cords in order for vocalisations of any sort to emerge. Lips and tongues move and flex to make words that might (or might not) be understood by adults. This book joins a growing body of research interested in foregrounding the connection between children's moving bodies and their talking, vocalising, mark-making, creating, and various other ways of communicating. Movement of many different kinds is essential to children's language.

Dominant notions of talk consider language as a primarily cognitive process that "fl[ies] between lips and brain" (Hackett, 2021, p. 16) of an individual child. Connected to this perspective is much of the research on the so-called 'word gap', a problematic explanation for marginalised children's perceived 'lack' of vocabulary, which lays the blame on parents and home environments. It imagines that words are 'banked' inside an individual brain, to be retrieved and 'produced' via the mouth and throat at any given opportunity. Yet, this banking metaphor and the emphasis on cognition overlook the bodily-ness of talking, the importance of how bodies feel and function differently, the importance of how children feel, and the political relationship between language and place.

When young children are not enthusiastic to talk in a particular way in a particular place, it is rarely because they have insufficient vocabulary 'banked' in their brains. Assumptions such as these are damaging to children and to communities, first because they point in unhelpful directions that engender deficit discourses about what children cannot do and what professional interventions may be needed to support children. As Ruth Churchill Dower (2022b) puts it, we can end up with a "language-based solution for a complex, heterogeneous [body]-based situation" (p. 142). Second, these assumptions open the door to the pathologisation of families and communities, who get 'blamed' for what they apparently have not previously done (in terms of ensuring their children are banking the correct kinds of vocabulary in the correct way).

Expecting or desiring children to speak in particular ways (confident, elaborated, individualised statements), regardless of the context in which they find themselves (atmosphere, unspoken rules and relationships, (un) familiarity) or their developing sense of identity (which may not cohere with the kind of mainstream, *white* language identity that such talk requires them to enact), can be experienced as an exorbitant demand on a young speaker. It is hardly surprising that the lonely burden of speaking in institutional contexts, even for adults, is often accompanied by anxiety (Jones, 2013; Thiel, 2015) and often registers in the *body*: in the gut, the pulse, the dry mouth, the invisible film of sweat on the skin.

Questions to consider

- What types of movements do our spaces invite, encourage, or make possible?
- How do (or could) children experiment with what their bodies can do in the different places where they play?
- Time to move: how does time limit or open up sense-making when thinking about language in early childhood?

Place and language co-constitute each other

Place (and the stuff in place) is never just the backdrop to what unfolds: it shapes and inspires children's play, learning, and movement. We could say, then, that learning to talk is not just a matter of mastering a system of sounds and abstract rules under the encouragement and guidance of adults. It is fundamentally a matter of getting involved in the world, creatively and politically. This includes joining in with other people and with the more-than-human world. One way we can imagine this is to think about opportunities for children to 'join in with place'. If, as adults, we want to make irresistible invitations for children to join in, we need wide, expansive possibilities for what joining in with place could look like, including joining in with place in unplanned ways. And we need to create atmospheres in which joining in, whether that be through vocalisations, movement, making, or any other kind of multimodal literacy, feels comfortable and easy.

When we think about place in relation to children's language, we must always be mindful of the power relations and histories involved and what Sara Ahmed has called "the angle of [one's] arrival" (2014, para 4). That is, the same spaces are not experienced in the same way by everyone. How we experience the politics of place depends on our sense of identity, our previous experiences in similar places, and the effect these have on how they make us and our bodies feel.

The political-ness of place is an important distinction between the ideas we discuss in this book and the narrower notion of the Home Learning Environment (HLE) (e.g., Rowland et al., 2020), which has been used to understand how place and wider context might influence nursery/school learning. HLE research has found correlations between different aspects of the immediate family context, neighbourhood characteristics, and children's language development (see Iruka et al., 2015, for a review). These findings have been interpreted into actionable and 'empowering' guidance for parents, suggesting that by changing their home practices and behaviours they can better support their children's language and consequently achieve upwards social mobility for their children. Yet, for this logic to cohere, place and language must be regarded as discrete and modifiable variables. These deficit-centric portrayals of children's capacities and their home learning environments run counter to the view of place we offer in this book. Here, we explore how children, bodies, language(s), and the more-than-human are deeply entangled, temporally as well as spatially, and cannot be neatly separated out or neatly correlated. In addition, we encourage readers to beware of making unjustified associations between economic deprivation, 'poor' quality environments, and children's language use: these discussions frequently reinforce racialising and classist corporeal hierarchies that are not borne out by rigorous research (c.f. Basit et al., 2015; Li et al., 2022).

Questions to consider

- *What else* (in terms of objects, spaces, atmospheres, and so on) might be important to children and their language practices in our contexts?
- What might 'joining in with place' look like in our contexts?
- How might we create irresistible opportunities for joining in, which are welcoming and relevant for all children?

Language is not a simple process of transmitting and receiving meaning

Western education systems have historically relied heavily on the assumption that learning is a process of transferring skills and knowledge from one person to another or from one situation to another. This transmission model has led to functional approaches to learning and the belief that language – as a medium for representing things, ideas, or feelings through words, in ways that are clearly understood – is central to learning. Following this logic, the absence of language has been pathologised. However, neither learning nor communication are such straightforward processes. Language does not simply transmit meaning like a radio mast. Rather, it reflects the identity of the language user (e.g., their age, gender, race, culture, status) and language use involves a complex interplay between power relations, asymmetrical relationships, systems of communication, and activities, which all unfold in different places.

Communicating meaning also involves affective and sensory forces that can arise independently of signification and are expressed through bodies as well as through words. All language includes breaths, coughs, sniffs, or giggles that may not be strictly equated with meaning (MacLure, 2013), and children's language often involves language play, musicality, experimentation, and vocalisations that are not easily recognised as words. Instead of seeing these aspects of children's language as irrelevant or in need of improved pronunciation, grammar, or sentence formation, what would it mean to honour the "ongoing, everyday, moment-by-moment, autotelic, intra-active, seemingly pointless or *meaning-less*" qualities of children's talk (Horton & Kraftl, 2018, p. 929).

There is an alarming predicament hidden just beneath the surface of this culture in the West of measuring children's ability to meet developmental goals to ascertain whether they are physically, cognitively, emotionally, or socially 'normal' (as if this were a real thing). The pressure to conform means that educators, parents, and carers can feel obliged to ignore, even to stop, the *meaning-less* in children's play. There is an increasing sense that there is no space or time to play without *purpose*, without it ticking at least some of the 'developmentally appropriate' boxes, and certainly not if these meaning-less expressions might indicate something is 'wrong' (Burman, 2017). Educators and parents alike are stuck in a cleft-stick situation of trying to meet their professional (or dutiful) expectations whilst still honouring children's expressions of who and how they are. In this context, improvisation can be a powerful conceptual frame. It is a means of acknowledging the productive agencies of young children with their obscure and varied body languages in relation to the world around them (Arculus & MacRae, 2022).

Recognising young children as skilled improvisors can, in turn, inform what Arculus and MacRae (2022) have called pedagogies of improvisation. These approaches challenge the dogma requiring structured plans for specific learning outcomes, and they resist anticipating the spontaneous expressions that are produced when new flows of thought and action are opened up. Often these involve what Olsson (2009) calls a "bodily logic" as opposed to conscious thinking (p. 55). Oftentimes these "unpredictably experimenting" lines of flight (Olsson, 2009, p. 74) are set off by imperceptible but culturally important minor gestures (Manning, 2016). The space opened up by pedagogies of improvisation is ripe for expressions, movements, gestures, and signs that may be suppressed in more formal environments (Taguchi et al., 2016). Improvisation allows bodies and minds to travel in surprising directions, releasing a complex web of entangled identities and creative imaginaries that may never be apparent otherwise. It offers children and their grown-ups "different ways of communing, affecting, and tuning in with each other and the material world which might make a difference to how they, and we, think about communication" (Churchill Dower, 2022a, p. 77). In this way, improvisation can open up new languages of multiple identities that resist the partial definition, reduction, and representation that can dominate early childhood environments (Hackett & Rautio, 2019; Olsson, 2009; Taguchi et al., 2015).

In addition to valuing language and communication as involving connection, energy, surprise, and motion, we encourage readers to consider the political importance of something that Viruru (2001), drawing on the work of Glissant (1997), has called children's 'right to opacity'. There is often an assumption that children ultimately *want* to convey exactly how they feel to adults and that enabling children to express their feelings and desires is *always* empowering or emancipatory. However, in the work of Glissant (1997), the idea of rendering another person completely transparent and knowable involves reducing or simplifying the other person.

Opacity, or the right *not* to be fully transparent and knowable, should be everyone's entitlement. As adults, we can respect children's feelings, actions, and language *even when* (especially when) we do not fully understand the meaning. The right to opacity is an important principle which upends many of education's assumptions about what language is for and how it is experienced in childhood. The concept of opacity informs many of the ideas in this volume, including the 'rights of the talker' manifesto with which we end this book.

Questions to consider
- How can we plan for the unpredictable?
- How can we make space for things we have not yet imagined?
- How can we value opacity and resist demanding fixed meanings and clear logics?

Why use this book?

Children's language has long been associated with educational success, social mobility, and economic prosperity. How children talk (nicely, clearly, appropriately, and preferably in a language the educator can understand) is increasingly seen as evidence of children's 'proper development' and an indicator of their future success. From this standpoint, early interventions to fix and correct their talk, and stimulate the most desirable kinds of talk, are sometimes viewed as benign practices that are 'for children's own good'. We also note how requirements to still the body, fix meanings, and comply with dominant hegemonies of communication intensify as a child moves through school. We see back-and-forth effects of these requirements during a child's (supposedly linear) progression through the educational system. Practice in early childhood settings is foreshadowed by the pressure to make a child 'school-ready' (still body, clear speech, dominance of the English language), and children in primary school or beyond who are deemed lacking are described as 'behind' or 'operating at the level of a X-year-old'. The way in which these ideas about language, place, and the body ripple through infanthood, early childhood, and primary schooling (and beyond), with differential effects and consequences, was the rationale for a book that looks across the first 11 years of childhood.

One of the key things we hope that readers will take from this book is that thinking about children's language as more-than-human will prompt them to rethink many of the assumptions and hierarchies that abound in policy and curriculum about what counts as language and what kinds of language practices are preferred in education environments. For example, the rationale set out in one language-screening package makes clear the sheer weight of societal and educational concern that has come to be attached to young children's language: "By targeting preschool children, the aim is to increase school readiness and decrease the risk of poor literacy, behavioural difficulties, mental health difficulties, criminal activity, and unemployment that are associated with poor early communication skills" (RSPH, n.d.).

Not-speaking, then, is viewed as undesirable and troubling. It is pathologised like an illness that can best be remedied by professional intervention. Vocalisations that are not easily recognised as words (by the adults listening) are categorised as pre-language, with potential for improvement (Hackett, 2022). A child who remains silent in an educational context risks being read as either defiant or pathological (MacLure et al., 2010). However, these logics about defiance, pathology, and future success, and the essential/normal/natural character of certain kinds of talk, only hold up if we conceptualise language as purely human, residing in the brain, and separable from place.

The more-than-human helps us to rethink these assumptions that locate the fault in the individual human child. Words are not 'banked' in a child's brain to be pulled out in each and any future context if they so choose. Instead, language can be understood as something collective that moves through bodies, emotions, relationships, and atmospheres. Often, children creatively improvise with sound and movement in order to see how something might feel, or what it might do or set into motion, for both other humans and the more-than-human world they are constantly exploring, such as enjoying the sounds of an echo. Children's improvisations with sounds and words do not unfurl in a vacuum but in places that are loaded with the far-reaching politics of culture, power, and belonging.

So, we repeat our invitation to readers to understand the more-than-human as an invitation to ask *what else*? and to foreground what children themselves value or are interested in. We hope this will offer a refreshing contrast to the oft-felt constraints of curriculum and practice where there is pressure to focus on predetermined criteria of what 'quality' talk or 'appropriate' language development looks like. These predetermined criteria are known to be particularly damaging to children of colour, working-class children, bilingual children, and indeed all marginalised communities (Baker-Bell, 2020). As Yoon and Templeton (2019) have pointed out, in neoliberal educational spaces where certain behaviours and responses are valued over others, we need tools to help us really listen to children and to 'hear them out' (p. 55). We hope that more-than-human theories of children's language may be one such tool. In this sense, we would argue that the more-than-human is not *actually* about decentring the human but rather about decentring a particular kind of human, one who is rational, sensible, stationary, who always talks in complete sentences, who does not actually exist, and who is not doing any favours for children or the adults who work with them.

We hope that this book will be useful for anyone working with or spending time with children. It is for anyone who would like to create spaces and moments for children, where moving, playing, communicating, storytelling, disrupting, experimenting, surprising, and confusing will feel easy, comfortable, and right.

References

Ahmed, S. (2014, September 15). Atmospheric walls. *Feministkilljoys*. https://feministkilljoys.com/2014/09/15/atmospheric-walls/

Anzaldúa, G. (1987). *Borderland / La Frontera: The New Mestiza*. Aunt Lute.

Arculus, C., & MacRae, C. (2022). Clowns, fools and the more-than-adult toddler. *Global Studies of Childhood*, 12(3), 209–223. https://doi.org/10.1177/20436106221117569

Badwan, K. (2021). *Language in a Globalised World. Social Justice Perspectives on Mobility and Contact*. Palgrave Macmillan.

Baker-Bell, A. (2020). Dismantling anti-black linguistic racism in English language arts classrooms: Toward an anti-racist black language pedagogy. *Theory Into Practice*, 59(1), 8–21. https://doi.org/10.1080/00405841.2019.1665415

Basit, T. N., Hughes, A., Iqbal, Z., & Cooper, J. (2015). The influence of socioeconomic status and ethnicity on speech and language development. *International Journal of Early Years Education*, 23(1), 115–133. https://doi.org/10.1080/09669760.2014.973838

Björk-Willén, P. (2016). The preschool entrance hall: A bilingual transit zone for preschoolers. In A. Bateman, & A. Church (Eds.), *Children's Knowledge-in-Interaction: Studies in Conversation Analysis* (pp. 169–187). Springer.

Burman, E. (2012). Deconstructing neoliberal childhood: Towards a feminist antipsychological approach. *Childhood: A Global Journal of Child Research*, 19(4), 423–438. https://doi.org/10.1177/0907568211430767

Burman, E. (2017). *Deconstructing Developmental Psychology* (3rd ed.). Routledge.

Churchill Dower, R. (2022a). Contact improvisation as a force for expressive reciprocity with young children who don't speak. *LEARNing Landscapes*, 15(1). https://doi.org/10.36510/learnland.v15i1.1065

Churchill Dower, R. (2022b). Too much kin in the game? The intimate reciprocities available in not speaking. *Cultural and Pedagogical Inquiry*, 14(1), 139–151. https://doi.org/10.18733/cpi29656

Dean, B. (2021). Spontaneous singing in early childhood: An examination of young children's singing at home. *Research Studies in Music Education*, 43(3), 434–450. https://doi.org/10.1177/1321103X20924139

Fashanu, C., Wood, E., & Payne, M. (2020). Multilingual communication under the radar: How multilingual children challenge the dominant monolingual discourse in a super-diverse, Early Years educational setting in England. *English in Education*, 54(1), 93–112. https://doi.org/10.1080/04250494.2019.1688657

Flewitt, R. (2005). Is every child's voice heard? Researching the different ways 3-year-old children communicate and make meaning at home and in a pre-school playgroup. *Early Years*, 25(3), 207–222. https://doi.org/10.1080/09575140500251558

Frieson, B. L. (2021). Remixin' and flown' in centros: Exploring the biliteracy practices of Black language speakers in an elementary two-way immersion bilingual program. *Race Ethnicity and Education*, 25(4), 585–605. https://doi.org/10.1080/13613324.2021.1890568

García, O., Flores, N., Seltzer, K., Wei, L., Otheguy, R., & Rosa, J. (2021). Rejecting abyssal thinking in the language and education of racialized bilinguals: A manifesto. *Critical Inquiry in Language Studies*, 18(3), 203–228. https://doi.org/10.1080/15427587.2021.1935957

Glissant, E. (1997). *Poetics of Relation*. University of Michigan Press.

Hackett, A. (2021). *More-Than-Human Literacies in Early Childhood*. Bloomsbury.

Hackett, A. (2022). Beyond transparency: More-than-human insights into the emergence of young children's language. *Literacy*, 56(3), 244–252. https://doi.org/10.1111/lit.12297

Hackett, A., MacLure, M., & McMahon, S. (2021). Reconceptualising early language development: Matter, sensation and the more-than-human. *Discourse. Studies in the Cultural Politics of Education*, 42(6), 913–929. https://doi.org/10.1080/01596306.2020.1767350

Hackett, A., & Rautio, P. (2019). Answering the world: Young children's running and rolling as more-than-human multimodal meaning making. *International Journal of Qualitative Studies in Education*, 32(8), 1019–1031. https://doi.org/10.1080/09518398.2019.1635282

Horton, J., & Kraftl, P. (2018). Rats, assorted shit and 'racist groundwater': Towards extra-sectional understandings of childhoods and social-material processes. *Environment and Planning D: Society and Space*, 36(5), 926–948. https://doi.org/10.1177/0263775817747278

Iruka, I. U., Curenton, S. M., & Gardner, S. (2015). How changes in home and neighbourhood environment factors are related to change in black children's academic and social development from kindergarten to third grade. *The Journal of Negro Education*, 84(3), 282–297. https://psycnet.apa.org/doi/10.7709/jnegroeducation.84.3.0282

Jones, S. (2013). Literacies in the body. *Journal of Adolescent and Adult Literacy*, 56(7), 525–529. https://doi.org/10.1002/JAAL.182

Li, Q. K. W., MacKinnon, A. L., Tough, S., Graham, S., & Tomfohr-Madsen, L. (2022). Does where you live predict what you say? Associations between neighborhood factors, child sleep, and language development. *Brain Sciences*, 12(2), 223. https://doi.org/10.3390/brainsci12020223

MacLure, M. (2013). Researching without representation? Language and materiality in post-qualitative methodology. *International Journal of Qualitative Studies in Education*, 26(6), 658–667. https://doi.org/10.1080/09518398.2013.788755

MacLure, M., Holmes, R., Jones, L., & MacRae, C. (2010). Silence as resistance to analysis: Or, on not opening one's mouth properly. *Qualitative Inquiry*, 16(6), 492–500. https://doi.org/10.1177/1077800410364349

Manning, E. (2016). *The Minor Gesture*. Duke University Press.
Maybin, J. (2012). Towards a sociocultural understanding of children's voice. *Language and Education, 27*(5), 383–397. https://doi.org/10.1080/09500782.2012.704048
Murris, K. (2016). *The Posthuman Child: Educational Transformation Through Philosophy with Picturebooks*. Routledge.
Olsson, L. M. (2009). *Movement and Experimentation in Young Children's Learning: Deleuze and Guattari in Early Childhood Education*. Routledge.
Richardson, T., & Murray, J. (2017). Are young children's utterances affected by characteristics of their learning environments? A multiple case study. *Early Child Development and Care, 187*(3–4), 457–468. https://doi.org/10.1080/03004430.2016.1211116
Rowland, C. F., Theakston, A., Ambridge, B., & Twomey, K. (Eds.) (2020). *Current Perspectives on Child Language Acquisition: How Children Use Their Environment to Learn*. (Trends in Language Acquisition Research; Vol. 27). John Benjamins Publishing Company. https://doi.org/10.1075/tilar.27
Royal Society for Public Health (RSPH) (n.d.) Early years communication and language pathway in Manchester. *Royal Society for Public Health*. https://www.rsph.org.uk/static/uploaded/c66c80e5-b305-46c7-9c7d1225aea29b89.pdf
Saavedra, C., & Esquierdo, J. J. (2020). Platicas on disrupting language ideologies in the borderlands. In F. Nxumalo and C. P. Brown (Eds.), *Disrupting and Countering Deficits in Early Childhood Education*. (pp. 37–52). Routledge.
Taguchi, H. L., Palmer, A., Gustafsson, L. (2015). Individuating 'sparks' and 'flickers' of 'a life' in dance practices with preschoolers: the 'monstrous child' of Colebrook's Queer Vitalism. *Discourse: Studies in the Cultural Politics of Education: Fabulous Monsters: Alternative Discourses of Childhood in Education, 37*(5), 705–716. https://doi.org/10.1080/01596306.2015.1075710
Thiel, J. (2015). Shrinking in, spilling out, and living through: Affective energy as multimodal literacies. In G. Enriquez, E. Johnson, S. Kontovouki, & C. Mallozzi (Eds.), *Literacies, Learning, and the Body* (pp. 106–120). Routledge.
Tizzard, B., & Hughes, M. (1984). *Young Children Learning*. Harvard University Press.
Viruru, R. (2001). Colonized through Language: The case of early childhood education. *Contemporary Issues in Early Childhood, 2*(1), 31–47. https://doi.org/10.2304/ciec.2001.2.1.7
Wells, G. (2009). *The Meaning Makers. Learning to Talk and Talking to Learn*. Multilingual Matters.
Yoon, Y. S., & Templeton, T. N. (2019). The practice of listening to children: The challenges of hearing children out in an adult-regulated world. *Harvard Educational Review, 89*(1), 55–84. https://doi.org/10.17763/1943-5045-89.1.55

SECTION II
Language as bodily and material

2a

LANGUAGE AS BODILY AND MATERIAL

Rosie Flewitt, Rachel Holmes, and Christina MacRae

This chapter introduces theory and scholarship that look at how language emerges in young children through their bodies, movements, and encounters with the material world. Our starting point is to question the enduring tendency for language to be considered as something that sits primarily within the brain (de Freitas & Curringa, 2015; MacLure, 2013; Shannon, 2020). We unpick how the historical tendency to view cognition as separate from the sensory and motoric body has led to a mind/body split in education policy in the UK and globally. In turn this has fuelled the persistent policy focus on the 'language gap' between children in terms of their socio-economic context. Such deficit discourses tend to locate language as words 'banked' in the brain (Avineri et al., 2015; Cushing, 2022; Grainger, 2013; Lareau, 2003). In countering these perspectives, we draw on recent more-than-human and feminist scholarship and pay attention to the 'feeling' body (Dernikos et al., 2020), an approach that liberates the body from its subordination to the mind (Grosz, 1994). This 'affective turn' in the scholarship "highlights the openness and vulnerability of human bodies: the inexplicable ways we move between and attach to bodies (writ large), ideas, sensations, things and even other affects" (Dernikos, 2020, p.138/139). It proposes imagining a "bodily logic of potentiality through affect", rather than assuming that all learning "[takes] place through conscious thinking" (Olsson, 2009, p. 49). Acknowledging that language involves a sensing and moving body, not just the brain, enables a focus on how bodies *feel* in spaces and situations and how, crucially, this shapes children's language (Enriquez et al., 2015; Saavedra & Esquierdo, 2020; Wynter-Hoyte & Boutte, 2018). Finally, we pick up on a rich seam of scholarship that recognises the disavowal of children's bodies as problematic (Leander & Boldt, 2013; Tobin, 1997, 2004). Here we explore how language can be animated by bodies' "unceasing movement" that "exceed[s] capture by reason and meaning" (MacLure, 2023, p. 213). We conclude by looking to the potential of unruly moving bodies to resist the over-privileging of language.

In Chapter 1, we invited readers to consider these questions:

- What types of movements do our spaces invite, encourage, or make possible?
- How do (or could) children experiment with what their bodies can do in the different places where they play?
- Time to move: how does time limit or open up sense-making when thinking about language in early childhood?

All the chapters in this section of this book help us explore some possible responses to these questions. In this introductory chapter, we highlight a body of research in the early education field that attends to ways the mind/body split continues to haunt and play out in early childhood education contexts (Murris et al., 2020; Van Laere et al., 2014). We do this with a view to prompting the reader to think (and practise) in more capacious and productive ways in relation to young children and language. The contributors to this section are inviting the absent body back in, in terms of how we conceptualise early language and also in the practices we enact in the context of education and speech and language provision for young children. By highlighting "the ways in which language tangles with matter and movement and sensation, and lodges in the body" (MacLure, 2023, p. 213), our aim is to foreground research that counters the trend to represent language as an investment in resources that are 'banked' in the brain. In the following chapters, the contributing authors draw on their own experiences of working with young children to offer up a more capacious, generous view of language as embodied.

Stilled bodies, schooled minds

The absenting of the body in favour of the mind, a bias that seeps through education and curriculum discourse, is a legacy of the mind/body dualism associated with the Enlightenment philosophies of Descartes. In education, this dualism accompanies other binary oppositions, such as rationality/emotionality, objectivity/subjectivity, and language/matter, which are all infused with this Cartesian thinking. The developmental preparation of young children for school, as ideal learners, focuses on the rational, the objective, the linguistic – and involves the stilling of the body, as we go on to explain.

Over 100 years before Tobin (2004) lamented the disappearance of the body in early childhood education of the 1990s, there were anxieties about the stilling effect of schools on the body. The concerns were articulated by Friedrich Froebel as he began to re-envision early childhood education away from formal, seated classrooms towards the notion of 'kindergarten'. He promoted the idea that we should focus on self-led activity as the primary site of learning for the young child. He warned that thinking, moving, and feeling should not be separated and that the effect of schooling on children was to "neglect the plastic expression of ideas" (Froebel, 1887/1906, p. 37). As Karin Murris and colleagues note, from the position of a developmental theory of knowledge, the child's maturation process is completed when "the child's mind is scientific and rational, that is, thinks like an adult" (2020, p. 5). bell hooks discusses how the mind/body dualism in education "dictates that instruction should take place solely between minds, which leaves no place for acknowledgment of the body's role in teaching and learning" (1994, p. 17). Scrutinising this model of the developing, rational, and objective human being, Karen Barad argues that "language has been granted too much power" (2007, p. 132). This privileging of language became unhelpfully tangled up with colonial ideas about humans as an exceptional species set apart from others and at the expense of other ways to attune with and respond to the rest of the world (Finnegan, 2002; García et al., 2021; Gurney & Demuro, 2022; Hackett, 2022). The ideal of the school child has become one that insists on the still, articulate body as the learning body, able to separate thought from action and mind from body (Ingold, 2004, p. 323). This body of the ideal learner is distinct from other bodies that need to be more mobile, even fidgety – bodies that "intrude into the disembodied space of being-educated minds" (Paechter, 2011, p. 311).

In the current climate of assessment and metrics, children at ever-younger ages are subject to preparation for school and to adults' notions of the school-ready body and mind. The separating of minds from bodies, and the idealisation of the still body, is resurgent in a landscape of neoliberalised early childhood education (Moss & Roberts-Holmes, 2021). Contemporary anxieties about perceived lack of school readiness often focus on language development, with an assumption that 'fixing' language 'delay' will produce children who are better ready for school (Hackett et al., 2020). Following this questionable logic, still and docile bodies become an essential goal of formal education.

Before returning to our focus on language emergence as bodily, we turn to the influence of colonialist, racist, and ableist norms in the notion of the ideal body and its relationship to the mind. The relevance to how bodies (and language) are viewed in contemporary classrooms will become clear. Kašparová et al. (2023) remind us that we have been "socialized under modernity to believe we are a composition of a (separate) physical body and an abstract mind" (p. 144). Modernity has privileged the white, European ideal of the body as an abled, gender-conforming, conventionally attractive, and reproductive body, one that is not only separate from the mind but also under its control. According to Loeser et al. (2018), the Cartesian tradition has been influential in defining the white male body as 'bounded' (i.e., independent and separate) and therefore 'normal' in Western societies. Non-conforming bodies are deemed 'Others' and seen as sources of disruption to the operations of education. There is therefore a relationship, both historically and today, between the influences of colonialism, anti-blackness, and ableism and the emphasis on controlling and schooling the body. Normative assumptions about the body are particularly enforced on people of colour, people who are neurodivergent, and people who are LGBTQ+. (For more on these historical developments, see Butler, 1990, 1993; Davis, 1995, 1997; Fuss, 1991; Gatens, 1996; Grosz, 1994; Petersen, 1998; Shilling, 1993.) Cervenak captures the problem succinctly in the observation that "black movement is, more often than not, *read* as disruptive physicality" (2014, p. 5).

The belief that the mind governs the body has a long history, and it takes on new formations when coupled with post-structural notions of 'disciplinary power' over the body, to use Foucault's term. If we consider children in school, the "school's disciplinary measures render the body docile and useful to itself as well as to others through a mastery of the mind" (Pawelski, 2022, p. 164). Relatedly, Tobin (2004) notes how disembodiment becomes the *goal*, rather than simply being the byproduct of the suppression of the body's pleasure and desire in exchange for docility. Tobin examines the well-worn phrase "use your words" (so familiar to those who spend time in early education settings) and notes that it implies "and not your body" (2004, p. 117). In Maya Leela's chapter (2d), we hear how as a speech therapist she is deliberately moving away from measuring children's language abilities according to universal assessment metrics, scales, or scores. Instead, she asks families "to bring multiple video recordings of their child to the appointment" and guides them about specific scenarios to capture, such as the child playing with materials like water, sand, or mud or engaging in outdoor games involving running, jumping, or climbing. In Maya's chapter, we glimpse the anxieties felt by parents in the face of an increasingly competitive environment for gaining places in schools for young children, in the specific context of India, together with the effects of the creeping marketisation of 'edu-care' in early childhood – a trend which is recognisable around the world. Maya's discussions with parents reveal that the pressure to get their young children school-ready is fuelling their worries about the children's speech. Those worries translate to a specific wish – not simply that Maya can help their children to talk but that they will talk *whilst sitting still*.

The material dimension of language in early childhood

A recent body of literature has started to pay much closer attention to how the 'bodymind' is entangled in "processes of minding (the body) and bodying (the mind)" (Kašparová et al, 2023, p. 143). Feminist theorists have challenged the dualism of mind/body, arguing that "the mind is always embodied or based on corporeal relations, and that the body is always social, political and in-process rather than natural" (van Laere et al., 2014). In order to re-situate language in more bodily terms, we signpost readers to research that foregrounds the material relationships between language, body, and movement in relation to children. For example, Hackett and Somerville (2017) help us to notice the active and lively part played by the more-than-human world as children respond expressively to places, materials, and things through movement and sound-making. Drawing on observations of children engaged in play with mud and water, the authors argue that the ways children occupy space and are occupied by their material encounters constitute world-forming communicative practice: in these encounters, "words fail" because much of the practice "occurs at the limits of language where vocalisations are not words or are so entangled with water, play and voice that they are not distinguishable" (Hackett & Somerville, 2017, p. 384). They talk about this world-making as an ongoing emergent process that is driven by children's affective responses to encounters with other bodies, matter, and space. In the play events discussed, there is a sense that "story, imagination, movement and gesture are inseparable from the simultaneous actions of mud and water" (p. 384). Research has highlighted the way things and materials have a vibrancy that is sensed rather than reducible to rational thought and words (MacRae, 2020; Thiel, 2015). If 'things' are seen this way, we can start to re-frame the idea that conversations are necessarily something that happens between human beings and recognise that conversations can also happen with the 'stuff' in the more-than-human world, as Charlotte Arculus demonstrates in her chapter in section (2c). She writes that these are conversations with "less emphasis on defining what everything is (with words) and a lot more emphasis on improvising and experimenting with things". Such conversations can also be seen as a way of "answering the world" (Hackett & Rautio, 2019).

Bessie Dernikos, who does research on the teaching of reading in early years education, makes a point of actively seeking out what she calls "the 'fleshy' frequencies" that permeate classroom spaces, in order to "awaken us to those social worlds that already always exist alongside the 'normative' space-times that often serve to colonize literacy learning and denigrate students from diverse communities" (Dernikos, 2020, p. 135). Her work highlights *affects* as "the forces (intensities, energies, flows, etc.) that register on/with-in/across bodies to produce and shape personal/emotional experiences" (Dernikos et al., 2020, p. 5). It goes on to explore how these forces reverberate on different bodies in different ways in the particular context of the educational spaces that young children find themselves in. This work is a reminder that what *moves* us is also a deeply political matter, as gender, race, and class vibrate through our responses to other bodies, materials, and spaces.

The politics of what moves us is picked up by Williams and Shannon (Chapter 2b) as they consider the intersectional experiences of Black and neurodivergent children in their classroom. They point out that in the UK and internationally, there is evidence of a pattern where students racialised as Black are "over-represented in judgement-based categories of need, while underrepresented in provision for sensory and physical support". They also note that the narrowing of the curriculum is coupled with the narrowing of what might be considered as neurotypical. In the context of the early years curriculum in the UK, they observe how policy and curriculum expectations construct the neurotypical child as one who is "able to control [their] passions, interests, and bladder well enough to participate in formalised, desk-based literacy and maths instruction from the age of four". As a means to resist this requirement for still, docile bodies, Williams and Shannon carefully curate multisensory environments where they experiment with more 'visceral' forms of mutuality – ones which invite bodies to move. This approach also aligns with Hackett and colleagues' research on the language development of two-year-olds in a nursery setting: the authors suggest that "early language development might be better supported by paying less attention to words, grammar and meaning, in favour of fostering participation in dynamic, multisensory, collective events" (Hackett et al., 2020, p. 913).

Moving and wild bodies

We now turn our focus to the potential of unruly moving bodies to stubbornly resist the over-privileging of language. To counter our deep-seated "wordism" (Blum, 2015) as adults, we look to alternative practices of listening and attunement that pay attention to what bodies in motion might be saying, for example when they gesture, insist, refuse, rest, laugh, drag, or shrug. We can describe this as kind of a 'wild discourse', a kind of communication or connection that happens on the boundary of language and body, "restoring language to the open potential of becoming" (MacLure, 2013, p.171). In Chapter 2e, Adam Power-Annand describes theatre-making and storytelling practices which are offered to schools as a way to enable more relational, collective, and embodied forms of communication. This work highlights that storytelling is not necessarily a skill based narrowly on verbal expression (as it so often becomes in the school context) but that when storytelling is enlivened through theatre, we can make ourselves intelligible in 'more-than-words' and bodily ways. Working within the field of theatre practice opens up a more experimental space for children where a 'whole-bodied' approach is the starting point for communicating something. In theatre, communication is recognised as "largely embodied, concerned with physical and facial gesture, rhythm, sound, pause and proximity" (see also Cremin et al., 2017). This is an approach that does not insist on words and one that suggests that the practice of silence might make us better speakers.

Likewise in Chapter 2c, the artists who work with Magic Acorns understand that their conscious effort to get adults to reduce their words is an "invitation to listen" and an "invitation to be present". Inspired by Bronwyn Davis (2015), the artists strive to "listen to children with all our senses". They see this as a mutual process where their own improvisational skills as adults and artists are honed by the children's expressiveness, which better supports them to tune into children's ways of knowing the world. In Section IV of this book, Ruth Churchill Dower similarly proposes a practice of 'body-listening', to be open to body-languages that are "unpredictable, intense and immeasurable" (Chapter 4c). It is this very unpredictability of how a body might respond that means we are never quite sure where the 'conversation' of a child engaged in world-making might go. The Magic Acorns artists (Chapter 2c) urge adults to "make friends with awkwardness and uncertainty" and to "[let] things become what they want to become", as a way to make space for these unpredictable conversations with the world.

Maya Leela points out in Chapter 2d that there is an irony about the silence of classrooms where children are sitting at desks, in contrast to the rich sounds of communication filling playgrounds where children are in a constant state of movement. We propose that the practices presented in Section II of this book all variously reframe the 'wildness' of children's playground bodies – as bodies that are relevant and productive in their emerging language practices and world-building.

Conclusion

We note with a degree of wariness that despite a lineage of pedagogies that have attempted to bring bodies back into early childhood education, it is the stilled, docile, schooled body that currently casts a shadow on early years provision (Moss & Roberts-Holmes, 2021). We note how the effects of these policy and curriculum discourses are negatively felt by all children but fall in especially heavy and punitive ways on bodies that are differently raced, classed, and gendered (Saavedra & Marx, 2016). Su-Ming Khoo points out our complicity with the silencing around these realities for some bodies, rendering the silence "an outcome, a symptom, as well as a root cause of oppression and injustice" (2024, p. 146). Let's support and join all the practitioners in the field committed to disrupting those silences with their ever-expanding repertoire of anti-complicit practices. In this chapter, we have highlighted the potentiality of the body as expressive and as a site for knowing the world and communicating with other bodies (both human and more than human). Nevertheless, the idea that language and literacy are divorced from the body, and that mind presides over matter, continues to dominate school and policy discourses in ways that stubbornly uphold a Cartesian legacy.

As an antidote to the wariness we feel about the neglect of the body in education, we are heartened by the collective counter-practices that are emerging in classrooms and other places. In these practices, the body is a site of resistance to the normativity and whiteness of developmental progress. We also note that there is scholarship that does recognise and affirm the unruly body: studies that show how children's unruly bodies are a means of resisting the straitening effects of the classroom (Galman, 2015; Hackett, 2022; Thiel, 2020) and research that points to ways that practitioners themselves are working more productively, rather than oppressively, with unruly bodies (Nxumalo, 2021; Ovington, 2023). In Chapter 2b, Williams and Shannon, both teachers with backgrounds in special education, share their collective classroom practice in a multisensory special educational provision for children in Year 1 and Reception in a primary school in Leeds. Resisting the tendency to describe children's (and particularly Black children's) unruliness as a behaviour problem, they propose that unruliness can be reframed as communication and language provision: a joyful act of resistance in the face of the narrowing of neurotypicality.

To end, we remind ourselves of the neoliberal capitalist context that early years settings are operating within. We turn to Alexander Means whose work honours the countless numbers of teachers and practitioners "who show up and struggle every day for dignity, connection, and community within schools, despite the historical determinations that are often quite intolerable" (2024, p. 484). As the practice in some settings reclaims the body as a site of resistance to the normativity and whiteness of developmental progress, *despite* the prevailing neoliberal education discourses, Means highlights that the institutions themselves are important 'sites of struggle'. Within those institutions, it is important to find and value those unruly spaces "where the work gets done" (Harney & Moten, 2013, p. 26). These are the spaces where potentialities play out in what Means describes as the many acts of care and resistance, the labour of activism, as we strive to transform all young children's lives.

References

Avineri, N., Johnson, E. J., Brice-Heath, S., McCarty, T., Ochs, E., Kremer-Sadlik, T., & Paris, D. (2015). Invited forum: Bridging the "language gap". *Journal of Linguistic Anthropology*, 25(1), 66–86. https://doi.org/10.1111/jola.12071

Barad, K. (2007). *Meeting the Universe Halfway: Quantum physics and the Entanglement of Matter and Meaning*. Duke University Press.

Blum, S. (2015). "Wordism": Is there a teacher in the house? *Journal of Linguistic Anthropology*, 25(1), 74–75.

Butler, J. (1990). *Gender Trouble: Feminism and the Subversion of Identity*. Routledge.

Butler, J. (1993). *Bodies that Matter: On the Discursive Limits of 'Sex'*. Routledge.

Cervenak, S. J. (2014). *Wandering: Philosophical Performances of Racial and Sexual Freedom*. Duke University Press.

Cremin, T., Flewitt, R. S., Mardell, B., & Swann, J. (2017). *Storytelling in Early Childhood: Enriching Language, Literacy, and Classroom Culture*. Routledge.

Cushing, I. (2022). Word rich or word poor? Deficit discourses, raciolinguistic ideologies and the resurgence of the 'word gap' in England's education policy. *Critical Inquiry in Language Studies*, 20(4), 305–331. https://doi.org/10.1080/15427587.2022.2102014

Davis, L. (1995). *Enforcing Normalcy: Disability, Deafness, and the Body*. Verso.

Davis, L. (Ed.) (1997). *The Disability Studies Reader*. Routledge.

De Freitas, E., & Curinga, M. X. (2015). New materialist approaches to the study of language and identity: Assembling the posthuman subject. *Curriculum Inquiry*, 45(3), 249–265. https://doi.org/10.1080/03626784.2015.1031059

Dernikos, B. P. (2020). Tuning into 'fleshy' frequencies: A posthuman mapping of affect, sound and de/colonized literacies with/in a primary classroom. *Journal of Early Childhood Literacy*, 20(1), 134–157. https://doi.org/10.1177/1468798420914125

Dernikos, B., Lesko, N., McCall, S., & Niccolini, A. (2020). Feeling education. In B. Dernikos, N. Lesko, S. McCall, & A. Niccolini (Eds.), *Mapping the Affective Turn in Education: Theory, Research, and Pedagogy* (1st ed.). Routledge. https://doi.org/10.4324/9781003004219

Enriquez, G., Johnson, E., Kontovourki, S., & Mallozzi, C. (2015). *Literacies, Learning and the Body: Putting Theory and Research into Pedagogical Practice*. Routledge.

Finnegan, R. (2002). *Communicating: The Multiple Modes of Human Interconnection*. Routledge.
Froebel, F. (1906). *The Education of Man*. (W. N. Hailmann, Trans.). D Appleton & Company. (Original work published 1887). https://doi.org/10.1037/12739-000
Fuss, D. (1991). Inside/out. In D. Fuss (Ed.), *Inside/Out: Lesbian Theories, Gay Theories* (pp. 13–31). Routledge.
Galman, S. C. (2015). Mischief-making of one kind/and another: Unruliness and resistance in rural preschoolers' free play. *Ethnography and Education*, 10(3), 310–324. https://doi.org/10.1080/17457823.2015.1050684
García, O., Flores, N., Seltzer, K., Wei, L., Otheguy, R., & Rosa, J. (2021). Rejecting abyssal thinking in the language and education of racialized bilinguals: A manifesto. *Critical Inquiry in Language Studies*, 18(3), 203–228. https://doi.org/10.1080/15427587.2021.1935957
Gatens, M. (1996). *Imaginary Bodies: Ethics, Power and Corporeality*. Routledge.
Grainger, K. (2013). 'The daily grunt': Middle-class bias and vested interests in the 'Getting in early' and 'Why can't they read?' reports. *Language and Education* 27(2), 99–109. https://doi.org/10.1080/09500782.2012.760583
Grosz, E. (1994). *Volatile Bodies: Toward a Corporeal Feminism*. Allen & Unwin.
Gurney, L., & Demuro, E. (2022). Beyond coloniality and monolingualism: Decolonial reflections on languages education. *Teaching in Higher Education*, 27(4), 502–511. https://doi.org/10.1080/13562517.2022.2035350
Hackett, A. (2022). Unruly edges: Toddler literacies of the Capitalocene. *Global Studies of Childhood*, 12(3), 263–276. https://doi.org/10.1177/20436106221117575
Hackett, A., MacLure, M., & McMahon, S. (2020). Reconceptualising early language development: Matter, sensation and the more-than-human. *Discourse: Studies in the Cultural Politics of Education*, 42(6), 913–929. https://doi.org/10.1080/01596306.2020.1767350
Hackett, A., & Rautio, P. (2019). Answering the world: Young children's running and rolling as more-than-human multimodal meaning making. *International Journal of Qualitative Studies in Education*, 32(8), 1019–1031. https://doi.org/10.1080/09518398.2019.1635282
Hackett, A., & Somerville, M. (2017). Posthuman literacies: Young children moving in time, place and more-than-human worlds. *Journal of Early Childhood Literacy*, 17(3), 374–391. https://doi.org/10.1177/1468798417704031
Harney, S., & F. Moten. (2013). *The Undercommons: Fugitive Planning and Black Study*. Minor Compositions.
hooks, b. (1994). *Teaching to Transgress: Education as the Practice of Freedom*. Routledge.
Ingold, T. (2004). Beyond biology and culture. The meaning of evolution in a relational world. *Social Anthropology*, 12(2), 209–221. https://doi.org/10.1017/S0964028204000291
Kašparová, I., Scutaru, B., & Millei, Z. (2023). 'When the body speaks back': Socialization of body-mind dualism in body memories of Cold War childhoods. *Journal of Childhood, Education & Society*, 4(2), 142–155. https://doi.org/10.37291/2717638X.202342278
Khoo, S. (2024). Response to policy and practice call on development education silences: Reflections on a pedagogy of non-silence – Resisting the politics

of hopelessness. *Policy & Practice: A Development Education Review, 39,* 145–158.

Lareau, U. (2003). *Unequal Childhoods: Class, Race, and Family Life.* University of California Press.

Leander, K., & Boldt, G. (2013). Rereading "A Pedagogy of Multiliteracies": Bodies, texts, and emergence. *Journal of Literacy Research, 45*(1), 22–46. https://doi.org/10.1177/1086296X12468587

Loeser, C., Pini, B., & Crowley, V. (2018). Disability and sexuality: Desires and pleasures. *Sexualities, 21*(3), 255–270. https://doi.org/10.1177/1363460716688682

MacLure, M. (2013). Researching without representation? Language and materiality in post-qualitative methodology. *International Journal of Qualitative Studies in Education, 26*(6), 658–667. https://doi.org/10.1080/09518398.2013.788755

MacLure, M. (2023). Ambulant methods and rebel becomings: Reanimating language in post-qualitative inquiry. *Qualitative Inquiry, 29*(1), 212–222. https://doi.org/10.1177/10778004221106756

MacRae, C. (2020). Tactful hands and vibrant mattering in the sand tray. *Journal of Early Childhood Literacy, 20*(1), 90–110. https://doi.org/10.1177/1468798420901858

Means, A. J. (2024). Beyond epistemic exodus in educational studies: A response to Jordi Collet-Sabé and Stephen J. Ball. *Journal of Education Policy, 39*(3), 480–489. https://doi.org/10.1080/02680939.2024.2328616

Moss, P., & Roberts-Holmes, G. (2021). Now is the time! Confronting neoliberalism in early childhood. *Contemporary Issues in Early Childhood, 23*(1), 96–99. https://doi.org/10.1177/1463949121995917

Murris, K., Smalley, K., & Allan, B. (2020). Postdevelopmental conceptions of child and childhood in education. *Oxford Research Encyclopedia of Education.* https://doi.org/10.1093/acrefore/9780190264093.013.1425

Nxumalo, F. (2021). Disrupting anti-Blackness in early childhood qualitative inquiry: Thinking with Black Refusal and Black Futurity. *Qualitative Inquiry, 27*(10), 1191–1199. https://doi.org/10.1177/10778004211021810

Olsson, L. M. (2009). *Movement and Experimentation in Young Children's Learning: Deleuze and Guattari in Early Childhood Education.* Routledge.

Ovington, J. (2023). The "Unruly" snowflake: (Re)imagining school readiness for two-year-old children. *Cultural and Pedagogical Inquiry, 14*(2), 61–73. https://doi.org/10.18733/cpi29681

Paechter, C. (2011). Gender, visible bodies and schooling: Cultural pathologies of childhood. *Sport, Education and Society, 16*(3), 309–322. https://doi.org/10.1080/13573322.2011.552573

Pawelski, M. (2022). Michel Foucault's figure of *les corps dociles* following a critique of the Cartesian *Cogito. French Studies Bulletin, 43*(164), 10–13. https://doi.org/10.1093/frebul/ktac017

Petersen, A. (1998) *Unmasking the Masculine: 'Men' and 'Identity' in a Sceptical Age.* Sage.

Saavedra, C., & Esquierdo, J. J. (2020). Platicas on disrupting language ideologies in the borderlands. In F. Nxumalo & C. P. Brown (Eds.), *Disrupting and Countering Deficits in Early Childhood Education* (pp. 37–52). Routledge.

Saavedra, C. M., & Marx, S. (2016). Schooling as taming wild tongues and bodies. *Global Studies of Childhood*, 6(1), 42–52. https://doi.org/10.1177/2043610615627929

Shannon, D. B. (2020). Neuroqueer(ing) noise: Beyond 'mere inclusion' in a neurodiverse early childhood classroom. *Canadian Journal of Disability Studies*, 9(5), 489–514. https://doi.org/10.15353/cjds.v9i5.706

Shilling, C. (1993). *The Body and Social Theory*. Sage.

Thiel, J. J. (2015). Vibrant Matter: The intra-active role of objects in the construction of young children's literacies. *Literacy Research: Theory, Method, and Practice*, 64(1), 112–131. https://doi.org/10.1177/2381336915617618

Thiel, J. J. (2020). Red circles, embodied literacies, and neoliberalism: The art of noticing an unruly placemaking event. *Journal of Early Childhood Literacy*, 20(1), 69–89. https://doi.org/10.1177/1468798420901816

Tobin, J. (1997). *Making a Place for Pleasure in Early Childhood Education*. Yale University Press.

Tobin, J. (2004). The disappearance of the body in early childhood education. In L. Bresler (Ed.), *Knowing Bodies, Moving Minds. Landscapes: The Arts, Aesthetics, and Education* (pp. 111–125), vol. 3. Springer.

Van Laere, K., Vandenbroeck, M., Roets, G., & Peeters, J. (2014). Challenging the feminisation of the workforce: Rethinking the mind-body dualism in Early Childhood Education and Care. *Gender and Education*, 26(3), 232–245. https://doi.org/10.1080/09540253.2014.901721

Wynter-Hoyte, K., & Boutte, G. S. (2018). Expanding understandings of literacy: The double consciousness of a black middle class child in church and school. *Journal of Negro Education*, 87(4), 375–390. https://dx.doi.org/10.7709/jnegroeducation.87.4.0375

2b

MAKING TIME FOR UNRULINESS IN THE SPECIAL EDUCATION CLASSROOM

Resisting the narrowing of neurotypicality in England

Yvonne Williams and David Ben Shannon

Introduction

In every primary school classroom, there are always bodies defined as 'unruly', whose movements and vocalisations seem both uncontrolled and uncontrollable. Yet, in the afterlives of the COVID-19 pandemic, an epidemic of unruliness seems to be unfolding in schools in England. More and more teachers seem to be identifying an increase in highly disruptive pupil behaviours. While we're very conscious of how the media and politicians like to complain about children's behaviour in schools, even we find it difficult to deny the significant shift in the wake of the COVID-19 pandemic. Based on anecdotal evidence from our own teaching practices with young children, and those of our friends and colleagues, and also commentaries by education professionals on social media, and by the mainstream press (Moss & Dunkley, 2024; Weale, 2023), we feel confident in stating that schools are dealing with a wave of unexpected and often unwanted unruliness. This is consistent with official data indicating a 57% rise in the rate of fixed-term school exclusions over pre-pandemic levels (bringing the rate of fixed-term exclusions to their highest since records began: Department for Education, 2024c). Plenty is already being said in policy, research, and practice about how to resist this wave of unruliness. In this chapter, we want to think about unruliness a little differently.

For a time, the authors of this chapter taught together in a multisensory special education provision in a mainstream (or 'integrated') primary school. At some point, we read Fikile Nxumalo's (2021) "Disrupting Anti-Blackness in Early Childhood Qualitative Inquiry" together, and its ideas resonated with our experiences of working in education. Nxumalo draws from her research with kindergarten children and their play at a local creek in Texas. She discusses how the word 'unruliness' is often used to describe Black children in schools in racist ways. To contest this, Nxumalo uses the word unruliness with the "intention" to "create fissures in conformity and normativity" and their inherent entanglement with "anti-Black logics that normalize the subjection of Black children's ways of being with the world to unrelenting surveillance" (p. 1197). In this way, Nxumalo writes about unruliness as a hopeful refusal of hierarchies that racialise both bodies and gestures.

Like Nxumalo, we want to resist the tendency to describe children's (and particularly Black children's) unruliness as a behaviour problem, to be solved by behaviour tsars, purchasable emotional-regulation learning schemes, or shallow performances of wellbeing. Instead, we want to think about the importance of unruliness as a key aspect of communication and language provision: a joyful act of resistance in the face of what we will term the 'narrowing of neurotypicality'. Below, we will trace some of what we think is at stake in national conversations around unruliness in the afterlives of the COVID-19 pandemic. We then draw from a few fictionalised examples of how our practice deliberately curates moments for unruliness. We argue that this commitment to 'making time for unruliness' is an important part of our speech and language practice in three ways: (1) that unruliness can be communicative; (2) that unruliness can be a shared experience; and (3) that unruliness can be an important antecedent to other learning.

The narrowing of neurotypicality in schools in England

We are both teachers with backgrounds in special education. Yvonne is a Black British woman of Jamaican heritage. She has taught in early childhood autism provisions for most of her teaching career and has also researched in an autism provision during her master's degree. David is a white British man. He taught primary and special education in mainstream schools until he started his PhD in 2017, and then again from 2020 until 2022. For a while, we taught together in the same multisensory special educational provision for children in Year 1 and Reception in a primary school in Leeds. David set up the provision when he started teaching at the school in September 2020; this was also the first time all children had been in schools together after many were closed for most pupils during England's first COVID-19 lockdown. Yvonne started working in the provision in March 2021, immediately after the second set of COVID-19 school closures. While working together, we shared a keen attention to issues of inclusion and equity. Our school serves a community that is richly diverse but subject to significant socioeconomic deprivation. Given the make-up of our cohort of pupils, and also our prior teaching experiences and our understanding of wider national and international issues of disproportionality, we were also invested in Black children's access to autism provisions. We discuss the matter of disproportionality in the next paragraph.

Nationally, issues of disproportionality have long shaped the access of racialised children to special educational provision. Black African Caribbean children, in particular, remain over-represented in the communication and interaction area of need compared to white children (Department for Education, 2024a). This reflects both a national and international pattern of students racialised as Black being over-represented in judgement-based categories of need but under-represented in provision for sensory and physical support. While the resurgence of the movement for Black lives in the aftermath of George Floyd's murder in 2020 had prompted schools in England to perform easily tweetable gestures of solidarity with anti-racist, decolonial causes (Gaztambide-Fernández et al., 2022), we were unconvinced as to how effective these gestures would be in reducing the number of school exclusions of Black African Caribbean children, which remain disproportionately high compared to exclusions of white British children, and in addressing the unequal access of Black African Caribbean children to special educational provision (Department for Education, 2024a; see also No More Exclusions, 2024; Strand & Lindsay, 2009).

As discussed elsewhere in this book, the emphasis on speech and language pathology has increased dramatically in the afterlives of the COVID-19 pandemic. Consequently, education settings target an ever-widening group of children for intervention to bring their communication and language practices in line with a narrower version of normal. However, we are conscious that this seems to reflect a more widespread pattern of narrowing what it means to be typically developing in the education system in England – what we're terming a narrowing of neurotypicality. With this term, we are referring to how, in recent years, pedagogy, behaviour expectations, and modes of assessment have become ever more unilateral, giving teachers less and less room to differentiate and try out alternative practices for their children. Scholars of critical disability studies, such as Jasbir Puar (2017), Alison Kafer (2013), Mel Chen (2012), and Kathryn Runswick-Cole (2014), have long argued that typicality and divergence, ability and disability, and capacity and debility do not "signify monolithically" (Sedgwick, 1993, p. 8). In other words, what it means to be disabled or to have a disability is flexible, existing in relation to a specific social, historical, geographical, and infrastructural context (Puar, 2017), whereby divergence (or neurodivergence) is the result of "events, actions, and encounters between bodies, rather than simply entities and attributes of subjects" (Puar, 2012, p. 58). Scholars have applied these ideas to understandings of speech and language pathology, whereby what it means to have disordered speech development has changed incrementally over time as expectations of 'normal' have shifted (St. Pierre, 2022). Specifically concerning education in England, we're arguing that to be neurotypical is to be recognised as possessing the neurotype, communication and sensory profile, and learning abilities and disabilities considered most valuable, most productive, and most closely associated with the idealised capacities of the capitalist, white, English-speaking child (Broderick & Roscigno, 2021; Shannon, 2020).

As pedagogy, curriculum, and assessment have become more heavily prescribed and more tightly focused in England since 2012, so too has the range of neurotypes for whom those pedagogies, curricula, and assessments are intended to *work*. For instance, since 2012, to be neurotypical means to have sufficient verbal working memory, rapid recall ability, and phonemic processing ability to (a) learn to read using systematic synthetic phonics and (b) achieve a score of 32 out of 40 in the statutory Phonics Screening Check (Department for Education, 2016). Having the abilities to learn to read using methods other than synthetic phonics, or to learn less systematically, or to refuse to read the fake words that make half of the word list in the phonics screening check, renders children as neurodivergent. Similarly, since 2017, to be neurotypical increasingly means to be able to control one's passions, interests, and bladder well enough to participate in formalised, desk-based literacy and maths instruction from the age of four (Ofsted, 2017). Since 2019, to be neurotypical means to have sufficient rapid recall ability and sufficiently normative executive function to pass a timed, computer-based multiplication tables check (Department for Education, 2020). Passing these assessments and learning through these techniques require increasingly specific configurations of ability and capacity: in this chapter, we're calling this increasing specificity the narrowing of neurotypicality. To be clear, we are not talking here about the raised expectations on pupils and teachers in terms of the *content* of the 2014 National Curriculum (although that's definitely part of it too). Rather, we are speaking specifically about how teachers are enabled to teach and assess that content. The consequences of this ever-narrowing, highly contextualised version of neurotypicality in England include the steep increase in the proportion of children and service users requiring funded special educational support.

In England, funded special education support takes two forms. First, there is a statutory process called an Education, Health and Care Plan (EHCP), which was introduced in 2015 to replace an earlier system called a Statement of Special Educational Needs. Despite previously being stable at around 2.8%, the proportion of students in England requiring a Statement or EHCP has increased by around 10% each year since 2017, reaching 5.3% in January 2025 (Department for Education, 2024b, 2025). A similar pattern is evident in the proportion of children accessing 'notional' school-level funding for SEN (Special Educational Needs) Support. Like the EHCP, SEN Support was introduced in 2015 to replace the older School Action system. The proportion of children accessing School Action had been *falling* for years prior to 2016 but began increasing again in 2017, reaching 14.2% in 2025 (Department for Education, 2024b, 2025). This rapid, long-term increase in the proportion of children requiring funded special education support has placed considerable pressure on school and local authority resources, prompting the Department for Education (2023) under the then Conservative government to admit that despite an "unprecedented" 50% increase in funding between 2019 and 2024 (p. 15), the system is both ineffective and "financially unsustainable" (p. 15). Consequently, in March 2024, the Department for Education (2024d) announced they were offering new places for up to 60,000 children in special education schools and nearly doubled the total number of special education schools (from 108 to 200) at a cost of £850 million. While there are likely numerous causes of the current funding crisis in special and inclusive education in England, we suspect that the shifting (i.e., narrowing) expectation of what it means to be typically developing (i.e., neurotypical) is contributing to the increasing proportion of children and young people who require additional 'special' educational funding to be able to access mainstream learning.[1]

To summarise our discussion so far, we think that children in schools in England are being subjected to a narrowing understanding of what it means to be typically developing: in other words, teaching and assessment approaches are designed for an increasingly narrow version of the neurotypical child. Consequently, more and more children find their learning styles and sensory practices labelled as non-neurotypical and rule-breaking: in other words, unruly. Little is being said, it seems, about the implications of this narrowing for special education funding or about its implications for *behaviour*. Rather than decry the present situation, our argument now pivots to think about how our practice together invests in children's unruliness as a practice of resistance against the narrowing of neurotypicality. Specifically, we want to think about the ways in which unruliness is a communicative practice and an integral part of our speech and language provision. We draw from examples from our own teaching experience that illustrate how we activate a commitment to unruliness.

Setting the scene for unruliness in our practice

Our multisensory provision catered for groups of up to six children from different year groups. The classroom was very spacious. It was dimly lit despite having windows on both sides. It was situated on the Early Years Foundation Stage (EYFS) corridor between two Reception classrooms, with direct access to the playground. The classroom itself was roughly divided into four themed quarters: (1) a carpeted area near the interactive white board (for stories, computer work, or one-to-one learning); (2) a desk-based area, partially screened off from the rest of the classroom by a bookcase (for fine motor skills work: threading, tweezers, and pre-handwriting formations with chalk, paint, and pencils); (3) a sensory area with a blackout tent, a glowing bubble tube filled with plastic fish, large felted cubes, balance and movement equipment, and various other sensory toys; and (4) a messy area with a large patch of laminated flooring and a table (for paints, water play, etc.). The walls were sparsely decorated: a number line ran the whole length of one wall and large pieces of sugar paper with pre-handwriting formations were stapled to a pushpin board next to the playground door. A row of red vertical Velcro task strips, each with a small 'done' bin and a picture of a different child's face, ran underneath the window looking out onto the EYFS corridor.

Unruliness as communicative (but not communication)

When discussing children's early language and communication practices, we think it's important to distinguish between what is *communication* and what is *communicative*. *Communication* is directed towards somebody else, for the purpose of informing them of something: for instance, communicating the need to use the toilet. However, children's or service users' practices can also be communic*ative*, even when they're not specifically intended to communic*ate:* for instance, signing the word for toilet just because you enjoy the motion might communicate your contentment to someone who knows you well. Teachers and other workers can develop deep, nuanced familiarity with children's or service users' individual 'vocabularies', which not only combine gestures, words, and intonations but also involve times of day and patterns of activity. In other words, the children may have specific practices that are communicative because of staff's familiarity with that individual's whole, unruly self. The practice anecdotes that follow illustrate some of these communicative practices and how they invite us to make time for their unruliness.

> **PRACTICE ANECDOTE 1: JUMPING AND LANDING ON ONE'S HEELS**
>
> Sometimes, moments of unruliness are preceded by subtler, more nuanced unrulinesses. For instance:
>
> - Jumping and landing hard on one's heels before pausing, as if to feel the shock ripple through the body.
> - Dragging one's bottom along the window sill or shuffling alongside sideways, like a crab, clicking one's heels together.
> - Tugging ever more firmly on a tooth.
> - Moving in some new and unexpected way, never before seen and never to be repeated.
>
> Ignoring these minor unrulinesses is likely to prompt further and usually more major unrulinesses!

Bodies need motion and some bodies need more than others. The kinds of movement described here are unruly in that they don't meet the definition of neurotypicality in those instances, which might be more likely to prioritise stillness, quietness, or 'walking sensibly'. They are also unruly in that they might not repeat, meaning they are difficult to prepare for and respond to. However, they are also deeply communicative for those who are familiar with those young people. We are not suggesting that bottoms are dragged or teeth are tugged for our benefit, in order to tell us something (i.e., communication). Rather, unruly behaviours are communicative of the need to behave, and unruly movements are communicative of the need to move. Those who are sufficiently familiar with children and service users and their preferences can interpret those gestures, and so the onus is on us as practitioners to bend our schedules and pay more attention in order to make time for unruliness. As discussed across the chapters in this section of this book, language and communication are sometimes thought of as above or higher than the body. The kinds of communicative practices we describe here might otherwise be thought of as too unruly, not just because they fail to meet the increasingly narrow expectations of neurotypicality that we associate with school but because they are visceral: entirely within and for the body, and perceived as altogether too removed from the realm of the 'neuro'. These examples run in one direction: we as practitioners are reading something off the visceral, embodied gestures of our young people. In the next section, we examine a more reciprocal kind of viscerality.[2]

Unruliness as a shared experience: intensive interactions

In our practice, we both use Intensive Interactions (Hewett et al., 2012), which is an approach for developing the fundamentals of communication. Rather than trying to teach children or service users to use spoken or gestural vocabulary, Intensive Interactions involve echoing or mimicking the other participant. If the service user finds your contribution relatable, they might echo it back to you again. Oftentimes this echoing gets a little louder, a little more exuberant. Over time, Intensive Interactions can often amplify minor unruly gestures into quite major ones. The practice example below is from David's PhD research project, which took place in a mainstream school with an adjacent special education provision.

> **PRACTICE ANECDOTE 2: SHARING IN SOME GRUMBLING**
>
> Abdulkadir (not his real name) tended not to bother himself with David very often. However, on this occasion, David joined him squatting on the carpet. Abdulkadir was tapping the floor in front of himself with the flat of his open hand, gently but repeatedly. David joined in with him, tap-tap-tapping with the flat of his hand. As Abdulkadir looked over, towards David, his hand turned, so that the sides and then the back of his fingers struck the floor instead: the slapping turned into a knocking, which David joined in with. He vocalised a single haughty laugh, and the knocking grew louder. He began to use his second hand to knock too, leaving short pauses, and David likewise joined in. This double knocking seemed to draw him forwards slightly, which David echoed and amplified until they found themselves scrabbling across the carpet together, giggling and vocalising.

In many ways, Intensive Interactions is quite a normative practice: it still encourages back-and-forth turn-taking and the kind of human-focused reciprocity that we associate with communication in its most normative forms. However, we also find that Intensive Interactions give the teacher or support worker an opportunity to join a young person in their own activity, such as the tapping, scrabbling, and giggling in the practice anecdote above. Moreover, this communication is without clear rules or boundaries and without a clear purpose or learning goal in mind. This resembles what Shannon and Hackett (2024), drawing from Édouard Glissant's (1997) concept of opacity, call "opaque reciprocity": exchanges between two participants with no clear outcome, which, "while 'meaningless', are mutually enlivening" (p. 127). In this way, our use of Intensive Interactions ever so slightly decentres the emphasis and expectations around words and vocabulary and makes space for a different way of communicating. For a few moments, the interaction actively resists the narrow and narrowing expectations placed on speech and language provision in the classroom, broadening what it means to be neurotypical for those few moments (Shannon, 2020). We encourage you to look at other examples of Intensive Interactions on YouTube to see how it might work in your own practice.

So far, we have discussed children's unruly communicative practices and an example of a shared unruly communication. In the final section of this chapter, we will discuss children's unruly engagement with sensory activities and how these feed into discussion of communication and language.

Unruliness as an antecedent to learning

Sensory activities are often thought of as a preparation for, or a break from, more formalised learning. From this point of view, sensory provision is understood as something worth investing in *because* it improves concentration or attainment in more conventional notions of learning. However, in the practice anecdotes below, we describe how the sensory activities of sprinkling and spinning are an antecedent to learning: more than just preparing children to access the learning, we suggest they are an integral prelude to the learning.

> **PRACTICE ANECDOTE 3: SPRINKLING AND SPINNING**
>
> Each morning, Yvonne lays out two or three trays of sprinkling resources. Children squat down in front of the tray, grabbing large handfuls of whatever is on offer, lifting their hands high above their heads and then sprinkling it back down: pencils, clattering on top of each other; fusilli pasta, tumbling like heavy rain; or grains of rice, trickling through fingers as they are rubbed together. Bare toes, fingers, faces, and sometimes even whole bodies scrunch up in a kind of glee, before pausing a moment and then diving back in for a second go: sometimes from a different tray (plastic keys or felt-tip pens over here, sand or balls of playdough over there) but never mixing them up.
>
> Elsewhere, some children like to spin, twirling on their toes for minutes at a time. On a table by the door, in the messy area, is another tray, this time filled with colourful plastic picture frames, with the transparent plastic

> 'glass' removed. Inserting an index finger through the frames allows them to be twirled around in a tight circle.
>
> These activities and others like them might happen before anything else, or they might accompany other, more formalised learning: for instance, twirling while singing the counting song, sprinkling while rehearsing phonics sounds.

Sprinkling might not immediately seem like the most obviously unruly habit, although really that depends on what you want to sprinkle. The clatter of heavier objects reverberates off hard floors and passes through thin walls. At the same time, the soft pittering of falling rice grains or the silent trickling of grains of sand is usually accompanied by vocalised sounds of approval. Likewise, spinning is its own kind of unruliness: spinning bodies take up space, while spinning picture frames risk spinning loose and flying across the room! However, spinning and sprinkling are also necessary work.

First, when the children engage in these kinds of sensory activities, it sets them up to carry on into the more formal learning activities that follow. For many children, these joyful, unruly practices are a necessary precursor to the more formalised learning that is now a big part of mainstream classroom practice. But these unruly activities are also an important prelude in that they inject some aspect of the children's interests and felt experience into their educational provision. This is different from the idea of using sensory activities to prepare children for learning, which requires that the activity makes some change in the child, for example sprinkling to calm down or spinning to 'get the wriggles out'. Shannon (2020) argues that this is the problem of inclusion: that it always relies on the malleability of the child that we wish was different, rather than on us changing our expectations of what it means to be neurotypical.

Likewise, the prioritising of certain kinds of sounds (sensible, reasonable talk as part of a dyad) over others (sprinkling, spinning, gleeful vocalising) in certain spaces and at certain times is based on a series of expectations around bodily capacities that for some children will never be appropriate. Yet, in reality, these expectations are unrealistic for everyone, because no body is or could be silent. Instead, in our practice, we try to facilitate children and young people to set the tone of their learning through pursuing their sensory interests. Wynter-Hoyte and Boutte (2018) use W. E. Du Bois' notion of double consciousness to explore how a black middle-class girl code-switches between church and school in order to disguise certain aspects of herself.[3] They argue that this prevents her from bringing her whole self to her formal education. In contrast, sprinkling and spinning, as examples of the highly specific interests children bring to our practice setting, allow them to bring their whole selves – moving and sounding and unruly – to the classroom.

Conclusion

In this chapter, we have described the importance of creating moments for unruliness in education: unruliness as communicative, as shared, and as a prelude to learning. Specifically, we have argued that unruliness can be communicative of the need for further unruliness, can be shared in mutually enlivening ways, and can help children insert some aspect of their personalities into the classroom.

Perhaps, in some respect, making unruliness part of the schedule stops it from being unruly: we'll leave it to you to decide whether or not that's acceptable. However, in times where neurotypicality is becoming ever narrower, hemmed in by unilateral approaches to learning and assessment, it's inevitable that more and more children will find their behaviours being labelled as unruly (where what is unruly is anything that is not neurotypical). Consequently, we argue that making unruliness an integral part of learning is an important social justice commitment.

Moreover, this increasing unruliness will doubtless be framed in racialising ways. In this chapter, we have tried to resist describing how this raciality unfolds in our practice experience. As Nxumalo (2021) argues, bringing attention to racial injustice is vital but also risks "perpetuat[ing] rather than disrupt[ing] deficit pathologizing frames of young Black children" (p. 1192). In other words, repeatedly describing instances of anti-Blackness in the classroom risks repeatedly inscribing them. Instead, we have argued for the importance of curating space for this unruliness in ways that have the potential to avoid or evade racialising frameworks. For some children, these curated pockets of unruliness will be necessary precursors, accompaniments, or interludes that are planned into more mainstream curriculum activities. For other children, the pockets of unruliness will be ad hoc, woven into the day as you realise that they're needed.

Despite embracing the virtues of unruliness, planned or unplanned, we are conscious of how unruliness of all kinds can be challenging for teachers. The unruly classroom is increasingly taken as evidence of the ineffective teacher, and teachers who can't rein in children's unruliness may feel self-conscious, or stressed, or that they can't get down to the business of 'proper learning'. We are also conscious that, as practitioners in a special education classroom with a higher adult:child ratio, we perhaps have more capacity to curate these moments for unruliness. Consequently, we finish this chapter with a few questions that might provide some ideas on how to make time for unruliness in your own practice:

- Can you make time for safe, manageable unruliness? If not, why not?
- Reflect on unruliness: did it work? If so, why? If not, why not?
- If children's unruliness happens at a time that's inconvenient, ask why: why did it happen now? But also, why is it inconvenient now? Is it *actually* (ever) inconvenient? If so, can you identify less inconvenient times for that unruliness?
- In unruly moments, teachers can often feel under scrutiny: ask why. Is anyone actually scrutinising you? If so, talk to them about it. Explain what's happening.
- How will you make moments for yourself to be unruly in the classroom?

Notes

1 We don't think this increase can be attributed entirely to COVID-19. First, the rise in funded SEN Support dates back to 2017, and local authorities were struggling to cope as early as 2019. Moreover, schools typically need two terms' worth of evidence before they can apply for an EHCP, and the EHCP writing process takes at least 20 weeks (although over 50% miss this deadline, taking up to 146 weeks in some local authorities: again, due to the sheer numbers of children requiring support). Consequently, we suspect that even the very earliest pandemic-influenced EHCPs could not have been finalised until autumn 2021 and could not have been reflected in census data until June 2022.
2 You can find more discussion and examples of the difference between communication and communicative practices in Chapter 4b, written by Willow Spencer, Jess Clarke, and David Ben Shannon.
3 See the Section 3 introduction (Chapter 3a) to learn more about code-switching.

References

Broderick, A. A., & Roscigno, R. (2021). Autism, inc.: The autism industrial complex. *Journal of Disability Studies in Education*, 2(1), 77–101. https://doi.org/10.1163/25888803-bja10008

Chen, M. Y. (2012). *Animacies: Biopolitics, Racial Mattering, and Queer Affect*. Duke University Press.

Department for Education (2016). *Statutory guidance: Phonics screening check administration guidance*. Gov.uk. https://www.gov.uk/government/publications/key-stage-1-phonics-screening-check-administration-guidance

Department for Education (2020). *Multiplication tables check: Information and guidance about the multiplication tables check*. Gov.UK. https://www.gov.uk/government/collections/multiplication-tables-check

Department for Education (2023). *Special Educational Needs and Disabilities (SEND) and Alternative Provision (AP) Improvement Plan. Right Support,*

Right Place, Right Time. GOV.uk. https://www.gov.uk/government/publications/send-and-alternative-provision-improvement-plan

Department for Education (2024a). *'FSM, Ethnicity and Language, by Type of SEN Provision and Type of Need -2016 to 2024' from 'Special Educational Needs in England'* (Permanent data table). GOV.uk. https://explore-education-statistics.service.gov.uk/data-tables/permalink/933cb2df-a4b4-48e3-4105-08dce44cbd16

Department for Education (2024b). *'Pupils in All Schools, by Type of SEN Provision - Including Independent Schools and General Hospital Schools -2016 to 2024' from 'Special Educational Needs in England'* (Permanent data table). GOV.uk. https://explore-education-statistics.service.gov.uk/data-tables/permalink/043bc41d-efc7-44d1-519b-08dca27efdd7

Department for Education (2024c). *'Suspensions and Permanent Exclusions - Full Year by Characteristic' in England between 2006/07 and 2022/23* (Permanent data table). GOV.uk. https://explore-education-statistics.service.gov.uk/data-tables/permalink/3520194c-2ba8-4b98-d50f-08dd12dee30d

Department for Education (2024d). How we're improving support for children and young people with special education needs. *The Education Hub.* GOV.uk. https://educationhub.blog.gov.uk/2024/03/26/improving-support-children-young-people-special-education-needs-send/

Department for Education (2025). Academic year 2024/25 Special educational needs in England. GOV.uk. https://explore-education-statistics.service.gov.uk/find-statistics/special-educational-needs-in-england/2024-25

Gaztambide-Fernández, R., Brant, J., & Desai, C. (2022). Toward a pedagogy of solidarity. *Curriculum Inquiry, 52*(3), 251–265. https://doi.org/10.1080/03626784.2022.2082733

Glissant, E. (1997). *Poetics of Relation.* (B. Wing, Trans.). The University of Michigan Press.

Hewett, D., Firth, G., Barber, M., & Harrison, T. (2012). *The Intensive Interaction Handbook.* Sage.

Kafer, A. (2013). *Feminist, Queer, Crip.* Indiana University Press.

Moss, L., & Dunkley, E. (2024). Pupil behaviour 'getting worse' at schools in England, say teachers. *BBC News.* https://www.bbc.co.uk/news/education-68674568

No More Exclusions (2024). Transforming education. In J. Virasami (Ed.), *A World Without Racism: Building Anti-racist Futures* (pp. 18–31). Pluto Press.

Nxumalo, F. (2021). Disrupting anti-Blackness in early childhood qualitative inquiry: Thinking with Black refusal and Black futurity. *Qualitative Inquiry, 27*(10), 1191–1199. https://doi.org/10.1177/10778004211021810

Ofsted (2017). *Bold Beginnings: The Reception Curriculum in a Sample of Good and Outstanding Primary Schools.* [URN 170045] https://www.gov.uk/government/publications/reception-curriculum-in-good-and-outstanding-primary-schools-bold-beginnings

Puar, J. K. (2012). "I would rather be a cyborg than a goddess": Becoming-intersectional in assemblage theory. *PhiloSOPHIA, 2*(1), 49–66. https://doi.org/10.1353/phi.2012.a486621

Puar, J. K. (2017). *The Right to Maim: Debility | Capacity | Disability*. Duke University Press.

Runswick-Cole, K. (2014). 'Us' and 'them': The limits and possibilities of a 'politics of neurodiversity' in neoliberal times. *Disability & Society, 29*(7), 1117–1129. https://doi.org/10.1080/09687599.2014.910107

Sedgwick, E. K. (1993). *Tendencies*. Duke University Press.

Shannon, D. B. (2020). Neuroqueer(ing) Noise: Beyond 'mere inclusion' in a neurodiverse early childhood classroom. *Canadian Journal of Disability Studies, 9*(5), 489–514. https://doi.org/10.15353/cjds.v9i5.706

Shannon, D. B., & Hackett, A. (2024). Opaque reciprocity: or theorising Glissant's 'right to opacity' as a communication and language praxis in early childhood education. *Discourse: Studies in the Cultural Politics of Education, 45*(1), 118–130. https://doi.org/10.1080/01596306.2023.2273336

St. Pierre, J. (2022). *Cheap Talk: Disability and the Politics of Communication*. University of Michigan Press.

Strand, S., & Lindsay, G. (2009). Evidence of ethnic disproportionality in special education in an English population. *The Journal of Special Education, 43*(3), 174–190. https://doi.org/10.1177/0022466908320461

Weale, S. (2023). Headteachers in England tell of worsening behaviour of pupils – and parents. *The Guardian*. https://www.theguardian.com/education/2023/nov/28/headteachers-tell-of-worsening-behaviour-of-pupils-and-parents

Wynter-Hoyte, K., & Boutte, G. S. (2018). Expanding understandings of literacy: The double consciousness of a black middle class child in church and school. *Journal of Negro Education, 87*(4), 375–390. https://doi.org/10.7709/jnegroeducation.87.4.0375

2c

LETTING THINGS BECOME WHAT THEY WANT TO BECOME

Uncertainty, improvisation, and resisting the tyranny of talk

Charlotte Arculus

Introduction

I am a co-director and founder member of Magic Acorns, a collective of improvising artists working with very young children. A characteristic of the projects I work on with Magic Acorns is that there is never a clear idea of where things are heading. Instead, we endeavour to hold possibilities open. Working with objects, music, and movement, and taking a playful, artful, and experimental approach, my fellow artists and I use very few words in our practice and instead find other ways of connecting and listening. This way of being becomes an invitation to other adults also to limit their words. Our working with fewer words has come as a response to the way in which words tend to pin the world down to a particular kind of certainty. I have found through my work with Magic Acorns that reducing words opens up the creative and expressive ambiguity of the world.

Our guiding principle, *letting things become what they want to become*, within set parameters (such as limiting words), relates to the concept of the *enabling constraint* (Manning & Massumi, 2014). Enabling constraints (such as, in our practice, reducing spoken language) create conditions for open-ended experimentation and emergent production. Taking the theme of this book, I discuss how body, place, and language might *become what they want to become* and what kinds of pedagogical and artistic practices and conditions enable this. Thinking about language in relation to Le Guin's 'carrier bag' theory (Haraway, 2016; Le Guin, 1989), I suggest that language is contained, containing, juxtaposed, woven, and related with everything else in the world. Carrier bag theory resonates in our work materially, with the many actual bags involved with Magic Acorns' practices, as I describe later in this chapter.

Magic Acorns spaces are places of adult uncertainty, places where adults don't know best. As such, they potentially act as decolonising spaces (Arculus & MacRae, 2022) as they actively resist what Cannella and Viruru (2004) identify as (Western) adults' profound lack of interest in the actual knowledges and abilities of young children. While children are excellent improvisors, adults can be very unsettled by not knowing what is going on. Resisting the pressure often felt by adults to always be certain, I want to discuss the ethical, pedagogic, and aesthetic potential of improvisation to *care* for adults as we *wonder and wander-with* children.

Introducing Magic Acorns

Magic Acorns is a 25-year-old collective of artists working with very young children. The company grew out of a visionary children's centre in Great Yarmouth in the East of England. I began working regularly as an artist facilitator at this children's centre in 2008, continuing the work of my colleague and fellow Magic Acorns director Jessica Pitt. When I joined the children's centre, its music and arts work was in dialogue with the emergence of the Early Years Foundation Stage curriculum in England and the roll-out of free nursery places for two-year-olds from low-income households. The centre was looking at how arts practice fitted with this new curriculum for children from birth to five years and how it supported children's development. However, the creative work that I and my fellow artists were involved with at the children's centre was understood as more than supporting development. The ubiquitous narrative of development that is attached to children's education tends to become the justification for arts funding. Nearly two decades on, I can argue that this development discourse, which focuses on *what children must become next*, tends to negate the idea of young children *in their present state* as citizens and art makers in their own right. At the children's centre, however, the arts work from the very beginning was grounded in social justice and an ethics of care for children and families. In addition, the Magic Acorns collective tended to resist the idea that art should be useful or instrumental, although we engaged with development narratives pragmatically when necessary.

When the children's centre went into liquidation in 2019 due to cuts and austerity, Magic Acorns managed to slowly and painstakingly establish itself as an independent organisation and now has its own dedicated arts space for children under the age of three. Although our existence is highly precarious, we no longer have to justify what we do in terms of children's development. We can care for families and emerging artists and offer a different kind of early childhood community space that is not about school readiness or discourses around talking. Instead, we can create artistic work where the fascinating ways in which young children know and experience the world can be made tangible to adults and valued for its creative potency. We open up 'present time' and explore what is possible when children, parents, carers, educators, and artists come together.

As a community of artists, Magic Acorns recognises the generative creative potential of working with young children. Our work aims to encounter the world alongside very young children, learning about what very young children are capable of *from* very young children themselves. We also learn what our own arts processes and practices do, through listening to and exploring with children. We recognise that arts practice and the state of childhood are intimately related. The ways in which young children think, sense, and experience the world are states of being which inhabit us "in parallel with all other self-formations [that] haunt the adult's poetic, amorous and oneiric experiences" (Guattari, 1995, p. 66).

Perhaps we can remember our own states of early childhood and how time and space felt very different. I have vivid childhood memories of texture, feelings, senses – a magic that is at the heart of my aesthetic expressions. Perhaps art helps us to remember how time, and place, felt when we were children? Perhaps young children help us to reanimate a different relationship with the world, where places are deeply resonant and materially felt and where time is experienced rather than measured. Researcher and author Heesoon Bai writes:

> Many of us may recall how in our childhood the world seemed like an enchanted place, not because anything extraordinary or spectacular happened, not because we felt we were very powerful and could make things happen at will, but because we could feel the pulse of life and mystery of being in every thing and every being that surrounded us.
>
> *(Bai, 2009, p. 141)*

An exciting and vital element of Magic Acorns' work is growing our community of artists. Our associate arts practitioners are drawn from across different arts disciplines and their voices offer fresh and ongoing perspectives on creativity and childhood knowing. It is fascinating to witness the invigorating effect that young children have on creative thinking when we open up the space and time to listen and connect.

Resisting narratives on word gaps and school readiness

As you can probably gather, Magic Acorns takes the state of childhood and our young child collaborators very seriously. This is a political stance as well as an arts practice. Our academic and creative outputs work to disrupt the story of children as adults-in-waiting – the child who will be completed only by reaching adulthood. It is really, really difficult, perhaps impossible, for adults to do this, but imagine if we could somehow stop constructing and talking about children as adults-to-be. Instead, we could take seriously the way in which children understand and experience the world, as a valid and vital way of knowing that is different to, but not less than, an adult's way of knowing.

There is a current focus on the so-called 'word gap' in early years. The word gap is a popular ideology, with questionable roots in its historically biased and assumptive research (see Cushing, 2022; Flores 2021). That there is some kind of word gap is treated as a fact and is cited in educational literature, government policy, and public-facing literature. Funding is rolled out and programmes are introduced that affect two-year-old children, their families, and educators. It is under (or in response to) these deficit narratives around 'disadvantaged' children that arts projects such as Magic Acorns are funded. In an era of neoliberal accountability (and cost saving) in early years practice, the professionalisation discourses of early childhood education are also creeping into and infecting parenting discourses (MacRae & Arculus, 2020). It becomes the task of parents to ensure their children are school-ready by fixing or improving their perceived deficits – such as lack of words – to secure a frictionless (low cost, high production) journey through state education. The perspectives of the young children themselves, what they are capable of, and how they understand the world are absent from the prevailing discussions around the word gap. The greater the independence (or distance) that our arts practice has from these discourses, the more we can support and advocate for adults working with young children and the more we can resist the domination of word-oriented discourses that eclipse implicit, bodily, and materially attuned ways of relating to the young child.

The idea that children are somehow incapable of expressing themselves before they have learned to 'use their words' is commonplace. We refute this at Magic Acorns. Instead, we advocate for the idea that children are inherently competent in making language. Expressiveness is always more-than-words, and babies and toddlers express themselves all the time to anyone who is listening and attending. With Hackett (2021), I suggest that children's language (spoken and non-spoken) arises out of creative relationships with the world. I suggest that rather than attempting to formally 'teach' homogenised skills of (verbal) communication to children, adults might start watching and listening to the ways in which young children already competently express themselves. We might begin to notice how language arises through the myriad and very different ways children engage with the world. Many linguistic anthropologists who are looking widely at different cultural practices – for example, Baugh (2017), Burman (2017), and Sperry et al. (2018) – argue that there is no explicit understanding of how adult talk relates to how children acquire language. In other words, we don't know very much at all, although a global perspective shows that there are many non-Western cultures where adults do not directly address young children and yet children gain language effortlessly (Avineri et al., 2015). Yet the UK state seems intent on rolling out multiple interventions aimed at encouraging parents and educators to be talking more to children at the exclusion of alternative approaches that are less heavily focused on talk. These interventions are directed particularly at what are commonly termed 'disadvantaged' families. Behind this term are racially and economically minoritised children, their families, and their communities (Cushing, 2022). Disadvantaged is an othering term that glosses over matters of class, race, and social injustice. Through my work with Magic Acorns, I have found that the label disadvantaged conceals the generative potential of rich cultural differences, parenting practices, aspirations, and forms of resilience that families bring to a creative space.

Magic Acorns' practice with young children has found that reducing our own adult talk is an extremely useful tool in stepping sideways into a place where different kinds of conversations can take place. It is an invitation to the other adults to listen and attend that is modelled sensitively by artist practitioners, never presented as a rule. It is an invitation to be in present time. Following Bronwyn Davies (2015), we strive to listen to children with all our senses, and, in turn, this hones our adult improvisational skills and attunes us to the way in which children know and understand the world.

I have noticed how children's conversations with the more-than-human world sometimes exceed the capacity of adults for such conversations (Abram, 2010). I understand, through hanging out with babies and toddlers, that communication and conversation do not privilege verbal speech acts but instead foreground a "mutually transformative sense of unfolding collective action" (MacRae & Arculus, 2020, p. 43).

Finding new ways to listen (to language)

During a Magic Acorns group, over time – which can be over regular sessions or a single event – a culture is mutually formed between parents, artists, and children. There is a rich sensual aesthetic to working without words; our senses are drawn beyond the explaining, narrating, describing, and naming the world that removes our attention from being of the world. By letting go of words, we become part of an emerging, multi-modal improvisation which words would distance us from. We have found that overly talking about things tends to stop this incipient co-produced improvisation in its tracks.

Our approach to language is that it comes in many forms. Words come out of a whole load of other, experimental stuff and cannot be separated out from those things. They might come – and this is an example I recently experienced – from a child who has been standing for 15 minutes at the edge of the room, appearing to be doing very little. If you are *listening* and *sensing*, the felt attention between the child and his parent becomes palpable. You can sense, and the child's parent can sense, that the child does not need to have any kind of intervention, does not need to be cajoled or verbally instructed. Parent and artist can take time to witness his exquisite, slow watching/thinking as he is pulled, drawn, allured, invited – all of these things – to move into the room, an exquisite encounter and conversation with, say, a roll of cardboard on the floor, as his hands touch and feel the corrugation of the cardboard and then meet with an artist's hand that has been waiting and attending.

We can think of these things as conversations. The etymology of conversation is to 'turn with' and the etymology of facilitation is to 'make easy'. Setting the conditions for easy and abundant conversation can start with touch, movement, and the body. Children will come to multiple Magic Acorns sessions, taking their time to have long conversations with the stuff in the room over weeks, months, and sometimes years. This might mean moving around the space, dipping in and out, or being in one place with a few things. In many ways this is like any early childhood education setting, but with our practice there is a lot less emphasis on defining what everything is (with words) and a lot more emphasis on improvising and experimenting with things. *Letting things become what they want to become.*

Where a child puts their energy, and what inspires them, may not always be about what adults or other humans expect, and that is ok. We want to work with that. We also strive to make Magic Acorns spaces very special for adults too – to care for and inspire children's adults and to open up 'present time' for them also.

Project examples

THE BEACH

We did a piece of work in autumn 2023 on the beach. It was exciting to be working outside, as we usually work inside. The beach space became a massive presence in what was happening. We brought a few items – steel bowls that reflected the sky and pieces of fabric that we could play with. These things combined with the wind and the wide-open skies – that was enough. It was almost too much, taking away those walls, that containment. The roaring presence of the world. Beaches as edgelands. Artists learnt so much from the children: how every child had different ways of being with the world, the beach, and us; how the children engaged with materials in a myriad of ways; and what happened with time. This was a tuning into the children's ways of knowing and being. It was also, for adult artist and adult carer, a tuning into our own childhood ways of being on the beach.

FIGURE 2c.1   Magic Acorns beach session set-up

IN BETWEEN SPACES

As another example, Magic Acorns' In Between Spaces project explored the aesthetic qualities of a huge disused department store in 2021, as families were emerging from lockdown. We worked with a vast space, light and shadow, acoustics, movement. Into this space we invited a single family at a time to explore and play in an unstructured way. We created an aesthetic experience that was spacious, communicative, and emergent. Every session was different; every child or baby provoked radically different bodily conversations with the materials and space. These conversations further invited us to experiment with each other and with the installation space we had created. We recognised that doing hardly anything was so often a powerful act of improvisation because it let things become what they wanted to become. We understood that the giving of space, both physically and temporally, to

> family groups was absolutely critical during this project. The doing of hardly anything became our expression of being present. This allowed us to sense connections through present time and offered space, stillness, and attentive distance. Because there is no rush, there is space to listen, and stillness to move into: an out-breath, an expanding of present time. Not knowing what will happen next forced us to reside in the present moment and the present moment unfolds into a deep space of connection and encounter.

What does participation look like?

Participation can look like doing hardly anything at all. We can reframe doing hardly anything at all as a generative act that resists the way in which children are rushed towards their futures. A child who stands by the door for 15 minutes is taking the world in – an inhalation, if you like – and we grown-ups cannot make assumptions about what they are feeling or what they should be doing. To wait and attend is to be-with, to slow down, to be curious. What might the child be hearing, watching, smelling, or feeling? To ask these questions is to experience the world, time, and space differently, to open up its magic.

In the example of the child standing by the door for 15 minutes, the child's mum left him by the door and sat somewhere comfortably. She was closely attending to him even though she was not talking at him. She was not narrating or reassuring verbally, but somehow her attention was felt by the child. They felt okay. There was no hurry. She didn't put any pressure on him by encouraging him to move into the room. Both child and grown-up took their time. Sometimes the drive to talk – or to be seen talking – comes at the expense of being present and at the expense of listening. Because, in this example, everyone waited and listened, the multi-modal conversation that gradually emerged between child and cardboard and artist and parent was beautiful, felt, and full of meanings and senses that were beyond words.

Parameters for emergence (and bags)

When we are setting up our spaces of invitation and care, we do not have fixed expectations about what the children will do. Instead, we think of it as setting the *parameters for emergence*. This relates to Erin Manning and Brian Massumi's idea of the *enabling constraint*, which I introduced earlier in this chapter. For example, reducing talk enables different (bodily, material) conversations to emerge. Or having an empty room enables different kinds of movement of bodies to emerge. The aesthetics of the space are important for creating these parameters; they inspire and affect how people (including adults) are in the space.

We work with the idea of magic: an experience that might be a shock out of the everyday, a shock out of habits. Ruby Holness, fine art student and Magic Acorns associate artist, writes about preparing to work with young children:

> We have been practicing a state of not knowing, working against the tide of certain teleological thought. For the artist, it is developing a readiness, creating the germinal conditions where something unanticipated may arise. Working with young children, it is obvious that the precarity and improvisation in play comes naturally and without thought. As an adult, the liminal space of not knowing is not inherently productive but is experience untainted by knowledge and we must practice receptivity to its potential for outcomes that are authentic and spontaneous.
>
> *(Holness, 2021)*

Bags are also important to our work. Carrier bag theory (Haraway, 2016; Le Guin, 1989) resonates in our thinking. We have so many actual bags and containers that are constantly emptied, packed, re-packed, re-ordered.

FIGURE 2c.2 Setting the space as questions

Transported. Bag contents are collated differently to set different parameters in the spaces where we practise. Bags somehow contain and restrain what can happen (and our thinking) while offering huge possibilities in the way they mix and reveal heterogeneous elements. We expect a mess to be made. *What are we preparing for to happen?* Or *How will the bags be unpacked (or repacked)?* is a better question than *What do we hope children will learn?*

In a way, everything is a question, not the sort of question that can be answered, but the sort of question that leads to further interesting questions.

How to reanimate a space

It can be hard work to reanimate an existing space or a practice, because it is easier to do things the way you have always done them. Our best advice would be to make friends with awkwardness and uncertainty. They are the portals that open up to something different. Dwell with awkwardness because connection and change lie within that feeling of discomfort. If something new is introduced to a regular group or setting, it might not work 'well' the first time. It will probably feel awkward, maybe out of control. It may not be interesting. It will almost certainly never go the way you expect it to. Make uncertainty your creative inquiry. Repeat, experiment, and work out what is interesting and expect that it will change. Keep changing things. You don't have to change everything all at once. Even with the same materials or room set-up, you might experiment with changing how you listen and attend to children. Can you attend with all senses? Can you (re)consider what is happening? Maybe you could have ten minutes in your setting where the adults don't talk (unless someone really needs to). It doesn't have to be a long period of time. What happens? What changes?

FIGURE 2c.3 Empty room, movement, and shadow

Can you introduce materials or objects with a more open-ended sense of what they are for or what a child might do with them?

Reflections from our collective of artist associates

The following quotes from Magic Acorns associate artists are taken from project blogs on our website. In these artist reflections there is a sense of (re)learning from children and (re)discovering different states of being. Magic Acorns' work also aims to foreground this child-time for parents, a place to play and relax, a space that offers a break from anxieties and the rights and wrongs about children's development that have somehow crept into the work of being a carer.

> Entering onto a child's wavelength takes breaking out of the adult world which revolves around unspoken rules, time and expectations.
> *(McSherry Birley, 2024)*

> Time disappears, this is what it must be like for a child playing.
> *(Watson, 2021)*

Similarly, musician and Magic Acorns artist Bella Askew writes of entering the child's space-time:

> I was […] no longer functioning as an adult or teacher equipped with training and academic theories but joyfully embodying a toddler and tapping into my innate spontaneity, imagination, creativity and playfulness. It was liberating.
> *(Askew, 2021)*

Composer Chris Dowding writes about 'small ecologies' emerging, rather than having a single point of focus – a characteristic of Magic Acorns' work:

> I think the immersive environment that we made lent itself really well to groupings and smaller ecologies. […] I don't think these kind of small group experiences would happen in a 'session' centred around one leader.
> *(Dowding, 2023)*

Small ecologies that work upon each other, generating creative, communicative, and affective resonance, are potentially a way in which language can also be conceptualised: words as one of many ecologies entangled with senses, materials, relationships, and feelings. However, to refrain from being an adult 'leader' who holds forth with words, spinning the world into existence and knowability with words, is not an easy practice. Musician Charley Jolly writes on (re)learning to improvise:

> I felt liberated. But it wasn't easy, on the first day I had to learn to let go of inhibitions and how to be silly, authentic and uninhibited with a group of people I had only just met. It made me realise that to truly engage in non-verbal play with young children you have to let your guard down and connect very quickly. But it showed me that if my focus is entirely on what is offered by young children, that it is always unimaginably fruitful.
>
> *(Jolly, 2022)*

Closing words

How might education, rather than being shaped by perceived deficits, be shaped by children's space-time, towards the not-yet imagined? How might children's wild conceptual and communicative capacities, which are always bound to the material and sensorial realm, shape their own language-making? How can we *think-with* children through moving, experimenting, and playing? What opens up?

I propose that arts projects in early education have the potential to become ongoing experimental conditions that pose questions without answers. They have the potential to become pedagogies of improvisation that bring children's ways of knowing to their own educations: this requires valuing the fertile intersection between arts and education and other early childhood practices (Arculus, 2024).

Letting things become what they want to become is a practice of creativity and improvisation in conversation with the world. It is what socially engaged artists do even though their work is chronically undervalued. Rather than justifying this work in terms of outcomes for children's literacy, behaviour, and cognitive development, we might begin to value what artists, educators, children, and parents are capable of doing together when they improvise together and how this will always be unique, situated, and unknowable.

Language is so much more than its ability to name, describe, and direct the world. Perhaps the ways in which preverbal children converse with the world can help us to begin to acknowledge the complexity and unknowability of the linguistic process. Perhaps we can begin to sense how words arise through time, out of encounters with matter and bodies. The language of adulthood can affect our relationship with the magic of the world. This is what words in adult mouths so often do: they teach us to stand outside the world and name it. Perhaps hanging out with young children has the potential to re-enchant the world – and the materiality of language itself.

I think about how children are constantly hustled through adult-made agendas of development and curricula, their time and space colonised, homogenised, standardised. This is a tyranny of rushing towards the future, reducing present time until we hardly notice it at all. As artists working in the early childhood field, Magic Acorns recognises not only the importance of aesthetic richness but also the ethical imperative to meet children in their own time and space, with curiosity and respect. I suggest that taking our foot off the accelerator pedal, finding our friendship with not-knowing, doing hardly anything, and resisting the urge to talk and control are *creative* practices with an inherent ethics of care and the potential to open up present time.

Whatever word games we might play with our funders, arts practices cannot be aligned with the predominant neoliberal discourses of developmental goals and targets or standardised measurements, because it is our difference from these things that matters. Our work is about resistance to these things, about embracing childhood itself as a wild, unknowable, embodied, more-than-words way of thinking and understanding the world.

References

Abram, D. (2010). *Becoming Animal*. Vintage.
Arculus, C. (2024). More-than-words: Reconceptualising two-year-old children's onto-epistemologies through improvisation and the temporal arts. [Doctoral thesis, Manchester Metropolitan University]. MMU Research Repository. https://e-space.mmu.ac.uk/view/creators/Arculus=3ACharlotte_Kathleen=3A=3A.html
Arculus, C., & MacRae, C. (2022). Clowns, fools and the more-than-adult toddler. *Global Studies of Childhood*, 12(3), 209–223. https://doi.org/10.1177/20436106221117569
Askew, B. (2021, December 17). Submitting to the present moment. *Magic Acorns*. https://www.magicacorns.co.uk/post/submitting-to-the-present-moment
Avineri, N., Johnson, E. J., Brice-Heath, S., McCarty, T., Ochs, E., Kremer-Sadlik, T., Blum, S., Zetella, A. C., Rosa, J., Flores, N., Samy Alim, H., & Paris, D. (2015). Invited forum: Bridging the "Language Gap". *Journal of Linguistic Anthropology*, 25(1), 66–86. https://doi.org/10.1111/jola.12071
Bai, H. (2009). Reanimating the universe: Environmental education and philosophical animism. In M. McKenzie (Ed.), *Green: Restorying Culture, Environment, and Education* (pp. 135–151). Hampton Press.

Baugh, J. (2017). Meaning-less differences: Exposing fallacies and flaws in "The Word Gap" hypothesis that conceal a dangerous "language trap" for low-income American families and their children. *International Multilingual Research Journal, 11*(1), 39–51. https://doi.org/10.1080/19313152.2016.1258189

Burman, E. (2017). *Deconstructing Developmental Psychology* (3rd ed.). Routledge.

Cannella, G. S., & Viruru, R. (2004). *Childhood and Postcolonization: Power, Education and Contemporary Practice.* Routledge.

Cushing, I. (2022). Word rich or word poor? Deficit discourses, raciolinguistic ideologies and the resurgence of the 'word gap' in England's education policy. *Critical Inquiry in Language Studies, 20*(4), 305–331. https://doi.org/10.1080/15427587.2022.2102014

Davies, B. (2014). *Listening to children: Being and becoming.* Routledge.

Dowding, C. (2023, November 9) The nest-games, guides and groupings. *Magic Acorns.* https://www.magicacorns.co.uk/post/the-nest-games-guides-and-groupings

Flores, N. (2021). Raciolinguistic genealogy as method in the sociology of language. *International Journal of the Sociology of Language, 2021*(267–268), 111–115. https://doi.org/10.1515/ijsl-2020-0102

Guattari, F. (1995). *Chaosmosis: an Ethico-aesthetic Paradigm.* Power Publications.

Hackett, A. (2021). *More-Than-Human Literacies in Early Childhood.* Bloomsbury.

Haraway, D. J. (2016). *Staying with the Trouble: Making Kin in the Chthulucene.* Duke.

Holness, R. (2021, December 10). Practicing a state of not knowing. *Magic Acorns.* https://www.magicacorns.co.uk/post/practicing-a-state-of-not-knowing

Jolly, C. (2022, January 8). Sonic possibilities: Remembering the arts of play. *Magic Acorns.* https://www.magicacorns.co.uk/post/sonic-possibilities-remembering-the-art-of-play

Le Guin, U. K. (1989). The carrier bag theory of fiction. In *Dancing at the Edge of the World: Thoughts on Words, Women, Places* (pp. 165–170). Harper & Row.

MacRae, C., & Arculus, C. (2020). Complicité: resisting the tyranny of talk. *Global Education Review, 7*(2), 43–57.

Manning, E., & Massumi, B. (2014). *Thought in the Act: Passages in the Ecology of Experience.* University of Minnesota Press.

McSherry Birley, A. (2024, March 13) Connecting with my silliness. *Magic Acorns.* https://www.magicacorns.co.uk/post/connecting-with-my-silliness

Sperry, D. E., Sperry, L. L., & Miller, P. J. (2018). Language *does* matter: But there is more to language than vocabulary and directed speech. *Child Development, 90*(3), 993–997. https://doi.org/10.1111/cdev.13125

Watson, H. (2021, November 9). Time disappears, this is what it must be like for a child playing. *Magic Acorns.* https://www.magicacorns.co.uk/post/time-disappears-this-is-what-it-must-be-like-for-a-child-playing

2d

FACILITATING EXPRESSIVE LANGUAGE THROUGH BODY MOVEMENT

Clinical implications

Maya Leela

In this chapter I share my journey, as a private speech-language therapist based in Trivandrum, Kerala, India, in which children taught me the importance of body movement for language acquisition, especially for verbal expression. I set out the observations I made, the lessons I learned, the methods I adapted, and the results achieved.

I work primarily with children whose first language is Malayalam. In Kerala, children are usually exposed to multiple languages, typically Malayalam and English, or Tamil, Hindi-Urdu, among others. In my experience, students struggle more with acquiring literacy in Malayalam, Hindi-Urdu, or Tamil than in English. Children with delayed speech and language skills were found to acquire English vocabulary faster than other languages. One of the possible factors here, based on my observations, is that the vocabulary associated with playtime/leisure time tends more to be in English – for example, the names of the toys and play equipment, and in entertainment such as cartoons/videos. In more formal environments, such as school, children hear more words in Malayalam. For example, it is the medium of instruction for actions like sitting down, following instructions, and obeying commands. It seemed to me that the place of language use made a difference in the acquisition of vocabulary. My students showed me that the language used while playing is acquired and retained better than the language that was used to limit them. These observations, and events and experiences in my speech therapy practice, inform this chapter.

Having trained and practised in a predominantly ableist society where 'talking' is the only accepted form of communication in early childhood development, I found that opportunities to explore alternative methods

DOI: 10.4324/9781032677927-7

were scarce. In India, the emphasis on making a child 'talk' during therapy still prevails. This is partly because families often switch between speech therapists until they find the one who can make their child talk. So, in order to be a successful therapist, there was nothing else to consider other than 'make the child talk'. We assessed, diagnosed, and rehabilitated children with that ultimate goal. If they didn't talk, their families were dissatisfied and the therapy was deemed a failure. Often, these children were not accepted by society. The purpose of speech and language therapy was to make children produce verbal behaviour that was acceptable by adult standards. It seemed we could not escape the 'tyranny of talk' (MacRae & Arculus, 2020) in which spoken language is the preferred mode of communication, one that requires a still or compliant body – as I go on to discuss.

In the early stages of my career, I was taught that building children's 'sitting tolerance' was a primary therapy goal. It was seen as a prerequisite to pre-linguistic skills and was implemented rigorously. We would make children sit and label flashcards or stack blocks, expecting verbal language to emerge. To even entertain the idea that early language learners use their bodies and environment as part of communication, we had to deviate from the sole focus on verbal skills. During my practice, I serendipitously observed that my students improved their communication when they had freedom of movement and less pressure to articulate. They often communicated effortlessly when there was an organic need. Even so, as an enthusiastic therapist, I used this newfound insight to continue pursuing my goal of getting children to 'speak in sentences'. Finding that children were more verbal when they could move freely, I began advising primary caregivers to encourage communication during movement-focused activities, rather than making two- and three-year-olds sit down to identify objects. I encouraged parents to let children explore their environment and initiate communication. The result was surprising. The children increased their verbal expression, both in quantity and quality. I didn't share this observation with anyone in my profession or make any official announcements. I wasn't even aware of the technical, medical, or biological terms typically used in Indian speech therapy academia to describe this phenomenon. From the evidence in my own practice of what strategies were successful for many of my students, I learned that language development is closely tied to body movement.

Here are some specific observations and reflections I recorded concerning movement and language:

- When encouraged to move more than usual, children with ADHD did not mix up the words 'look' and 'see' (words for towards and outwards direction were a major challenge for them).

- Dysgraphia and letter-mirroring generally improved when children wrote with their fingers in sand or flour or traced letters with their feet by running and jumping on letters.
- Dyslexia features lessened when children read while rocking or shaking their legs or when they had some object for stimming.
- Non-verbal children initiated verbal communication, starting with sounds of excitement and eventually words, when they chased bubbles or threw chickpeas on the floor and rolled with them.

Despite the substantial communication improvements that many children experienced through this approach, families found it difficult to accept. It appeared that prevailing notions of child development were focused on preparing young children for the 'adult-controlled space' (Yoon & Templeton, 2019) of school. Toddlers were taken to speech therapy to initiate verbal communication as a step towards school-readiness which included the ability to sit quietly. In this context, it seemed that speech and language therapy had an additional, less overtly stated goal. It was not just about supporting children's language but also about facilitating a separation between talk and movement, to encourage children's stillness during speaking and get them accustomed to being directed by adults on when to talk and what to say. My practice had developed differently, but the exhaustive work of helping caregivers to see and understand the importance of body movement and child-directed space for language development took up most of my practice time, leaving little time to research the topic. However, I continue to stand by my observations and learning and to insist that my students be allowed to move around as much as they like, with the rationale that this supports their language development.

So far, I have provided a short account of the evolution of my speech therapy practice with young children, in which speech is integrated with body movement. In the next section, I will look at two aspects in particular. First, I will report on the experiences that parents/caregivers shared with me about taking their child to a professional concerning speech delay. Second, I will talk more about what I observed in my therapy sessions when children were allowed to move freely and to direct their activities.

"Sir/Madam,[1] my child is not speaking like other children"

For most of my students, I was the second or third speech therapist the parents had consulted. These children had been taken to a hospital/clinic/institute with the primary concern that they were not speaking like their peers. This was followed by an assessment session, including a formal test, a diagnosis, and a recommendation for therapy. What happened in these assessments? Let me quote three of the parents verbatim:

> There were four people in the assessment team, they did not give my son time to settle down, they asked him many questions, but he did not answer. They gave him cubes to stack, but he did not understand the instructions and did not follow them. Altogether the assessment was finished in 40 minutes, and his verbal behaviour was different from that of at home.
>
> They did not interact with my son, instead they asked us questions, filled up forms, and gave a diagnosis. My son was very shy and quiet, he did not say hello or anything to them, which he usually does when someone comes home.
>
> I was made to sit outside; I saw them showing some pictures to my daughter and asking to name them. She did not name any of them even though she knew most of them. Then they gave her some blocks and asked her to make a tower. First, when my daughter entered, they said hello to which she did not respond, and they started the activities straight away.

Parents often said that their child grew withdrawn or quieter than usual, less responsive due to the new environment and unfamiliar people. Yet, it was the child who was seen as the problem by these assessors; the assessment report neglected the impact of surroundings and individuals on the child's verbal communication, and there was no follow-up session to evaluate the child in a more familiar setting. The child's unresponsiveness was simply attributed to their existing communication challenges. In India, healthcare resources are limited, making it impractical to demand prolonged interactions or extra sessions solely for assessment. These experiences are common in healthcare settings: a child comes in, and the practitioners assess the child using a standardised test, give a diagnosis, and recommend therapy.

How did my work with children change?

In my practice, I used to follow norms of speech and language development, and my assessments of children centred on a formal language assessment tool. With this, I measured each student's deviation from the 'normal' peer group. However, a one-size-fits-all approach failed in therapy. Each child's verbal behaviour was unique, because their speech and language development journey is personal and individual.

During the Covid-19 lockdown, I had an unprecedented opportunity to blend assessment results with therapy techniques in my practice. With sessions being online, I observed children in their familiar, comfortable surroundings, which allowed for their organic communication. I adjusted my assessment approach based on my online observations of the children's behaviours, tailoring therapy goals and techniques accordingly. My previous experience had made it clear to me that using a single template for assessment and therapy for a specific diagnosed disorder was ineffective and failed to honour the uniqueness of each child.

A key change in my assessment approach was requesting families to bring multiple video-recordings of their child to the appointment. I guided parents on specific scenarios to capture, such as the child engaging in activities like playing with water, Play-Doh, sand, or mud and participating in games involving running, jumping, climbing, or throwing, as well as story times, mealtimes, and an outdoor activity. These videos enabled me to observe how each child interacted with their surroundings through various sounds and gestures. I used these insights to offer children their preferred activities and toys in the therapy room, fostering a sense of familiarity and comfort. This method allowed me to evaluate children's verbal expressions and how these related to their environment and physical movements.

In raising the next generation, many in our society ask the question "why can't you be like others?". Two- and three-year-olds showed me a different perspective. They asserted their uniqueness through their verbal expression, through communication. Without me needing to delve into extensive readings or discussions, these children proved to me that their journey in language development was individual to each of them. When I attempted to categorise them based on age and gender, they would challenge the norms and make progress in their own way. I had to pause to grasp this concept and to ponder the daunting challenge of helping parents understand and embrace the idea.

Nowadays in my practice, the children I work with are not given scales or scores for their language abilities. I do not measure their language using any metrics. However, in my assessments and in therapy, I closely observe these children, noting their strengths, their challenges, and how they tackle those challenges. I believe that when assessments involve formal, artificial tasks, children lose interest. Without motivation and intention to communicate, children tend to avoid verbal expression. In contrast, when assessments are conducted in a playful manner – where there is no need for children to perform, and they can move freely and be themselves – the children show enthusiastic communication and eagerly include me in their world. Once the assessment is done and a child's strengths and preferences are profiled, then my therapy goals are set. The primary assumption on which I build therapy goals is that language is an expression of freedom and autonomy for children. My therapy approach seeks to create a space for them to feel that freedom and expand their communication.

The next section explores how this information changed the way I organise my sessions with children.

Let's move with the child and facilitate language

Allow me to share a story. I went for a trip with a friend's nine-year-old son, who was residing in the city and attending a prestigious school and whose teachers often complained about him talking excessively during class, causing disruption among teachers and classmates. Despite this, he is generally regarded as a well-behaved and compliant student. We took a trip to a nearby river, and he displayed a cheerful demeanour, engaging in conversation and singing during the journey. Upon reaching the river, he behaved in a remarkable way. Entering the shallow stream, he began splashing and immersing himself in the water, emitting a peculiar noise that resembled a joyful pigeon, cooing and grunting. This behaviour, unseen before, intrigued me, sparking my curiosity as to why he made such sounds only in this environment. The serene surroundings of the river seemed to awaken a unique vocal expression from within him, evoked by the coolness of the mountain stream, the echoes of the forest, the lush greenery, and the sense of absolute freedom.

This incident had a significant impact on my practice. It led me to reconsider the importance of physical freedom in verbal communication, the relationship between place, space, and language, and how to innovate in my therapy sessions. While I couldn't take all my students to a mountain stream for speech therapy, I could reassure them that they were free to move as they liked in the therapy space, and I could create conditions in that space to encourage child-led activity and movement.

Children being children

A child's environment is never tidy; it's often chaotic, with toys and objects scattered everywhere. A two-year-old rarely sits in one place to play; they are usually on the floor, table, or bed, engaging in various physical activities. Their verbal expressions naturally flow as they move. Sitting down is often linked to being quiet, even for adults. In Malayalam, the equivalent of 'shut up' is 'sit quietly' (*mindaathe irikk*). I now find this equivalence disturbing, as I had previously considered sitting still a pre-linguistic skill that children needed to learn. I have completely removed this pressure to be still from my practice and encouraged parents to let their children move freely, scatter toys, and take the lead in activities and games. For story time, I suggest that children sit on their caregiver's lap, prompting them to move their eyes and heads along with the adult's.

I have observed that moving speech therapy sessions to mats, and into occupational therapy rooms where children can run, jump, and climb, can lead to significant improvement in verbal communication development. However, for an independent practitioner without fancy equipment and limited space for therapy, incorporating movement into speech therapy sessions can be challenging. One effective strategy I have used is to scatter toys and books throughout the room, with mats on the floor for sitting, jumping, or lying down. Children can freely explore the room, interact with toys and books, and return to the mat for play or rest. All of these activities can promote children's language skills, by providing ample opportunities for joint attention, labelling objects and actions and interactions that encourage social communication.

What impact did this new approach have on my therapy outcomes?

- Children began to engage more with adults during sessions, showing recognition through gaze, head nods, and smiles. They patiently waited for their turn in shared activities, applauded the adults, and completed rhymes when prompted. They actively participated in communication using gestures and more words to request adult involvement in games.
- Children's enthusiasm for reading storybooks grew. They sat attentively on their caregivers' laps throughout story time, engaging interactively until the end. This was a significant improvement on their engagement level during the traditional table-chair settings.
- Over just four sessions, there was a notable increase in children's expressive vocabulary. They also demonstrated quicker learning of new action songs, mastering both lyrics and movements efficiently.

One of the most remarkable changes observed was the children's initiative to ask adults to repeat words or actions. For instance, while playing with bubbles, they would say 'pop' and then look to the adult for repetition. Similarly, when reading a storybook, they would point to a picture, name it, and then seek confirmation from the adult. This level of verbal communication dynamics had been particularly challenging to achieve previously.

I have often been told by parents that children must learn discipline early on, be made to sit still, and that verbal communication is the only normal form of communication. Some even threaten to find another therapist if I can't make their children talk. Despite this, I stand by my therapy methods. I continue to explore the relationship between language development and physical movement.

Conclusion

Children utilise language to express their intentions, needs, curiosities, and happiness. The way a child uses language varies depending on their environment and the people present. As children become more at ease with their surroundings and those around them, they become more inventive in their communication. The most common description about a child who is not interacting with the surrounding is that they are shy and once they get familiarised, they will open up. One could say that verbal expression is a personal and intimate behaviour that children reserve for people and places they are comfortable with. Unlike adults, children do not comply with social mandates on when and where to use speech and language. Language acquisition and development are not something that can be created within the standards of adults.

Children tend to use more language when they are in the playground. In a space where they can move freely, their body movement and verbal expression appear to be linked. Children scream, laugh, instruct, lead, follow, share, and enjoy themselves using language in the playground. When their bodies become quieter, such as when they sit down in a row or in the classroom, their learned stillness and discipline seem to trigger them to shut down and become passive listeners. Although this phenomenon is widely recognised, it has been largely overlooked in the practice of speech therapy in India. We typically have our students sit to participate in speech therapy sessions to work on their verbal skills. Given that young children tend to spontaneously vocalise and use language when they have the freedom to move their bodies, it seems counterintuitive not to have applied this principle to speech therapy sessions, which are usually structured as one-on-one language tutoring. Speech therapy in India has adopted a general approach where children sit and are guided through language facilitation techniques, similar to how they would sit for a pottery-making or calligraphy lesson. Moreover, we often use windowless basements or rooms that make the child feel restricted.

In recent years, my work has explored a different approach. As I write this and look back, my discovery seems like reinventing the wheel. However, if I hadn't been receptive to children's signals regarding the role of body and place in language development, I would not have gained this valuable insight. I would have remained convinced that language development can be dictated in an adult-controlled space and manner.

I changed my approach to assessment by observing children in their most secure and comfortable environments. I evaluated the language and communication they exhibited in that setting as their authentic language proficiency. I also evaluated these environments in terms of the extent, duration, quality, and freedom of movement children experienced. I adjusted my therapy methods and objectives to integrate these factors. I counselled parents and caregivers that it was a mistake to look to dominant, rigid norms of communication (St Pierre & St Pierre, 2018) and I emphasised that each child develops language uniquely and at their own pace. As a speech therapist, I strive to adapt the environment for each child, to encourage their communication and to deliver speech therapy in that context.

Let's conclude with the account of Kunjappi, a five-year-old who habitually apologises to his parents, believing he has done things wrong. Kunjappi, a late talker, struggles significantly with writing. Reading is relatively better, though still challenging. Teachers noted his underperformance compared to peers, urging parents to enforce more reading and writing practice at home. Internalising these critiques, Kunjappi now doubts his abilities in speaking, reading, and writing. He fears academic tasks and avoids literacy activities due to anxiety about failure. He shies away from participation, preferring silence. In response, Kunjappi's parents opted for a school change. They were invited for an admission assessment, and what follows is the parents' verbatim record of that experience:

> We took our son to a school for his kindergarten admission assessment. The room was small and had a steel almirah (cupboard) with charts, an office table with books and documents, and a table calendar with pictures of fish. Three rolling chairs were on one side of the table and one on the other end where the headmistress sat. They asked our son questions about his name, age, and asked him to identify pictures and colors on the table calendar. However, he refused to answer and turned his head away. The headmistress left to instruct a teacher to interact with him. At that time, he told us that the fish in the calendar was blue. Later, he was sent to the classroom where he was happy to see an aquarium and fishes swimming. However, he did not speak when asked to label things by the teacher or us. After the assessment, we were told that it was difficult to consider him for admission as he did not speak and looked troubled. We explained that he takes time to feel comfortable and only speaks when he feels safe. No recommendations were given. His behavior in public settings contrasts significantly with his behavior at home, where he fluently switches between English, Hindi, and Malayalam. While conversing with our domestic help in Hindi, he communicates with us in English or Malayalam, and with our parents, primarily in Malayalam during video calls. He adeptly distinguishes between the languages he uses. On the playground, his exuberance echoes throughout, even reaching our home on the third

floor. He particularly enjoys water activities. He engages freely with us, our parents, and his circle of friends, displaying a penchant for younger children. Kind and generous, he readily shares his toys with them. He extends his sociable nature to our adult friends, engaging in conversation if they show friendliness towards him. However, during evaluations, he turns notably quiet. After we came out from that school, he said sorry, as if he understood that he did something wrong that displeased the adults.

After this episode, I connected with Kunjappi through a Zoom session. He was in his safe and secure home environment, interacting with me naturally and effortlessly. He enthusiastically shared his toys, creating stories and scenarios with them. He moved around on the floor, playing with his toys, while expressing himself freely through language. Kunjappi crafted narratives and characters, eager for me to listen to his tales. I witnessed a child using his language skills in a situation where he was in control of his body and space.

Kunjappi's encounters with assessments and the challenges he faces at school have been deeply distressing for him. He is pressured to conform, displaying behaviours to please adults and meet their standards. Kunjappi was denied kindergarten admission due to not fitting the school's public image. Despite being agile, amiable, and vocal, he was quickly labelled as troubled and unsuitable for the school because he did not respond to the "what is this?" question in an artificial task, in a confined space, in front of an authority figure.

When grown-ups say we want young children to talk, it often emerges that we mean coherent speech – usually coupled with a still or compliant body, serving the purpose of school readiness. Kunjappi's story and my wider experiences doing this work bring into sharp relief the ways in which language, from a children's perspective, is so much more than this. Most importantly, language is inseparable from bodily movement, play, and the extent to which children feel accepted as themselves. We fail Kunjappi and many more children by forcing them to produce language on our terms and for the purpose of rating or grading their performance. In response, this chapter has proposed alternative strategies for creating spaces where children can claim and enact their authentic language capacities.

Note

1 In India we still use Sir and Madam when addressing others to show respect.

References

MacRae, C., & Arculus, C. (2020). Complicité: Resisting the tyranny of talk. *Global Education Review*, 7(2), 43–57.

St. Pierre, J., & St. Pierre, C. (2018). Governing the voice: A critical history of speech-language pathology. *Foucault Studies*, 24, 151–184.

Yoon, Y. S., & Templeton, T. N. (2019). The practice of listening to children: The challenges of hearing children out in an adult-regulated world. *Harvard Educational Review*, 89(1), 55–84.

2e

SPEECH BUBBLES

How play, joy, and storytelling open up expansive possibilities for language

Adam Power-Annand with Abigail Hackett

Introduction

How does communication affect how you feel?
How does how you feel affect how you communicate?

These questions lie at the heart of the work of Speech Bubbles, an organisation in England offering drama programmes in schools to support children's confidence and communication. Adam, the first author, is a theatre maker and the CEO of Speech Bubbles. In this chapter, we examine the Speech Bubbles approach, which focuses on the interconnection between feelings – of confidence, acceptance, joy, and belonging – and the ways that children and adults communicate with each other through movements, words, sounds, and bodies. The practice is grounded in the ethos that both confidence and communication depend on a positive environment for creativity. Starting with the environment, or how individuals feel and move in places, is the key to expansive communication possibilities.

At Speech Bubbles, we approach the question of 'What is communication?' as theatre makers. In theatre, the emphasis is not on vocabulary nor even only on words but on how we communicate with our bodies and with sounds. Words may be part of this but are not necessarily central or primary. Ultimately, we are interested in intelligibility – how do we understand each other best? Communication in theatre practice is also relational; rather than the onus being on an individual to make themselves intelligible, it relies on a collective effort to convey meaning. This leads us to a creative exploration of how children and adults can experiment and be open to expressing themselves and receiving information in many different ways. Children's capacities in relation to communication are not fixed – they depend on feelings, environment, and relationships. As adults, we see our job as providing the environment where children can experiment with communication in the most constructive way possible.

Developing the Speech Bubbles approach

Speech Bubbles started life as Speak Out, an Arts Council-funded research project in the London Borough of Lewisham in 2006, connecting primary schools and arts and theatre companies, with the aim of creating classrooms of children with confident speaking skills. Seeing the effectiveness of the practice, the next step was to structure the approach and the thinking in a way that was replicable and shareable. It involved asking the question 'What is making a difference here?' and as a result, the approach was refined and Speech Bubbles came into being.

In the current Speech Bubbles approach, a drama practitioner and a teaching assistant work with a group of 10 children long-term across 24 sessions throughout the year. We work predominantly with children aged five to seven years in mainstream schools. We also work in a range of education settings for children with additional learning needs, where we may well be working with children up to 11 years of age. The sessions draw on Vivian Gussin Paley's 'helicopter' technique (Cremin et al., 2017; Lee, 2016): children tell stories and adults scribe the stories, and then (bar safeguarding concerns or inappropriate content, which is rare) we act the stories out as a group. The stories are not collected or curated for future use – we celebrate them in the now. Over time and as the sessions progress, each group builds a storytelling culture of its own, and children tell stories they know their friends will love. In this way, the children create their stories for an audience. The audience they are creating for is their peers. There is a weekly flow of telling stories and acting them out, and the shared child-led development of the acting out, story themes, tropes, jokes, and relations, takes on great importance.

A whole-body approach to communication

As mentioned above, we approach communication as theatre makers and, in this sense, communication always involves more than words. Communication in theatre is largely embodied, concerned with physical and facial gesture, rhythm, sound, pause, and proximity. This whole-bodied approach to communication is nuanced and messy – why does one particular gesture work or one specific facial expression cause the intelligibility of the whole piece to fall into place? Approaching communication as embodied is often a challenge for educators, because it rubs up against the increasingly narrow ways that communication is defined and described in curriculum documents, and is difficult to measure in a standardised way.

Starting with the body necessitates a focus on feelings.
How we feel affects how we move.
How we hold our body is shaped by how we feel.
And because we are concerned with whole-body communication it is also true to say that:
How we feel affects how we communicate.
How we communicate is shaped by how we feel.

One of the things we are interested in is the relationship between well-being, self-esteem, and communication. We worked with Dr Jonathan Barnes, Canterbury Christ Church University, to explore this and evaluate what it was in our approach that was leading to children's effective communication (Barnes, 2020). Jonathan looked at the Speech Bubbles programme through the lens of personal and social well-being and its connection with communication. As well as session visits, and interviews with children, school staff, and drama practitioners, he studied the outward signs of well-being in participating children using an adapted Leuven Well-Being scale.[1] Jonathan's findings showed positive impacts of the programme on children's confidence, self-esteem, and empathy, as well as vocabulary and verbal and physical fluency. He pointed to the playfulness, the positive child-adult interaction, and the sense of a shared creative community as leading to those benefits.

Whole-body communication does not only involve an appreciation of the full range of affordances of the body and how it can be disciplined or used for communicative purposes. It is also always about feelings, identity, safety, and how children are taking up or rejecting the ways a certain context is positioning or narrating them. Importantly, keeping this exploration within a story world creates a safe and playful space for children. Instead of expecting children to talk about their own feelings, we can talk about characters, how the characters feel, and how their feelings might change how they move and communicate.

Some examples of this in practice would include:

- Movement games, where we encourage the children to move around the space with intention. Here we are giving the children the right to take up the space, all the while remaining thoughtful and considerate of each other.

- Mirroring games, because these involve paying attention to bodily communication by watching and reflecting how someone else is moving.
- Name games, inviting children to play with voice and physicality whilst saying their name. In a simple activity where everyone throws their name into a pretend bucket, we might practise throwing our name in our ordinary voice, in a huge voice, in a tiny voice and pairing that vocal quality with a matching physicality. To follow that up we would wonder with the children how else we might do this. The children are then free to come up with all their imaginative responses: like a robot. In a squeaky voice. Silly. Posh. Angry. And a million more!
- Games about body literacy. Can your body become different people or different things? If your body were a box, a car, a mountain, the sea, the sky, what would that look like and how would you move? Working together to take on being something different, by making those things with our bodies, leads us to a sense of shared representation and collective communication.

It's important to appreciate that this method of creation is exploratory and there isn't a single correct way of doing any of these things – rather, there is a whole spectrum of creative, personal responses. We are moving away from judgements of right or wrong.

Wondering and affirming

One important part of Speech Bubbles sessions is adopting the *I wonder* mode. This is best exhibited physically, with a wondering expression and stance as a prompt that seeks to elicit multiple answers or responses. Whilst it is not quite true that there are never any wrong answers, we try to ask questions that encompass lots and lots of possible right answers. *I wonder* removes the idea that there is only one possible answer to a question. For example, in one session, I was preparing the children to act out a story that included the line "the racing car that went so fast the paint turned from black to orange". Now that isn't an easy thing to represent! We wondered together: *How can we communicate this as a physical, bodily representation? How can we tell this part of the story with our bodies?* The group tried lots of different things and eventually settled on a physical and vocal representation of the extraordinary event. As the description was read out, all the children put their hands down to the floor – their hands began to shake on "the car went so fast", and when the narrative got to "the paint turned from black to orange" they raised their hands into the air showing their palms, with a roaring sound.

In this way, the starting point for communication is the body moving, and the end point is stories. The racing car story, like all the stories in Speech Bubbles, was collected by an adult scribe listening to the child author. The adult notes the story verbatim and then reads it back to the child to make sure they have got it right. Children can tell whatever story they want! The range of stories we hear is extraordinary: original tales, reworkings of known stories, wonderful mash-ups, as well as "what I did at the weekend", are all part of the mix. These stories are in the oral tradition; they are made for telling, acting, embodying; and they are not bounded by the rules of writing, grammar, or literary work.

A space for feeling comfortable

The essence of our approach is to provide a space for children to feel comfortable to communicate, a place to tell stories and have fun. Often, we are working with children who seem to use few words or who are selectively mute. In this context, our focus remains on creating a welcoming space, a place to belong, not on aiming to get them to speak. We might be thinking about body language, turn-taking, and asking ourselves: *Do the children look bright and engaged? Are their bodies open? What is their bodily communication saying?*

Often in school environments, we find children are withholding because there isn't a space where they feel listened to. For some children, the pace of learning in the Key Stage (KS) 1 classroom (Years 1 and 2 in England), with the pressure on curriculum delivery, can impact on their capacity to contribute. A busy KS1 classroom is also a challenging environment for the class teacher to give time and space to each child, especially children with communication needs who may require extra time to process instructions or to formulate and express a verbal response.

Accepting what children are bringing

Creating comfortable spaces for wondering and affirming is as much about the adult as it is about what children are doing. Our emphasis is on accepting what the children are bringing. All schools are unique, but with the move towards a 'knowledge-rich' curriculum and increased testing of that knowledge, there is less space for child-led or free-choice exploration. We work hard to demonstrate that in Speech Bubbles sessions we genuinely do want to hear what the children have to say, and we do not have a pre-intended, preferred response or answer.

Good questions to consider, as the adult facilitating a session, are:

- What is the relationship between the child's response and the question or provocation that I posed?

- How can my response, in return, accept and affirm whatever has been brought up?

For example, in one session, a group of children loved falling around on the floor. So, the practitioner Julie built the sessions around this, using activities that involved lots of falling on the floor, because that is how the children wanted to move and what they brought to the session. As the adult facilitating the session, it is important to look at how you work, as much as look at the children. Accepting what the children are bringing is really about the adult's mode. The freedom for the children comes from that.

The adult ear and the importance of listening to children

In education we often talk about children's voice, but it is also important to think about the 'adult ear'. We developed this emphasis on the adult ear after listening to Darren Chetty (2019) talk about his notion of the 'teacher ear'. He argues that the flip side of a focus on children's voices and engagement is that we also need to reflect on the role of the teacher ear. He asks us to think about to what extent teachers or other grown-ups are able to listen to the diversity of children's experiences – and whether having this listening teacher ear enables children to bring their whole selves into the classroom and into their stories. This is particularly important for white teachers working in diverse settings and for teachers working with a canon of children's literature and publishing which continues to consist largely of white authors writing about white protagonists. Chetty (2019) asks, "How do we, as teachers, listen to what children are bringing into the classroom, so as not to assume they have nothing to offer aside from what we give them?".

How do children feel listened to? Often, we need to work on training the adult ear more than we need to 'improve' the voice of the child, and sometimes this is a question of allowing enough time. We often find that children who appear to have communication needs actually require more time. They want to consider and arrange their response, and if we rush on too quickly there is not enough time and space for listening to them. The Speech Bubbles sessions aim to create a group ethos that understands this principle so that the group learns it is worth waiting. This can often be tricky, particularly for adults, and can involve a real shift to avoid the temptation to fill the silence or move things along. There can be an awkward phase or pause, but beyond that silence, if we wait, are new possibilities and ideas. We encourage adults to count silently in their heads. When you want to step in, to help, to move things along, give it another seven seconds. This strategy can be really helpful for an educator because it gives you something to do and provides an end-point to the waiting. It makes the wait purposeful.

Creating a space that is freeing

In the Speech Bubbles sessions, the drama practitioner and the educator (usually a teaching assistant) work together to deliver the programme over many weeks, building a professional working relationship. One of the things that we have had to consider is the fact that drama activity looks and feels different to many other things that happen in the classroom: it is physical, it takes up space, and it can at times be noisy. It asks children to behave in a different way than when they are at a desk. This is important because it frees the children up to move, make mistakes, make noises, experiment, and be playful. However, it can at times make school staff feel a little uncomfortable. One model we have found helpful for working with staff is Dan Hughes' (2017) PACE model (danielhughes.org). PACE is a framework of positive adult interaction which invites the adult to be:

Playful
Accepting
Curious
Empathic

As a model for educators, PACE is useful both as a way of creating a shared approach and as a way of checking in with each other at the end of sessions. We can ask each other:

- Did we demonstrate these qualities (playfulness, acceptance, curiosity, empathy) in our interaction with the children?
- Did we laugh during the session?

We don't teach vocabulary

Whilst we are aware that building children's vocabulary is increasingly high on the agenda for educational policymakers, as theatre makers we have a different relationship with words. As theatre makers, we love rich vocabulary and the power of words. However, in our work we start with what the children are offering in their stories, the physicality of what they offer, and then we consider how more words can get involved. For example, a child might tell a story of crossing a river as a dinosaur. We would start with the physicality of that and then ask what does it look like and sound like and, finally, how does language get involved in that?

Vocabulary has climbed educational policy agendas in large part because of the popularity of the theory of a 'word gap'. Originating from the work of Hart and Risley (2003), a small and heavily critiqued study of home language practices, the word-gap theory used data from 42 families to claim that working-class children have less exposure to vocabulary in the early years, leading to negative impacts on their communication and learning. The popularity of this theory has contributed to the direct teaching of vocabulary and in some cases the banning and policing of 'Tier 1' words[2] or words outside the scope of an academic notion of standard English. As the introduction to this book has outlined, research supporting the word gap is increasingly being challenged (Adair et al., 2017; Cushing, 2023; Kuchirko, 2017) and leading academics are beginning to explore whether, in fact, the bigger issue is how children's speech is perceived, assessed, and categorised. Our experience working with a wide range of children to co-create rich stories that start with bodies, feelings, movement, and play, before asking how sound and words might get involved, supports a view of language as being more complex, relational, and expansive than the word-gap theory and its focus on vocabulary might suggest.

We don't correct grammar

An important aspect of Paley's 'helicopter' method is retelling the story as it is given by the children. Schools are under increasing pressure to correct language and grammar, but this is something we resist. We often find we have to be extremely proactive about this, emphasising in training and in sessions that we *really do* collect the story how it is told.

There are important issues here about linguistic justice and the coloniality of schools being increasingly required to police and correct voice, to teach so-called standard English. This kind of policing is counter to the Speech Bubbles approach which, as we have described, is grounded in creating a comfortable and accepting environment for communication. There is an issue here of intelligibility and whether all parties are genuinely trying to understand each other: this is about the role of feelings of acceptance and belonging – for all voices – in positive communication and storytelling. As one of our advisory group, Warda Farah, says, "if the way I speak is accepted and valued, then I can belong. If you don't belong, why would you want to tell a story or contribute?".

In conclusion: "Tell me what you loved about it!"

In the Speech Bubbles induction session for participating school staff, we read out some children's stories and invite the adults to "tell me what you loved about it". This encourages a mode of being accepting and not critiquing. We also describe the children as artists. In this sense, it is not the job of the adults to improve children's stories. The adults' job is to engage with the story, value it, platform it, give it space. This mode of acceptance and engagement stands at odds with much pedagogical training which encourages educators to find the 'teachable moment' and 'scaffold' children towards ever bigger and better things (bigger and better according to an adult agenda).

We opened this chapter by wondering how communication affects how we feel and how our feelings affect how and what we communicate. In our work, we trace how best to facilitate the kind of whole-body communication that supports creative storytelling in an atmosphere of belonging and acceptance. Much of this is due to the stance adults take and the kinds of spaces and atmospheres they make available to the children, rather than due to children's individual competencies or skills. For example, we have found a great value in accepting and responding to what children bring, and fostering positive interactions, for their role in creating freeing spaces where children bring their whole selves. Reflecting on how (and if) we listen to children helps us make space and time for children to respond to the invitation to tell stories in their own ways and on their own terms. This involves thinking about language expansively, rather than over-focusing on vocabulary or grammar, and starting with the body and movement before asking how words could or should be involved. The success and longevity of Speech Bubbles, coupled with the richness of the work the children on our programmes produce, is a testament to how these kinds of approaches are not soft, fluffy, or optional niceties for working with children, language, and stories. They are the foundation from which the work emerges, starting with how bodies move and feel and culminating in joyful and playful communication.

Notes

1 https://learningjournals.co.uk/what-is-the-leuven-scale-and-how-to-use-it/
2 'Tier 1' words are vocabulary considered simple and frequent in everyday life. Sometimes teachers are encouraged to focus instead on 'Tier 2' words, which are considered more sophisticated and are more frequent in written texts than in oral language.

References

Adair, J. K., Sanchez-Suzuki Colegrove, K., & McManus, M. E. (2017). How the word gap argument negatively impacts young children of Latinx immigrants' conceptualizations of learning. *Harvard Educational Review*, 87(3), 309–334. https://doi.org/10.17763/1943-5045-87.3.309

Barnes, J. (2020). Improving children's social and emotional health by dramatising their stories. *Perspectives in Public Health*, 140(5), 255–256. https://doi.org/10.1177/1757913920927068

Chetty, D. (2019, June 28). *Beyond the Secret Garden* [Conference presentation]. The Thriving Child: The Royal Opera House Bridge Annual Conference, London, UK. Darren Chetty at 'The Thriving Child' – YouTube.

Cremin, T., Flewitt, R. S., Mardell, B., & Swann, J. (2017). *Storytelling in Early Childhood: Enriching Language, Literacy, and Classroom Culture*. Routledge.

Cushing, I. (2023). Word rich or word poor? Deficit discourses, raciolinguistic ideologies and the resurgence of the 'word gap' in England's education policy. *Critical Inquiry in Language Studies*, 20(4), 305–331. https://doi.org/10.1080/15427587.2022.2102014

Hart, B., & Risley, T. R. (2003). The early catastrophe: The 30 million word gap by age 3. *American Educator*, 27(1), 4–9.

Hughes, D. A. (2017). *Building the Bonds of Attachment: Awakening Love in Deeply Traumatised Children*. Rowman & Littlefield.

Kuchirko, Y. (2017). On differences and deficits: A critique of the theoretical and methodological underpinnings of the word gap. *Journal of Early Childhood Literacy*, 19(4). https://doi.org/10.1177/1468798417747029

Lee, T. (2016). *Princesses, Dragons and Helicopter Stories*. Routledge.

2f

COMING TOGETHER

Roundtable discussion on language as bodily and material

Charlotte Arculus, Rachel Holmes, Maya Leela, Christina MacRae, Adam Power-Annand, David Ben Shannon, and Yvonne Williams

This chapter takes the form of a roundtable conversation with different members of the editorial team (Christina, David, and Rachel) and chapter authors (Charlotte, Maya, Adam, and Yvonne). The discussion is framed around the following prompt questions (which are offered to readers in Chapter 1 in relation to this theme).

- What types of movements do our spaces invite, encourage, or make possible?
- How do (or could) children experiment with what their bodies can do in the different places where they play?
- Time to move: how does time limit or open up sense-making when thinking about language in early childhood?

Finally, we reflect on key messages and recommendations for action we hope readers might take away from this section of this book.

Reflecting on the chapter abstracts – what resonated in relation to your own work? What differed from your own work?

Adam: I just circled some words that resonated from each of them: *adults are quiet*; *improvisation*; *adult uncertainty* (which is something at the heart of our practice – we call it the 'I wonder' mode); and *space to move*. Improvisation is, of course,

	where my theatre-making background connects space for uncertainty.
Charlotte:	Can you say a bit more about the 'I wonder' mode?
Adam:	Yeah. So, I think it's a fairly standard approach in drama practice, which is to wonder rather than to question. It's that simple thing of wondering with the children, rather than asking them questions. Saying "I wonder what you were thinking?", "I wonder where we could go?", or "I wonder what that was?". Trying to wonder with the child, rather than asking them "what did you mean?" or "what do you know?". That opens up a much more exploratory mode which connected, for me, with adult uncertainty. Also, I really wanted to know more about *space for the unruly*.
David:	There was something in Charlotte's abstract that resonated with Yvonne's and mine – about the practice, but also the planning for that practice. It's like an oxymoron, right? Like you have to make a plan in order to improvise: planning time or space, or planning out the stuff that you need, so you can decide to do the unplanned things in the moment. Setting up the classroom, which is a really ordered space, in such a way that disorder can happen while keeping it functional. And that is the key tension around having those moments of what we call unruliness, after Fikile Nxumalo: from the outside, it might seem disorganised, but it can only happen because of the organisation of the space, the time, and the resources. Yvonne, you might have more to say about the difficulties of making space for 'unruliness' in our chapter, given that you're still actually in practice and facing these tensions. Things have definitely moved on even in the less than two years that I've been out of the classroom.
Yvonne:	Yes, David and I taught together in a multisensory, special education classroom and since he left the classroom, it feels even more like everything in schools – the planning, the space, the expectations – is moving towards what I call a box or a carbon copy. That's true for the children and the teachers. I explain it this way: I think outside the box, but you're trying to put me in the box. Then, if I'm being boxed, I start kicking out because it's not who I am. It affects the feel of the classroom and the children, so it becomes harder for them to have the space to be themselves, and to learn through the unruly moments in a more organised chaos. It's moving towards everybody having to be the same, which takes away the individuality of the

	children – because in my class there's six individual children, six individual mindsets, six individual ways of how they access things, which makes sense to me, and it makes sense to them. But, to move them away from that and put them into a more standardised way, to try to make them the same as everybody else in a mainstream setting, is going against who they really are. I'm having to deal with trying to put things in place to make them feel as comfortable as they can, but I'm finding it is getting more difficult for me.
David:	It's the same with classroom displays. You generally don't put too much stuff up on the walls when you're working in special education provision, you keep it fairly plain and favour a low-stimulus environment. But, increasingly, display policies don't allow teachers to make these kinds of choices. You end with the spread of carbon copies of the mainstream model.
Yvonne:	Yeah. The sector is definitely moving into standardising things like displays. There's less and less space for originality and tailoring your environment to your children.
Christina:	Maya, I saw you nodding a lot when Yvonne was talking about everything being the same and that issue of standardisation.
Maya:	Well yes, that is something that I'm fighting against. I'll have to literally use that word 'standards' with parents, with teachers, with government policymakers, whoever I am talking to. It's a cultural thing here in India. Everyone wants their children to be as competent as the next child, right? And speaking becomes one of those 'standards', as if there is no other form of communication. Linked with that, it becomes that there's no other way to behave, and there's no other way to be a child other than how everyone else is. Even very slight amounts of variation become an issue: let's say, eye contact. Again, and again, I have to tell people it's OK, the child is listening even if they are not looking at you. Parents will say "but he's not looking at me when I talk" – and I will say "they can still understand without looking at you", and I ask "why do you want him to look at you?". It's kind of a parental obedience thing: look at me when I talk to you, so the child has to look at the teacher or the parent when they talk. So, yes, that's why I was nodding. It makes me think of a new child I am seeing who sits in class and howls because he can't take it anymore. So yes, that is the box that he's been confined to.
Christina:	I'm conscious that Maya (as a speech therapist) and David and Yvonne (as teachers) are working much more with the weight

	of this standardisation. Whereas I guess for Charlotte and for Adam, they're coming in with an arts practice that can shake things up in a different way?
Adam:	Yes, one of the challenges is how to work in and with schools. It's important for us to work collaboratively. When one of our drama practitioners is working in a school, they work together with a teaching assistant (TA) to enable the TA and drama practitioner to work well together. We start the project off with a creative induction day that sets up the expectations and gives the two people a chance to connect. The different expectations and cultures of behaviour can be challenging: what does the school expect and what are the behaviours, or ways of being, that are effective in a drama workshop? What I have learnt in the more than 15 years of doing this work is that one way to overcome some of the tensions between those different expectations is when we approach the work as a task in common. With Speech Bubbles, it's about a group of people, children and adults whose task each week is to act out a child's story. It's the task that leads us; as long as the task is engaging and the children are interested in it, then you collectively work out what you need to do through doing the task. So, the question we are asking is what do we need to do to tell this story? This is different to individual learning tasks that might have a set of rules that seem external or abstract. This means we have to listen to each other and to work as a company. So, what might seem unruly in a school culture, for us might be everybody's ideas being taken up, being creative with them, trying stuff out and being imaginative. And when I say their 'ideas', I mean their movement ideas as much as their verbalised ideas.
Christina:	I really like the word company. At first when you used the word company, I thought of a business company, and then I suddenly realised, no, not in that sense, that what you were talking about was a kind of 'being in company'. That made me think back to what both Maya and Yvonne had described in relation to how they work with children. Maybe there's something about that idea of doing something 'in company' which gets erased in school environments?
Charlotte:	I think there's something about being in company that's not about a single adult or person leading. It's something that the young children that I work with are really good at, a kind of feeling into what's going on in the room. It's not a kind of dyadic thing, between two people, but more of a dispersed

attention. A kind of knowing in company. When you move with the company you are part of, then this takes on a life of its own and you're just a part of it. It's the sort of space that older children with special needs also get immediately. As well as unruliness I really like the phrase 'off-piste', because the moment it starts to go off-piste, I know I can start to relax, because what I have set out is working and so it's going OK. This means I'm out of control, so in that sense unruliness is a radical act.

There was also just one thing I just wanted to also chip in here, that connects to when Yvonne was talking about the box, which I really loved. Yvonne talked about the carbon copy of the mainstream model, rather than the individual, and how this boxes children in. It reminded me of a children's story that Toni Morrison wrote with her son, called the Big Box. I've only just discovered it, in an interview where she talks about ways that children are put in boxes, and about their capacities for resisting and getting out of them. She explains the effects of this boxed child in terms of:

The plight (and resistance) of children living in a wholly commercialized environment that equates "entertainment" with happiness, products with status, "things" with love, and that is terrified of the free (meaning un-commodified, unpurchaseable) imagination of the young.[1]

Maya, you talked about parental obedience. So, what are some of your strategies of managing that parental need for obedience on behalf of the child when you are working with children and their parents? It feels like you're kind of advocating, for the children?

Maya: What happens when they come to me is that in the hierarchy I'm above parents, right? I use my authority, I do this (*Maya points a wagging finger at an imaginary parent, and laughs*). But apart from that I make sure that either one of the caretakers or the parents is with me during the sessions: so, they see me with the child, rolling on the floor, and crawling and everything. They see how the child immediately transforms into a different person, and then they're fascinated. They want to know how that happens. So, actually, in some ways much of the time, my sessions are for the parents. I suppose it's kind of passed on through our generations – you have to obey the elders and the hierarchy is very rigid, and the expectation of speaking as directed by the adult. So, they see when I'm

	interacting with the child, that I don't really need the child to tell me anything in words: they're part of it, and I'm part of it. I tell parents this is the child directing the play, but even though they are the directors, I'm a choreographer. As the choreographer, I try to work with reciprocity so it always works both ways: I give them things and they do what they want with that and I gel with it. For example, I match my tempo of speech with the child's body movement: when they're jumping fast, I'm singing "Five little monkeys" at that pace. Then, when they're jumping slow, I'm singing at that pace. And I've had smart kids who would vary their movement tempo, speed, so they'll watch me to see if I'm going to change to match them. So, I'm always modelling other ways to interact with their child. I try to make sure that after three or four sessions parents come down with us on the floor and, yes, to be a companion, and to know that we are in company with each other.
Adam:	We try to have one open parent session during the year, when the parents are invited. We run the session the same, just with more people in the room. The task of acting out a story encourages the adults to join in and they invariably just want to have a go. It makes me wonder how much space there is for playfulness in many people's lives. I think the parents enjoy taking part and are playful because it's framed around us doing it for the children, but if we said "this is for you adults to have some play time", then that would be a different thing. So, the parents might be involved in acting out a story, and the six-foot guy is being the mermaid swimming in the sea. I think that puts them in company, even if it's for that very small moment – the adults in company with each other, with the children, and they just have fun. Even if we only have these open sessions once, it's still really important. So Maya, I'm really interested in what you were saying about how important it is to work with the adults in your setting. I am thinking about even if we only get a very small moment of it, it can make a big difference having that moment.

Time to move: how does time limit or open up sense-making when thinking about language in early childhood?

Rachel:	I think there's something really interesting around both the theme of time and of company which is important. Also, listening to everybody, words like 'rejection', 'refusal', 'resistance',

and 'unruly', and what came to my mind was a sense of all the possibilities within the children's anti-complicit practices. They seem to be almost resisting what we might understand as literacy, but this resisting opens up a broader sense and more radical edge of what literacy might look like. So, what young children help us to do, is to offer us subversive content – a more indeterminate and unruly aspect of literacy. I am thinking of the boy that Maya spoke about who was howling in the classroom because he had had enough, and other ways children use guttural sounds and other means to change the atmosphere, resist or respond to the demand to comply – and in this sense they are educating us, teaching us something different about how they need to express themselves, but often it can be us adults who are refusing to, or can't find a way, the time, or have the patience to really listen to them. So, yes, to return to that idea of time and company – giving ourselves time to be in company demands us keep 'unruly' spaces open so that we can stay attuned to what we might learn from these.

Charlotte: Yes, what Adam and Maya said also makes me pick up again on time, but in relation to resistance as well. It's like we're talking about small amounts of time or fleeting moments where things are changed somehow. These are moments where something is opened up, but also these small moments are kind of radical in the way that they change even though it is a small moment of time, like the six-foot dad being the mermaid.

Adam: In our work, time is very clearly marked out because we come into a school as a freelance practitioner and must work to the school schedule: the same time every week, with the same children. We offer 24 sessions across the school year, because we didn't want progress to be measured in short periods of time – like, "were they communicating by week six?". We wanted a period of time where they could really own the project, really know it, feel it, belong to it, and to develop it together. Often arts workshops in school are a one-off and, yes it can bring in an amazing moment, however having a lengthier engagement allows relationship-building – not only with the children, but with the TA who works alongside the drama practitioner. The TA comes to an induction day at the beginning of the year, works with the drama practitioner. Then through the year they're in there, they're modelling, they're doing all the things that children are doing. They're supporting us to understand the connection with behaviours, that school expectation, and cultures, sending messages back and forward to the teachers. Many TAs have talked about this creative time with the children being the highlight of their week and how it offers them a moment where they actually get to connect with the children in a completely different way.

I agree with Charlotte about those small moments that can be big: they can be real marker points. There is a child whose school attendance is appalling, and I was told that they only come into school on their Speech Bubbles day. That is because they want to be there, where things are given time. They are allowed to slow down, because all we do is we act out one story each week. Our drama practitioners haven't got a huge amount of curriculum to deliver to the children, so it can't go wrong in a way because we're not weighed down by this. You know, the curriculum doubled in Key Stage 1 over the last 15 years. No wonder everybody's stressed out. Now you're supposed to teach double the amount of information than 15 years ago. Of course you're stressed. If you as the adults are stressed, then the children don't stand a chance.

Yvonne: I think the thing about the curriculum is that before it was more free-flow for the children. On a typical Monday, we've got English phonics, play time, maths, lunch time, small chunks of time, and I've got to follow a certain plan. But now I try to make it my own for the children on Friday for English, because we have a whole hour. I work with music through the story, and with instruments. We push the tables back, sit on the carpet with all the cushions, with all the instruments in front. The children are happy, and all joining in. It could seem unruly, but they're actually following what the music session was planned for, and you have more verbalising coming from nonverbal children, more interaction between the verbal children, and also non-verbal children engaged through humming. A child who rarely speaks is now coming out confidently singing the songs and watching me play. She will stop; I stop; then she will start singing; and then I'll carry on. She's happily doing what she needs to do. The Friday session that I've incorporated is because it's for them in their realness, who they really are. It's a big opening for me, but it's about time – a time that I spend in my provision with my children doing what they need, away from all this rushing of the curriculum. It's a way for me to kick out of that box I spoke about before.

Adam: Yvonne, I wanted to ask you a question about how it feels to be the quiet subversive because it sounds to me like you're being quiet, but it's quite subversive what you're doing, from what you're talking about.

Yvonne: I feel like I'm on my own at times but also I'm the expert within my classroom, within the practice that I do. Like I said about the carbon copy and being in the box and the pressure to be like everybody else: I'm not that person. I'll do anything for those children and be their advocate. They cannot speak for themselves. Their parents are not at school. So, I'm the spokesperson for these six children, and I have to speak on their behalf. That's not being aggressive – it's me being passionate. Whilst they're with me, I'm kind of a signature on their life, if that makes sense.

Charlotte: It seems to me that you are listening to what they're capable of. You're listening to their capabilities and you're understanding what they're bringing to their own education. You're listening, and then you're advocating for that. That's a rare skill.

Christina: That idea of a different way of listening comes across so strongly across all four chapters. Adam's chapter talked about the 'adult ear' and trying to break that habit and to listen differently. How to listen to bodies and to move with bodies – that is what resonates for me in all of your different practices. Yvonne and David talk about it when they use Intensive Interaction techniques. And when Maya talks about moving with children's movements, it's a kind of responding as if it was a conversation of bodies. Charlotte's chapter talks about children having conversations with the world. That also chimes with Adam's chapter when he talks about how we feel affects the way we move, at the same time as how we move affects the way we feel. There's a kind of bodily reciprocity?

How do (or could) children experiment with what their bodies can do in the different places where they play?

Adam: Something about movement for us, is that because our collective task is to act a story out, we do this by moving. If we're going to act out being ducks or bats or mountains or whatever, we need to practise being all those things through movement. All those movements we practise build up a physical vocabulary through movements and emotion. We're always asking and showing in our moving: how are people feeling in this story? How are we going to show that feeling with our bodies? The other thing we do is we value copying – so, as the children are moving around, we'll encourage children to notice if others have a movement idea and if they like it, then copy it! It's quite a revolution. This is copying, a multiplying: copying is about connecting and being in company. For the children we work with who haven't been clinically diagnosed as having a communication need, but they're struggling in the classroom to speak, to understand and make connections: when they are in a different environment where they can move and make noise and say things that are maybe not completely on track, to be unruly for a moment or try an idea out, sometimes in that freer environment they can communicate effectively.

Charlotte: It's like movement as a kind of listening. The kind of movements and gestures that are produced in the flow of company, they are so often the kind of gestures that are sometimes cut short by the tyranny of curriculum. It feels like what we have in common is that what we're trying to create is a space where the movements can actually just flourish, a space where these gestures of bodies can actually take flight.

Maya: When I get a student for the first time and they are nonverbal, hand gestures are really important for me. For example, if they drop something, I make a sound "uh-oh" and then I make sure that I make the uh-oh sound every time something is dropped by anyone. Soon if somebody drops something, they make the sound uh-oh that goes with the hand gesture of picking something up. I make hand gestures for lots of things, and an accompanying sound, like with waving bye-bye, and chanting bye-bye in a sing-song way – even if it's not talking, there's a verbal expression going on there that accompanies the hand gestures.

Charlotte: Ah, yes – that kind of singing that emerges with minor gestures – that's what we call a micro-song in Magic Acorns. It's a really beautiful example.

Maya: I'm reframing and modelling to parents that movement is central. I also keep things a little far away from children, so they'll have to stretch and reach out. I might sit with them on the floor, facing them with toys. Then, after a while I will pick up everything and go and sit behind them, so they'll have to get up and change direction.

What types of movements do our spaces invite, encourage, or make possible?

Adam: How we organise space is important. We've already talked about hierarchy a lot. The first thing we do is we sit together in circles. Sometimes adults sit on chairs because they have a specific need, but on the whole, the adults will sit on the floor with the children. Even if the adult is sitting on the chair, there's very different ways of sitting on the chair as an adult: you can sit on a chair and lean in, or you can sit on a chair and sit back and be authoritarian. So, while we need to adapt around people's physical needs, the first point about a circle is that you connect with everybody in that circle – as long as the circle isn't too big, everybody sees everybody.

Rachel: Something that's coming across for me strongly is this idea about the importance of a kind of 'dwelling' that's typically overlooked. It partly goes back to time, and the speed of many of the settings, but it's also linked to the idea of the constraints of the setting that people find themselves working within – finding a place amidst what is often industrious and manic. I think Charlotte and Yvonne were talking about this so powerfully; it's about making a space where you can improvise as an adult. Yvonne and Maya are also resisting standards and norms by working with that sense of uncertainty and not knowing, by staying focused on being with the children. How do we live in that companionship for a while, dwell in it, when the pace of everything is so fast? How can we refuse clock time when we're not able to refuse it? Yvonne finds ways to do that.

Charlotte: The trick is always about how to open up those times: that's the magic of it.

Christina: Also, we have to remember that as adults it's important to create those spaces. We've heard so much from everybody about that pressure that's bearing down on us as adults, so maybe creating breathing space for us is necessary before we can begin to create that breathing space for children?

Adam: Yes, that connects to why I think having arts practitioners going into schools is important in creating that kind of breathing space. One of the hopeful things to hold onto every time they go into school, is that they go in with that 'artist' intention. But what I fear is that over the years, the drip, drip, drip of school environment and culture can eat away at that. The advantage of having practitioners from the outside and from

	an arts vantage point means they go into schools without that weight of the school week. They can come in with a new agenda: they don't know everything that's happened to that child; they don't know that that child was in trouble on Monday right through to Wednesday; so they can just receive them for that moment. One of the things that I try to do organisationally is find time for the Speech Bubbles practitioners to come together to talk and to remind each other of being artists, to shelter from that drip, drip, drip. There is a financial challenge, here, finding the time from that perspective, but it's so important.
Charlotte:	That coming together to talk is something that we build in now and we argue for it with our funders. I think it's about making the argument, isn't it – just as you would need for, say, clinical supervision? You need this kind of decompression time to really reflect on what's just happened and to discuss it with the people you're working with. This doesn't happen enough in schools of course, and always the question is how can more time be built in for this?
Christina:	Part of that idea of developing a different way of listening to children is about having this space to have those conversations at the end of sessions where we can pick out and share those small moments that are so big.
Charlotte:	Yes, it's almost a way of continuing the gesture and the movement through opening up fissures to keep those gestures in play, rather than the kind of staccato school-time where we move on to the next activity and the next. This intensive focus on separated-out time zones burns everybody out, and we're doing it to children. Teachers are doing it, and it's also a pressure that freelance artists become subject to. We need to find and open up those different temporalities, the openings, and fissures we create for ourselves and the children we work with.

Note

1 https://www.themarginalian.org/2013/07/15/the-big-box-toni-morrison-slade-morrison/

SECTION III
Place and language

3a

PLACE AND LANGUAGE

David Ben Shannon, Vishnu KK Nair, and Warda Farah

Introduction

This section of this book explores the complex relationship between young children's language and the places where that language happens. In Chapter 2a, we discussed the importance of materiality and children's bodies to their language use and development: for instance, how jumping, climbing, sand, and mud shape what children can or choose to say in any given moment. We introduced research and practice that showed how separating mind and language from the body and matter relies on racialising, ableist assumptions of what language is and who uses it. In this section, to build on these critiques, we will introduce research and practice perspectives that show how place is not merely a backdrop to talk but is deeply entangled with what and how children communicate.

Place is always political. Yet, it becomes depoliticised within the developmental psychology and psycholinguistics literature on language development in ways that result in punitive consequences for marginalised families. The work of Badwan (2021), Phipps (2019), and Flores and Rosa (2015), amongst others, helps us to think about the politics of how places are connected to identity and the importance of this connection to the relationship between language and place (Frieson, 2021; García-Sánchez, 2010; Martín-Bylund, 2018; Tatham-Fashanu, 2021). Within Euro-Western knowledge frameworks, language is usually seen as separate from place and capable of describing it. For instance, developmental psychologists Julie Dockrell and Chloe Marshall (2015) write that children's language "reflects an interaction between the intrinsic capacities of the child and the context in which he [sic] is developing" (p. 117). Here (and elsewhere), place tends to be understood as a backdrop (or 'context' or 'environment') to children's development and communication: this is a common understanding in policy frameworks and state-sponsored research. In this section, we want to push back against this dominant notion of place as only a backdrop to where talk happens and instead explore how using language is always an emplaced, *political* engagement with the world. Specifically, we argue that this dominant notion of place contributes to psychological and *physical* demarcations between the nation-state's 'standard' language and standardised forms (e.g., the Queen's English) and the practice of English and non-English home language(s). Following Flores and Rosa (2015), we describe this boundarying of place as *raciolinguistic*, in that it combines the policing of language with racialising logics. In Chapter 1, we posed three questions related to the entanglement of language and place:

- *What else* (in terms of objects, spaces, atmospheres, and so on) might be important to children and their language practices in our contexts?
- What might 'joining in with place' look like in our contexts?
- How might we create irresistible opportunities for joining in, which are welcoming and relevant for all children?

The chapters that make up this section of this book delve into research and practice that respond to these questions. Hackett and Shannon's chapter (3b) more extensively reviews some of the existing research into language and its relationship with place. Framing this relationship as the "entanglement of language and place", they explore how place shapes children's language, how children's language re-signifies place, and how place shapes the possibilities for listening to children. In this introductory chapter, we contextualise this work in relation to three themes in policy and practice: (1) the emphasis on blaming the Home Learning Environment for children's perceived language difficulties; (2) the English-centrism of classrooms in England; and (3) the normative understanding of the relationship between time and place. Crucially, across each of these three themes, we argue that place is often imbued with raciolinguistic ideologies, particularly when referring to the linguistic practices of racially minoritised, multilingual families.

Troubling the focus on 'Home Learning Environment'

The intensification of anxieties about children's speech, language, and communication development in the afterlives of the COVID-19 pandemic has largely been fuelled by concerns that parents and carers at home would be incapable of adequately supporting children's language development without the careful guidance of schools and other institutions and services. In other words, in policy and practice, some children's 'Home Learning Environments' are framed as substandard or insufficient to support learning, particularly in lower-income or culturally diverse communities. Underpinning this framing, as well as much research on Home Learning Environment (e.g., Department for Education, 2018),[1] is the idea that experiences in the Home Learning Environment shape language development in ways that might hinder or promote children's future language competence, with the implication that the responsibility ultimately lies with the families. While this might seem like common sense, we have two concerns: first, that it too narrowly configures what it is that place does for children's talk and, second, that it might too easily be used to reinforce deficit perspectives of children and families.

Language development is tied to developmental time in ways that tend to exclude or ignore place. When children's language is assessed in conventional ways, the assessment outcomes are assumed to show what exists *within* the child and *independently* of place, context, or the relationships between that child and others in the conversation: in other words, the child will demonstrate the exact same skills with a parent at home, a teacher in school, or a clinician in a testing facility. Similarly, place has been curiously absent in debates about the impact on language of COVID-19 lockdowns, during which children spent more time in some places (homes) and less time in others (classrooms, public spaces). Instead, there was a greater emphasis given to speculating on the presence or absence of dyadic interactions between adult and child in those places. Hackett et al. (Chapter 3c) unpick some of this complexity by looking at how "new encounters with different kinds of spaces and soundscapes" (p. 121) shaped the possibilities for language during families' visits to museum spaces in the afterlives of the pandemic. They take a view of language as relational-material: language is shaped by how bodies and minds encounter places and how they feel in those places. This is in stark contrast to how language is understood in education settings such as schools.

Education settings typically imagine place through ideologies of 'good languaging', where school comes to be thought of as a place for learning the ideal 'standard' language of the nation-state. Meanwhile, home and family contexts – particularly those that are translingual or multilingual – are devalued because they are understood as places lacking exposure to the standard language, especially the forms used in the education system (Flores & Rosa, 2015). Thus, the homes of minoritised families come to be understood as impoverished language environments, which frame minoritised children as 'deficient'.

Associating households with lack or deficit in this way exacerbates marginalisation and justifies surveillance. For example, some remedial approaches employ the Language Environment Analysis (LENA) audio-recording device, which can be physically strapped onto children as young as two months old in order to constantly monitor their language in different places. Described as a "talk pedometer" (LENA.org, no date), the LENA device is designed to count the different kinds of talk that children engage in, with the implicit assumption that the school ideal of 'standard' versions of language – including back-and-forth interactions with adults – should be universally reproduced in children's every environment (Nair et al., 2023). Remedial programmes and monitoring systems, such as LENA, and also more mainstream assessments, like the two-year-old check, are applied to minoritised families and children who are perceived to be lacking in 'quality' input (Figueroa, 2024), where 'quality' is equated with dominant and schooled language practices. In this way, raciolinguistic logics associate home with deficit and school with development. In the next section, we demonstrate how these logics infiltrate practice and policy for plurilingual children (or those labelled as 'English as an Additional Language').

Translanguaging, multilingualism, and 'English as an Additional Language'

According to national census data, a little over 20% of children in England are labelled as speakers of 'English as an Additional Language' (Department for Education, 2024): an increase of 2.8% since 2015. However, the framing of 'English as an Additional Language' downplays the complexity of what it is that children do when learning several languages at once. It can require children to switch between languages in different contexts: between English in the classroom and other languages at home, as well as between modes, cultural contexts, people, and their needs.

Classrooms in England are usually monolingual spaces where only English is welcome. Multiple examples from research illustrate that children often receive strong, raciolinguistic messages (both implicit and explicit) that English is the only language acceptable in the classroom (Anzaldúa, 1999; Badwan, 2021; Saavedra & Esquierdo, 2020; Shannon, 2020). Sometimes this is framed as beneficial for children, in that it teaches them what kinds of language are 'appropriate' for what places. The idea of 'appropriateness' simplifies how children often weave multiple languages together in complex ways, choosing between vocabulary, grammar, and syntax from across different languages to form new, hybrid languages that are often highly contextualised: this is called *translanguaging* (García et al.,

2021; Gurney & Demuro, 2022). Moreover, while the skill to use language 'appropriately' is often framed as an emancipatory practice that supports children to individual success, anti-racist researchers criticise this 'appropriateness' because it compels children to mask some part of themselves in order to experience and perform another identity for the benefit of the white gaze (Flores & Rosa, 2015; Nair et al., 2023). This illustrates what sociologist and civil rights activist W. E. B. Dubois (1903) and psychiatrist and philosopher Frantz Fanon (1952/1967) conceptualised as 'double consciousness'. Requiring children to set aside parts of their communicative repertoire in places such as classrooms gives children the message that their whole selves are not welcome in their schools (Baker-Bell, 2020). In Chapter 3e, Leala Holcomb explores the entanglement of signed language with place. Leala describes how places can become sanctuaries for people who use sign language. Importantly, they contend that some of these places are static (such as the home) but others are mobile (such as those created by signing together in public spaces), allowing signing families to bring their whole selves wherever they go.

Monolingual and raciolinguistic ideologies are further apparent when professionals in the UK use the term 'home language' to describe languages other than English spoken by plurilingual children. This framing requires neat separation of languages into English (associated with the classroom) and everything else (associated with home). Moreover, the term 'home language' is a singular form, not plural. It collapses the potentially multiple home languages into one assumed non-English language in the household. This undermines the acceptable or 'normal' linguistic practices of communities who use and combine multiple languages (Flores & Rosa, 2015). The neat, monolingual framing of the 'home language' associates non-English languages and home with deficit and lack: if school is the place of learning, and English is the language of school, then home is the place of neither. In Chapter 3d, Farah and Nair describe the potential impact of not welcoming children's whole selves to school and the role of place within this. Proposing the notion of 'spaces of reprieve', they recommend an embodied practice of "genuine connection and understanding" in order to make space for accepting children and their whole language repertoires. In this practice, the adult and child choose the physical space together, and the adult lets the child lead in the sessions: these are key ingredients in creating a space and relationship for deep listening and connection. Spaces of reprieve calls for a deeper interrogation of one's own ideologies in order to resist standard monolingual language ideologies imposed on minoritised children and families. In the final section of this chapter, we examine how these ideologies are tethered not just to place but to time.

Time and place

Disability and difference are often understood as related to time: the development of a skill at a surprising time (whether delayed, stalled, or too soon) points to a rupture between what and when was expected of a body and what and when those expectations ultimately arrived (Kafer, 2013). Likewise, age-related expectations are a temporal measure in that they associate a fixed point in the calendar year with an expected level of development. The language of 'developmental milestones', for instance, describes arrival at a predetermined destination, while the language of 'developmental delay' implies lateness in that arrival. St. Pierre and St. Pierre (2018) explain how early interest in speech correction was seeded from the post-industrial desire for rapid, clear communication and the avoidance of wasted time. Consequently, children are often required to communicate in ways that are efficient and do not take up unnecessary time, and their speech or speech development can be judged as moving too slowly or too quickly. Similarly, many of the concerns about children's speech and language development in the aftermath of the pandemic relate to time: whether children will hit their milestones *on time* after the *lost time* of the COVID-19 lockdowns. Deadlines for summative assessments frame children in time: the two-year-old check, the Early Years Foundation Stage (EYFS) baseline and end of EYFS judgement, the Year 1 Phonics Screening Check, and the Year 2 and Year 6 end-of-key-stage assessments all create deadlines by which children must achieve certain milestones in order to be deemed as developing at the 'expected standard'. Meanwhile, calculations of how children's language learning might improve over time are used to make targets (and, often, fatalistic predictions) for language development into the future. Some of these are anchored to each individual child's age, but most are attached to specific dates in the school calendar (e.g., the Phonics Screening Check always happens in early June). Importantly for our discussion of language and place, these understandings of progress over time are frequently tethered to metaphors of physical place. For instance, the terms 'milestone' and 'gap', which commonly circulate in education discourses, imply not only distance and time but also pace, place, and arrival.

Equally, concerns about the loss of *learning*, specifically language learning, through COVID-19 lockdowns are tethered to both time and place. The concerns rest on the understanding that hours spent in the home hinder the child's development while hours spent in the classroom expedite it. While these concerns might have reached fever pitch in the immediate aftermath of the pandemic, they continue in the form of alarm about children's school attendance levels. The attendance discourse is riddled with anxieties around time and place, which encourages schools to quantify individual pupils' absence in terms of hours of learning 'lost' by being away from school and to impose financial penalties on families to discourage future loss. Moreover, these narratives unfold disproportionately on children whose relationships with place are already contentious. One example of this would be the critique of families who take their children overseas to visit family during term time. The idea of a double deficit for these children animates much of the discourse: that learning progress is lost while the child is in a place that is not school and that (English) language progress is lost in the non-English-speaking society.

Conclusion

Dominant understandings and uses of place rely on normative ideas of *where* and also *how* and *when* children's speech and language skills should develop and be demonstrated (reproducible regardless of place and time). Each of the chapters in this section explores the complex and politically charged relationship between language practices and place. Understanding the role of place, and its politics, in children's language and communication is important because children who are deemed to have 'below average' language skills are likely to be subject to interventions that limit their interactions with other children and emphasise teacher-dominated interactions. This restricts children's opportunities to start or shape conversations, to use language in play, and to support each other. Farah and Nair (Chapter 3d) describe the impacts of judging and labelling a child as 'in need of' language remediation – a tag that proliferates in documents and practices over time, obscuring so many other facets of who the child is and what they can do. Likewise, Hackett et al. (Chapter 3c) describe how parents and other grown-ups can feel pressured into producing certain kinds of language practices in certain kinds of (public) spaces and the importance of hospitality for opening up a wider variety of ways for families to comfortably be together.

A recurring and common thread in this section of this book is to imagine bigger possibilities for how, when, and why children use language – possibilities that do not neatly fit into the linear and capitalistic versions of time that are predictable and only move in one direction. The section opens up interesting, complex, and expansive questions, including:

- How children use language in different ways at different times and places.
- How ableist assumptions of time are challenged when children diverge from linear developmental norms.
- How children can learn language at different paces and in different ways.

- How we can imagine futures that are inclusive and embracing of multiple temporalities (slow, fast, linear, circular, and many more) that prioritise care over capitalistic, productive, and disabling notions of time, place, and language.

Note

1 Research and policy related to the Home Learning Environment describe the importance of "physical characteristics of the home, but also the quality of the implicit and explicit learning support they receive from the caregivers" to the development of children's spoken language (Department for Education, 2018, p. 6).

References

Anzaldúa, G. (1999). *Borderland / La Frontera: The New Mestiza*. Aunt Lute.

Badwan, K. (2021). Unmooring language for social justice: Young people talking about language in place in Manchester, UK. *Critical Inquiry in Language Studies*, 18(2), 153–173.

Baker-Bell, A. (2020). *Linguistic Justice: Black Language, Literacy Identity, and Pedagogy*. Routledge.

Department for Education (2018). *Improving the Home Learning Environment: A Behaviour Change Approach*. Available at: https://www.gov.uk/government/publications/improving-the-home-learning-environment

Department for Education (2024). *'Pupil Characteristics - Number of Pupils by Ethnicity and Language' for Known or Believed to be English, Known or Believed to Be Other Than English, Non-maintained Special School, State-Funded AP School, State-Funded Nursery and 3 Other Filters in England between 2015/16 and 2023/24*. Available at: https://explore-education-statistics.service.gov.uk/data-tables/permalink/badd2b33-d42f-44be-a5f1-08dca1277804

Dockrell, J. E., & Marshall, C. R. (2015). Measurement issues: Assessing language skills in young children. *Child and Adolescent Mental Health*, 20(2), 116–125.

Du Bois, W. E. (1903). The Souls of Black Folk. Greenwich.

Fanon, F. (1967). *Black Skin, White Masks*. (3rd ed.) (C. Markmann, trans.). Pluto Press. (1952).

Figueroa, M. (2024). Language development, linguistic input, and linguistic racism. *WIREs Cognitive Science*, 15(3), e1673. https://doi.org/10.1002/wcs.1673

Flores, N., & Rosa, J. (2015). Undoing appropriateness: Raciolinguistic ideologies and language diversity in education. *Harvard Educational Review*, 85(2), 149–171.

Frieson, B. L. (2021). Remixin' and flown' in centros: Exploring the biliteracy practices of Black language speakers in an elementary two-way immersion bilingual program. *Race Ethnicity and Education*, 25(4), 585–605. https://doi.org/10.1080/13613324.2021.1890568

García-Sánchez, I. M. (2010). Serious games: Code-switching and gendered identities in Moroccan immigrant girls' pretend play. *Pragmatics*, 20(4), 523–555.

García, O., Flores, N., Seltzer, K., Wei, L., Otheguy, R., & Rosa, J. (2021). Rejecting abyssal thinking in the language and education of racialized bilinguals: A manifesto. *Critical Inquiry in Language Studies*, *18*(3), 203–228.

Gurney, L., & Demuro, E. (2022). Tracing new ground, from language to languaging, and from languaging to assemblages: Rethinking languaging through the multilingual and ontological turns. *International Journal of Multilingualism*, *19*(3), 305–324.

Kafer, A. (2013). *Feminist, Queer, Crip*. Indiana University Press.

Martín-Bylund, A. (2018). The matter of silence in early childhood bilingual education. *Educational Philosophy and Theory*, *50*(4), 349–358.

Nair, V., Farah, W., & Cushing, I. (2023). A critical analysis of standardised testing in speech and language therapy. *Language, Speech and Hearing Services in Schools*, *54*(3), 781–793.

Phipps, A. (2019). *Decolonising Multilingualism. Struggles to Decreate*. De Gruyter.

Saavedra, C., & Esquierdo, J. J. (2020). Platicas on disrupting language ideologies in the borderlands. In F. Nxumalo & C. P. Brown (Eds.), *Disrupting and Countering Deficits in Early Childhood Education* (pp. 37–52). Routledge.

Shannon, D. B. (2020). Neuroqueer(ing) noise: Beyond 'mere inclusion' in a neurodiverse early childhood classroom. *Canadian Journal of Disability Studies*, *9*(5), 489–514.

St. Pierre, J., & St. Pierre, C. (2018). Governing the voice: A critical history of speech-language pathology. *Foucault Studies*, *24*, 151–184.

Tatham-Fashanu, C. (2021). A third space pedagogy: Embracing complexity in a super-diverse, early childhood education setting. *Pedagogy, Culture and Society*, *31*(4), 863–881. https://doi.org/10.1080/14681366.2021.1952295.

3b

RESEARCHING LANGUAGE AND PLACE

What is the evidence base?

Abigail Hackett and David Ben Shannon

Introduction: the entanglement of language and place

What do we know about the connection between children's language and place? In 2022, we carried out a literature review to address this question. We drew from several different fields – primarily from scholarship in early childhood education, developmental psychology, and anthropology, as well as policy and curricula documents – to explore how early language emerges with and through children's embodiment in place. The review was funded by Manchester Metropolitan University and published in the journal *Critical Inquiry in Language Studies* (Shannon & Hackett, 2024).[1] In this chapter, we summarise some key themes and research findings that explore the complex connection between place and *when*, *why*, and *how* young children communicate: we theorise this complex relationship as *entanglement*.

We conducted this review of the literature for two reasons. First, within our own research and professional practice, we noted the significance of place and the body for when and how children use language. However, we found ourselves struggling for the theoretical tools necessary to make sense of this entanglement. Our aim in this review, then, was to identify scholarship from different disciplines that foregrounds the significance of place, in order to begin building a conceptual frame for how we might investigate the entanglement of place with language.

Second, we find that dominant discussions of early language tend to overlook how language practices are shaped by hierarchies such as racism, classism, ableism, and cis-hetero sexism. As anti-racist speech and language therapist Warda Farah has urged, "we need to actively de-centre white ways of conceptualising language" (Farah, 2022). We agree, and this impetus to reconnect language with the body and place in ways that re-politicise standardised talk (Flores & Rosa, 2015) was an aspiration underpinning our review.

WHAT DO WE MEAN BY ENTANGLEMENT?

Dominant theories conceptualise language as a process that "fl[ies] between lips and brain" (Hackett, 2021, p. 16) of an individual child whose subjectivity can be neatly separated from those around them. In contrast, in this chapter, we are using the word 'entanglement' to describe the ways that language is connected to a host of more-than-human entities that sit outside the body.

More-than-human theories explore how seemingly human social processes, such as language, emerge through and are mediated by a web of socio-material forces. These forces operate both above and below the threshold of human perception. In practical terms, this means attending to how children's language practices might be heard, detected, and felt, but also conditioned and evoked, by other humans, as well as non-human animals, non-animal life, and non-living matter. In this chapter, we pay particular attention to the entanglement of children's language with place.

Environment and place: what's the difference?

In language acquisition literature (which is mainly grounded in a medicalised and psychologised model of research), 'environment' is usually framed as anything outside the developing child (e.g., Rowland et al., 2020). Typically, researchers identify environmental features or behaviours within the immediate family context (e.g., Roulstone et al., 2011) and, less commonly, broader structural issues such as levels of state financial investment in local communities (see Iruka et al., 2015, for a review), as factors influencing children's language development. Thus, discussion often involves deficit-centric explorations of the impact of economic deprivation and 'poor-quality' home environments on language: these discussions frequently reinforce racialising and classist hierarchies (cf. Basit et al., 2015; Li et al., 2022). Sometimes these conclusions are presented as positive and empowering for families, with a message to parents that the power is in their hands to achieve social mobility for their children if they put enough effort into their parenting behaviour and home environment. Yet, in order for this logic to stand, environment/place and language must be regarded as separate and individually changeable.

Moreover, whilst developmental psychology research emphasises the significance of environment to the quality of children's language development, it also regards place as a troublesome factor that interferes with the quality of assessment of children's language (Camilleri & Botting, 2013). For example, Camilleri and Botting (2013) argue that children undertaking speech and language assessments are often extracted from their usual learning environments because the other sounds and experiences of the classroom are understood as negatively affecting children's performance: children are removed in order to assess their language in the 'purest' way possible, free of distraction. In contrast, early years educators point out that extracting children from their everyday learning environment to assess their language abilities means that such assessments do not reflect the children's everyday learning situations nor, therefore, their everyday *language* experiences (Duncan et al., 2020).

Across the literature on home learning environment and 'scientifically reliable' language assessments, we note a distinction between environment and place, where:

1 environment is a series of controllable and measurable factors that research is interested in modifying to draw conclusions about language development; and
2 place is a wild and unwanted variable that must sometimes be tolerated or considered as a limitation of the study in order to work practically with children, families, or practitioners.

It is this context within and against which we situate the present literature review.

Methodology: a narrative review

While we knew from the outset that there was likely to be only a small amount of literature that deliberately addressed the entanglement of language and place in education, we suspected that there would be other studies that touched tangentially on similar questions or that would complicate our review in ways that we had not expected. For this reason, we started without a clear sense of how an attention to place might emerge in papers we read.

A narrative review is a summary of a body of literature combined with "interpretation and critique" (Greenhalgh et al., 2018, p. 2). Thus, our purpose was not to produce an exhaustive review. For one thing, our review was limited to papers published in English. For another, as predicted, some of the articles only theorised place tangentially to their main argument, while the relevance of other articles to our topic only became clear when read alongside something else. So, the body of literature led us to a more nuanced approach to narrative reviewing that emphasises flexibility rather than reproducing a canon.

More detail on the search terms we employed and how we identified the literature is provided in our journal article in *Critical Inquiry in Language Studies* (Shannon & Hackett, 2024). In total we identified 50 articles for inclusion in the narrative review and we worked across them to identify the following three emerging questions:

1 How does place change children's language?
2 How does language re-signify or re-make place?
3 How does place shape the possibilities for listening to children?

We propose that these questions will support the building of a conceptual framework for scholars interested in researching the entanglement of place with children's language. In the next sections, we attend to each question in turn.

How does place change children's language?

In this section, we discuss the extant research exploring how place – as a physical, geographic context and a socially structured environment – changes what and how much children say.

It has long been understood that children's speech is changeable depending on the physical location. For instance, young children may speak much less in school or nursery than at home (Flewitt, 2005; Wells, 1979). Researchers have also found differences in the kinds of communication practices children use between contexts. For instance, early childhood communication scholar Rosie Flewitt (2005) used longitudinal video ethnography to explore how four 3-year-old children's language practices differ between home and pre-school. At home, the children drew from shared, carer-child understandings to structure their language. In pre-school, where these carer-child understandings are absent and where time for talking was prescribed by school staff, children talked less. Instead, they engaged in a variety of different, multi-modal communicative practices "negotiated through gaze, facial expression and body movement, supplemented by speech primarily to be specific" (Flewitt, 2005, p. 217). Flewitt contends that both school and home enrich children's communication in different ways, and neither should be understood as imposing limitations. Similarly, Bronya Dean (2021) explored how young children's singing changes between social contexts. Dean conducted non-participant observations of the singing practices of fifteen 3–4-year-olds using wearable microphones. Children wore the microphones for sustained durations. Dean found that the type of singing was shaped by where children were in the home, who they were with, and what was happening at the time. The most common kind of singing was improvised singing whilst playing alone, whereas children typically sang learnt songs or songs with clear words when interacting with others.

The scholars discussed above observed that children's speech changed between places. Likewise, scholars of early childhood education, Richardson and Murray (2017), identified significant differences in language use in unstructured 'natural' outdoor learning spaces compared with more formal indoor or outdoor 'classroom' learning spaces. Using a case study approach, they coded the language of four child participants aged four to five years. The researchers found that the children tended to use more verbs, exclamations, and adjectives in natural outdoor learning than in more formal classroom learning, while two children used more nouns in the formal classroom environments. Moreover, the children involved in outdoor learning preferred more onomatopoeic adjectives than those in the classroom (e.g., "'wriggly, 'sticky' and 'slimy'": Richardson & Murray, 2017, p. 465), suggesting that children experimented more with experiential language. The authors suggest that increased verb use might indicate greater action-focused learning, more exclamations might reflect more emotional engagement, and more adjectives might be rooted in the children's engagement with a greater range of sensory experiences. Similarly, Hackett et al. (2021) identified significant changes in the language practices of two-year-old children when their early childhood education setting adopted an outdoors-orientated pedagogy. Hackett and her colleagues argued that the shift to less structured learning outdoors "unsettled the customary assumptions about what counts as language" (p. 926), resulting in a freer experience (for both adults and children) of vocalising and experimenting with language and song. Moreover, their analysis of whole-cohort data indicated a dramatic reduction in the number of children referred for formal speech and language assessment when compared to previous cohorts from the same setting. Finally, MacRae and Arculus (2020) draw from the SALTMusic action research project to describe two 2-year-olds' improvisations during arts-based workshops, revealing the imbrication of place and music with language (you can read more about Arculus' work in Chapter 2c). The above scholars all build on earlier scholarship to show that the place where children's language happens changes that language, although they extend this work by also arguing that the social context further conditions the physical context.

Also relevant to our review are the socio-structural positions of children's cultures, languages, and literacies in how children use language in a given place. Place is invoked in the politics of how plurilingual students make space for their non-English languages in formal education contexts. This is because the classroom is "polycontextual" (Gutiérrez et al., 1999, p. 288) in that it operates across official and unofficial spaces that are often "characterized by their various and often oppositional discourses and social practices, [but] are also mutually constitutive and transformative" (p. 288). Language and literacy scholar Brittany Frieson (2021) explores how first-graders' use of African American Language in a bilingual immersion English-Spanish classroom interrupts standardised rules and teaching formats of 'formal' European languages. Likewise, learning and behaviour scholar Anna Martín-Bylund (2018) draws from her ethnographic research in a bilingual Spanish-Swedish pre-school to challenge the idea of the 'silent' phase, which many plurilingual learners are described as going through. Rather than posing the silent plurilingual child as lacking agency and needing extra intervention, Martín-Bylund takes an example of a child's silence when offered water to consider how silence might be used strategically to resist following adults' instructions. Similarly, drawing from her ethnographic research with a UK-based Reception class (whom she followed into Year 1), early childhood scholar Christina Tatham-Fashanu and her colleagues (2020) noted that children are more likely to speak non-English home languages in parts of the classroom where they feel unobserved. In this way, children self-regulate to switch between languages based on place: for instance, in the transition from indoor to outdoor spaces, when secreted away in a corner of the library, or during a lapse in the teacher's talk during 'lining-up time'. In Spain, Inmaculada M. García-Sánchez (2010) explores how first-generation Moroccan immigrant children employ hybrid language practices during play at home as a means to create a clandestine private space. García-Sánchez observed that the children organised and negotiated the play in Moroccan Arabic (their home language) but then enacted their characters in Spanish. This served to make the play less transparent to non-Spanish-speaking outside observers, including older siblings and parents. Rather than being a practice of code-switching, these translanguaging behaviours illuminate how child and place entwine as a way of resisting the dominance of institutional languages, whether the dominant language of the classroom or the dominant language of the home.

In this section, we have examined a body of research that grapples with the difference that place makes to the quantity and qualities of children's language. This research traces the ways in which the full repertoire of children's languages and meaning-making threads and oozes through place. In the next section, we consider how these linguistic behaviours (re)signify and (re)make places, including how plurilingual children demarcate place through the strategic use of different languages.

How does language re-signify or re-make place?

Freire (2017) contended that people transform the world by naming it. Taking up this contention, Margaret Somerville and her colleagues have portrayed young children's literacies as world-making (Hackett & Somerville, 2017; Somerville & Powell, 2019). In ethnographic fieldwork with one- to three- and four- to six-year-olds in early childhood education settings in New Zealand and Sweden, Bateman and Cekaite (2022) rethink the common presumption that place (or what they term 'context') is static. Instead, they consider how interaction in and with the environment, and particularly how children emphasise or accentuate aspects of it, shapes that environment – in other words, a child "talks the environment into significance" (Schegloff, 1992, cited in Bateman & Cekaite, 2022, p. 63). For instance, Bateman and Cekaite describe how children's narration of the properties of a patch of long grass reconstitutes the outdoor play space. Similarly, Gallagher and colleagues (2018), conducting 'sound walks' with three- to four-year-old children and their parents, describe how tall vegetation is talked into being a hiding place for speculative tigers. In this way, children's language-making practices redefine their relationships with space.

Children's language practices can add layers of meaning to places. Early childhood education scholar Polly Björk-Willén (2016) shows how the entrance hall of an early years education classroom becomes a 'transit zone' through which two children move between their non-Swedish home languages (Arabic, French, Albanian, and Greek) and the Swedish language of the classroom. Using video recordings, Björk-Willén observes the use of the home languages as transitional languages, for instance, when a carer leaves their child behind. She also notes that non-Swedish languages create privacy for carers and children in those spacetimes of transition for moments of intimacy or anxiety, to which the pre-school practitioners (who cannot speak those languages) are merely 'bystanders'. Moreover, Björk-Willén suggests that these transitions are possible due to the presence of material 'transition objects' (e.g., mitts and shoes) or embodied gestures (e.g., hugs and kisses) that provide focal points for language transition.

Emerging research shows how the process whereby language re-makes and demarcates place can also occur virtually, digitally, and across space. Martín-Bylund and Stenliden (2020) describe the ways that three transnational, multilingual families in China, each with children aged between three and nine, maintained proximity to relatives in European countries through the use of online video calls. The authors suggested that proximity and the language practices associated with proximity are mediated by physical objects in one or both of the physical locations. For instance, the camera on the video-calling device renders body(mind)s visible or invisible. Or proximity is mediated by objects that have transitioned between spaces, such as a bag gifted to one of the children by their grandparent. Similarly, Flewitt and Clark (2020) use a 'day in the life' style of ethnography to recount how two children (aged one and two) use digital technology to adopt new kinds of social practices. They explore how children's digital literacy practices operated across "material resources in actual and virtual social spaces" (p. 465), arguing that children's home literacy environments have permeable borders between physical and digital spaces and that these boundaries are made and remade through language.

Some scholars of bilingualism have mobilised Homi Bhabha's (2004) idea of 'third space'. For Bhabha, third spaces represent the hybridity that emerges when two people or cultures interact, thereby unsettling Euro-Western ideals of cultural homogeneity and sameness. Scholars have taken up this idea to explore how the 'first space' of "home, community, and peer networks" might re-constitute the 'second space' of "work, school, or church" (Moje et al., 2004, p. 41). For instance, education scholars Eisazadeh et al. (2017) conducted participant video ethnographic research with four-year-old Ojibwe children during their play in a small, remote, Indigenous community in Nishnawbe Aski Nation territory in central Canada. Although not the main purpose of the study, the authors briefly describe how the children formulate spaces that straddle Indigenous and popular cultures in their dramatic play: for instance, they fended off the "Minecraft guy" during a hunt and constructed a UFO that later evolved into an aeroplane to transport them to and from their remote community. These might be thought of as examples of third spaces, where play is formed from across different cultural spaces. Similarly, Christina Tatham-Fashanu (2021) draws from the idea of third space to suggest that the bridge between home and school languages and cultural practices might be rethought as a complex network of 'multiple bridges'. For example, she describes three children playing 'pirate ship' by throwing orange felted fabric at each other. The felt is then described as fire and then as confetti when one of the children yells "shaadi!". Although the Hindi word shaadi typically means 'wedding', the child explains an alternative meaning, 'party', and so the other two also start shouting "shaadi!" while pelting each other with fire/felt/confetti. In recounting this episode, Tatham-Fashanu illustrates not only how children make bridges from home languages into the classroom but also how third spaces are more than the sums of their parts: in this case, the construction of an alternative meaning and etymology for the word shaadi ('party' rather than 'wedding', via fire and pirates). Tatham-Fashanu suggests that an "appropriate metaphor for the third space might be an intersubjective 'spaghetti junction' with multiple entrances, exits, levels and connections" (p. 14), rather than a singular bridge between two cultures and languages. In this way, plurilingual children construct both shared and contested meanings that draw from linguistic and identity practices from across home and school and put them to work re-making and re-claiming place. So far in this review, we have discussed how researchers have explored the entanglement of children's language with place, considering how each shapes the other. In the final section of this review, we consider how 'listening' to children is mediated by place.

How does place shape the possibilities for listening to children?

We have emphasised in this chapter that place shapes how and what young children communicate. Importantly, place also shapes how adults are able (or willing) to 'listen' to children's communication. We use the word 'listen' here to stand in for a range of receptive communication strategies, including listening to spoken language, understanding signing and picture exchange, and discerning meaning in children's own personal communication styles. Frequently, in education – including in the use of speech and language therapy assessments – listening to children is framed as requiring silence, stillness, and a minimising of background inputs or influence. We feel that this conventional approach prioritises convenience for adults and the maintenance of school structures over the creation of a more accurate, if messy, portrayal of children's linguistic practices. Instead, we conceptualise listening to children in a more expansive way, even where that is difficult or inconvenient for the adults (Davies, 2014; Yoon & Templeton, 2019). Researchers have argued that the possibilities for adults to 'hear children out' (Yoon & Templeton, 2019) are filtered through curriculum or adult expectations of what children are supposed to say. Consequently, the limits of what the curriculum expects or is looking for, and what adults have learnt to habitually value or imagine, operate to shape and constrain the possibilities for listening to children (Olsson, 2013; Yoon & Templeton, 2019).

Scholars have explored how teachers' reception of pupils' speech is mediated by racial hierarchies (Bryan, 2020; Rosa, 2019; Thiel & Dernikos, 2020) and normative notions of ability and capacity (Shannon, 2020, 2022), with the result that teachers hear different groups of children differently. In a case study of two African American children from their own families, Boutte and Bryan (2019) identify the suppression in school of African American Language through the privileging of "White Mainstream English" (Baker-Bell, 2017, as cited in Baker-Bell, 2020), which they recognise as a mode of anti-Black violence in education. They argue that in certain school spaces, the relations between Black children's language, identity, and race are devalued, serving to disconnect grammar and linguistic features from lived reality and in effect reimposing the 'mastery' of white people. Drawing on critical race theory, Nathaniel Bryan (2020) unsettles idealistic white fantasies of the role of the playground in children's lives. Invoking the powerful imaginaries of what he calls the 'school playground-to-prison pipeline', he explores how adults adopt the logics of incarceration in their responses to Black boys' behaviour. Just as with the discussions of racism in the above papers, Flewitt et al. (2009) complicate what disability 'sounds' like by drawing on video ethnographic data from a small-scale study with three 4-year-olds attending early education settings. The authors consider how 'Mandy', a girl labelled with Special Educational Needs, unfolds her language practices differently across three settings: a children's centre, a playgroup, and home. At home and in the playgroup, Mandy engaged in multi-modal communication practices through a combination of vocalising, gaze, and bodily position, in addition to her use of a picture exchange communication system (PECS): in one instance, when a class reading included a birthday cake, Mandy "rocks excitedly to and fro, vocalising sounds in her excitement" (p. 223). However, the authors argue that such "intentional, idiosyncratic communicative competences" (p. 232) are squeezed out by the emphasis on Makaton signing or picture exchange in the more formal education context of the children's centre. In other words, formal disability accommodations intruded on Mandy's use of her personal, unique communication practices.

The above examples all describe how place changes how adults 'listen' to children. Concomitantly, disability studies in education scholar David Ben Shannon (2021) explores how place changes the ways that five- to six-year-olds listen to one another. Shannon recounts a series of experiments designed to prompt a kind of synesthetic 'listening'. In one episode, the children lay on their backs on a large, square carpet engaging in a "Deep Listening" activity (p. 14). Some children also wore sleep masks or ear defenders designed to alter their sensory experience. Following the episode, children reported how their perceptions of sounds were heightened, such as each other's "shouting" voices, "fidgeting", and breathing, but also indicating which senses were involved (for instance, one child reported "hearing the sun so bright"). In this way, the Deep Listening activity carved out a new 'place' in the classroom, in which sensory experience was remade. In all of these examples, scholars have identified how the socio-material construction of patterns of relation (and in some cases, systemic oppression) shapes how children are heard in education settings.

Conclusion

In conducting this literature review, we aimed to start a conversation on the entanglement of place with early childhood language, a field usually dominated by 'scientific' discourses of health and development that emphasise extraction from place and abstract notions of language competence. We identified a growing body of research that explores the entanglement of children's language with place. We explored this through three themes: (1) how place shapes language; (2) how language shapes place; (3) and how place shapes listening to children. This said, in comparison to the important and well-established body of scholarship resisting the pathologisation of families' language practices, we found much less literature that pays specific attention to language's entanglement with place and the politics of this. Indeed, in our review, we found that most discussion of children's language relies on some kind of extraction of children's language from place, reinforcing the idea that language is not emplaced. With this in mind, future research and practice should attend to how different places – outdoor or indoor spaces, different classrooms, different parts of the same classroom, or hybrid spaces – present different opportunities for different kinds of talk and different kinds of listening, with implications for what and who gets privileged.

Acknowledgement

The Entanglement of Language and Place in Early Childhood: A Review of the Literature by David Ben Shannon and Abigail Hackett taken from *Critical Inquiry in Language Studies* © 2024 The Author(s). Published with licence by Taylor & Francis Group, LLC.

This is an Open Access article distributed under the terms of the Creative Commons Attribution-NonCommercial-NoDerivatives License (http://creativecommons.org/licenses/by-nc-nd/4.0/), which permits non-commercial re-use, distribution, and reproduction in any medium, provided the original work is properly cited and is not altered, transformed, or built upon in any way. The terms on which this article has been published allow the posting of the Accepted Manuscript in a repository by the author(s) or with their consent.

Note

1 You can read the full review paper for free here: https://www.tandfonline.com/doi/full/10.1080/15427587.2024.2312142.

References

Baker-Bell, A. (2020). *Linguistic Justice: Black Language, Literacy Identity, and Pedagogy*. Routledge.

Basit, T. N., Hughes, A., Iqbal, Z., & Cooper, J. (2015). The influence of socio-economic status and ethnicity on speech and language development. *International Journal of Early Years Education*, 23(1), 115–133. https://doi.org/10.1080/09669760.2014.973838

Bateman, A., & Cekaite, A. (2022). Language as context: A case of early literacy practices in New Zealand and Sweden. *International Journal of Early Years Education*, 30(1), 55–70. https://doi.org/10.1080/09669760.2022.2029365

Bhabha, H. K. (2004). *The Location of Culture*. Routledge.

Björk-Willén, P. (2016). The preschool entrance hall: A bilingual transit zone for preschoolers. In A. Bateman & A. Church (Eds.), *Children's Knowledge-in-Interaction: Studies in Conversation Analysis* (pp. 169–187). Springer Singapore.

Boutte, G., & Bryan, N. (2019). When will Black children be well? Interrupting anti-Black violence in early childhood classrooms and schools. *Contemporary Issues in Early Childhood*, 22(3), 232–243. https://doi.org/10.1177/1463949119890598

Bryan, N. (2020). Shaking the bad boys: Troubling the criminalization of Black boys' childhood play, hegemonic White masculinity and femininity, and the school playground-to-prison pipeline. *Race Ethnicity and Education*, 23(5), 673–692. https://doi.org/10.1080/13613324.2018.1512483

Camilleri, B., & Botting, N. (2013). Beyond static assessment of children's receptive vocabulary: The dynamic assessment of word learning (DAWL). *International Journal of Language and Communication Disorders*, 48(5), 565–581. https://doi.org/10.1111/1460-6984.12033

Davies, B. (2014). *Listening to Children: Being and Becoming*. Routledge.

Dean, B. (2021). Spontaneous singing in early childhood: An examination of young children's singing at home. *Research Studies in Music Education*, 43(3), 434–450. https://doi.org/10.1177/1321103X20924139

Duncan, L. G., Gollek, C., & Potter, D. D. (2020). eLIPS: Development and validation of an observational tool for examining early language in play settings. *Frontiers in Psychology*, 11(July), 1–18. https://doi.org/10.3389/fpsyg.2020.01813

Eisazadeh, N., Rajendram, S., Portier, C., & Peterson, S. S. (2017). Indigenous children's use of language during play in rural northern Canadian kindergarten classrooms. *Literacy Research: Theory, Method, and Practice*, 66(1), 293–308. https://doi.org/10.1177/2381336917719684

Farah, W. (2022, November 6). We need to actively de-centre white ways of conceptualising language. Twitter. https://twitter.com/wfarahslt/status/1535527211461115904?s=61%26t=heosXYBos3XYzNq_wNRvhQ

Fashanu, C., Wood, E., & Payne, M. (2020). Multilingual communication under the radar: How multilingual children challenge the dominant monolingual discourse in a super-diverse, Early Years educational setting in England. *English in Education*, 54(1), 93–112. https://doi.org/10.1080/04250494.2019.1688657

Flewitt, R. (2005). Is every child's voice heard? Researching the different ways 3-year-old children communicate and make meaning at home and in a pre-school playgroup. *Early Years*, 25(3), 207–222. https://doi.org/10.1080/09575140500251558

Flewitt, R., & Clark, A. (2020). Porous boundaries: Reconceptualising the home literacy environment as a digitally networked space for 0–3 year-olds. *Journal of Early Childhood Literacy*, 20(3), 447–471. https://doi.org/10.1177/1468798420938116

Flewitt, R., Nind, M., & Payler, J. (2009). "If she's left with books she'll just eat them": Considering inclusive multimodal literacy practices. *Journal of Early Childhood Literacy*, 9(2), 211–233. https://doi.org/10.1177/1468798409105587

Flores, N., & Rosa, J. (2015). Undoing appropriateness: Raciolinguistic ideologies and language diversity in education. *Harvard Educational Review*, 85(2), 149–171. https://psycnet.apa.org/doi/10.17763/0017-8055.85.2.149

Freire, P. (2017). *Pedagogy of the Oppressed*. Penguin Classics.

Frieson, B. L. (2021). Remixin' and flown' in centros: Exploring the biliteracy practices of Black language speakers in an elementary two-way immersion bilingual program. *Race Ethnicity and Education*, 25(4), 585–605. https://doi.org/10.1080/13613324.2021.1890568

Gallagher, M., Hackett, A., Procter, L., & Scott, F. (2018). Vibrations in place: Sound and language in early childhood literacy practices. *Educational Studies: A Journal of the American Educational Studies Association*, 54(4), 465–482. https://doi.org/10.1080/00131946.2018.1476353

García-Sánchez, I. M. (2010). Serious games: Code-switching and gendered identities in Moroccan immigrant girls' pretend play. *Pragmatics*, 20(4), 523–555. https://doi.org/10.1075/prag.20.4.03gar

Greenhalgh, T., Thorne, S., & Malterud, K. (2018). Time to challenge the spurious hierarchy of systematic over narrative reviews? *European Journal of Clinical Investigation*, 48(6), e12931. https://doi.org/10.1111/eci.12931

Gutiérrez, K. D., Baquedano-López, P., & Tejeda, C. (1999). Rethinking diversity: Hybridity and hybrid language practices in the third space. *Mind, Culture, and Activity*, 6(4), 286–303. https://doi.org/10.1080/10749039909524733

Hackett, A. (2021). *More-Than-Human Literacies in Early Childhood*. Bloomsbury Academic.

Hackett, A., MacLure, M., & McMahon, S. (2021). Reconceptualising early language development: Matter, sensation and the more-than-human. *Discourse: Studies in the Cultural Politics of Education*, 42(6), 913–929. https://doi.org/10.1080/01596306.2020.1767350

Hackett, A., & Somerville, M. (2017). Posthuman literacies: Young children moving in time, place and more-than-human worlds. *Journal of Early Childhood Literacy*, 17(3), 374–391. https://doi.org/10.1177/1468798417704031

Iruka, I. U., Curenton, S. M., & Gardner, S. (2015). How changes in home and neighborhood environment factors are related to change in black children's academic and social development from kindergarten to third grade. *The Journal of Negro Education*, *84*(3). https://psycnet.apa.org/doi/10.7709/jnegroeducation.84.3.0282

Li, Q. K. W., MacKinnon, A. L., Tough, S., Graham, S., & Tomfohr-Madsen, L. (2022). Does where you live predict what you say? Associations between neighborhood factors, child sleep, and language development. *Brain Sciences*, *12*(2), 223. https://doi.org/10.3390/brainsci12020223

MacRae, C., & Arculus, C. (2020). Complicité: Resisting the tyranny of talk. *Global Education Review*, *7*(2), 43–57. https://ger.mercy.edu/index.php/ger/article/view/543

Martín-Bylund, A. (2018). The matter of silence in early childhood bilingual education. *Educational Philosophy and Theory*, *50*(4), 349–358. https://doi.org/10.1080/00131857.2017.1361820

Martín-Bylund, A., & Stenliden, L. (2020). Closer to far away: Transcending the spatial in transnational families' online video calling. *Journal of Multilingual and Multicultural Development*, *43*(7), 587–599. https://doi.org/10.1080/01434632.2020.1749643

Moje, E. B., Ciechanowski, K. M., Kramer, K., Ellis, L., Carrillo, R., & Collazo, T. (2004). Working toward third space in content area literacy: An examination of everyday funds of knowledge and Discourse. *Reading Research Quarterly*, *39*(1), 38–70. https://doi.org/10.1598/RRQ.39.1.4

Olsson, L. M. (2013). Taking children's questions seriously: The need for creative thought. *Global Studies of Childhood*, *3*(3), 230–253. https://doi.org/10.2304/gsch.2013.3.3.230

Richardson, T., & Murray, J. (2017). Are young children's utterances affected by characteristics of their learning environments? A multiple case study. *Early Child Development and Care*, *187*(3–4), 457–468. https://doi.org/10.1080/03004430.2016.1211116

Rosa, J. (2019). *Looking Like a Language, Sounding Like a Race: Inequality and Ingenuity in the Learning of Latina/o Identities*. Oxford University Press.

Roulstone, S., Law, J., Rush, R., Clegg, J., & Peters, T. (2011). *Investigating the Role of Language in Children's Early Educational Outcomes*. Department for Education. https://www.gov.uk/government/publications/investigating-the-role-of-language-in-childrens-early-educational-outcomes

Rowland, C., Theakston, A. L., Ambridge, B., & Twomey, K. E. (2020). *Current Perspectives on Child Language Acquisition: How Children Use Their Environment to Learn*. John Benjamins Publishing Company.

Shannon, D. B. (2020). Neuroqueer(ing) noise: Beyond 'mere inclusion' in a neurodiverse early childhood classroom. *Canadian Journal of Disability Studies*, *9*(5), 489–514. https://doi.org/10.15353/cjds.v9i5.706

Shannon, D. B. (2021). A/autisms: A "queer labor of the incommensurate": Holding onto the friction between different orientations towards autism in an early childhood research-creation project. *International Journal of Qualitative Studies in Education*, 1–19. https://doi.org/10.1080/09518398.2021.2003894

Shannon, D. B. (2022). Perversity, precarity, and anxiety: Tracing a 'more precise typology' of the affect of neuroqueer failure in an in-school research-creation project. *International Journal of Qualitative Studies in Education, 37*(3), 676–690. https://doi.org/10.1080/09518398.2022.2127023

Shannon, D. B., & Hackett, A. (2024). The entanglement of language and place in early childhood: A review of the literature. *Critical Inquiry in Language Studies*, 1–24. https://doi.org/10.1080/15427587.2024.2312142

Somerville, M., & Powell, S. J. (2019). Thinking posthuman with mud: And children of the Anthropocene. *Educational Philosophy and Theory, 51*(8), 829–840. https://doi.org/10.1080/00131857.2018.1516138

Tatham-Fashanu, C. (2021). A third space pedagogy: Embracing complexity in a super-diverse, early childhood education setting. *Pedagogy, Culture and Society, 31*(4), 863–881. https://doi.org/10.1080/14681366.2021.1952295

Thiel, J. J., & Dernikos, B. P. (2020). Refusals, re-turns, and retheorizations of affective literacies: A thrice-told data tale. *Journal of Literacy Research, 52*(4), 482–506. https://doi.org/10.1177/1086296X20966317

Wells, G. (1979). Describing children's linguistic development at home and at school. *British Educational Research Journal, 5*(1), 75–98. https://doi.org/10.1080/0141192790050109

Yoon, Y. S., & Templeton, T. N. (2019). The practice of listening to children: The challenges of hearing children out in an adult-regulated world. *Harvard Educational Review, 89*(1), 55–84. https://doi.org/10.17763/1943-5045-89.1.55

3c
RITUALS, VOCALISATIONS, AND CREATING COMFORTABLE SPACES

A spatialised view of young children's language in museums

Abigail Hackett, Christina MacRae, David Ben Shannon, Robert Chester, Lucy Cooke, Esther Hallberg, Georgina Simmons, Laura Smith-Higgins, and Sally Toon

This chapter describes a research collaboration between the Humber Museums Partnership (HMP) and Manchester Metropolitan University. HMP is a collaboration between different local authority museum services in the Yorkshire and Humber region of England, encompassing a wide range of indoor and outdoor museum and heritage sites. It comprises three participating local authority areas, where some of the authors work: Hull (Esther and Sally), East Riding of Yorkshire (Lucy and Robert), and North Lincolnshire (Laura and Georgina). HMP had previously worked with researchers from Manchester Metropolitan University (Abi, Christina, and David) to understand the experiences of young children and their families visiting museums (Hackett et al., 2018). Continuing these conversations, this study focused more explicitly on language and sound, seeking to understand more about how families and young children experienced museum places and how this might shape or inform language and communication during the visits.

Young children's experiences of language and place in the afterlives of COVID-19

Children come into museums with unique sets of previous experiences. For example, each child is likely to have had different experiences of being in groups, encountering strangers, spending time in public indoor and outdoor spaces, and more. However, one of the outcomes of the COVID-19 pandemic is that, in many parts of the world, including here in northern England, young children had unexpected and distinctive experiences of *place* during their earliest years. For many children, this might have included spending more time at home and less time in public spaces, playgroups, or nurseries or interacting with unfamiliar adults or other children. Moreover, with different levels of closure, lockdowns, and movement restrictions operating in different parts of the UK during 2020 and 2021, these unique and unexpected experiences of place dominated the first years of some children's lives, while for others the implications were less drastic. Consequently, in the afterlives of the COVID-19 pandemic, children were encountering aspects of museums and other spaces from a distinctive perspective.

Another outcome of the COVID-19 pandemic in England has been an intensification of concerns about young children's language development, which was already high on the agendas of many organisations working to support children and families. Since the pandemic, the statutory Early Years Foundation Stage framework (Department for Education, 2024) and non-statutory Development Matters curriculum guidance (Department for Education, 2021) have further emphasised the development of communication skills as 'underpinning' all other aspects of learning and development – specifically, they mean English language skills (with the notable removal of the requirement for supporting non-English home languages in the revised, 2024 guidance). Moreover, since the pandemic, news outlets run headlines such as "Lockdowns hurt child speech and language skills" (Jeffreys, 2021), whilst England's chief schools' inspector said the delay to young children's development was "particularly worrying" (BBC, 2021). Certainly, there seems to be concern from several quarters about young children's language but little consideration of experience of places and their potential relationship with language.

In this co-authored chapter, we share some of the things we learnt from the study, which was motivated by the following questions:

- What might it feel like for families to begin visiting museums in the afterlives of the COVID-19 pandemic?
- How might public places like museums shape children's language and communication?
- What role might HMP play in supporting children and families in this context?

Language as relational-material

The study took the perspective that language is *relational-material* (Hackett et al., 2021) and connected to place. From a relational-material perspective, we can think about places as a conglomeration of other humans, objects, ideas, how bodies feel and affect each other, and modes of engagement between these things. Each of us, adults and children, encounters places through the medium of how our bodies and minds feel and respond. When we describe language as being relational-material, we mean that language sits within this wider, multi-sensory, more-than-human conglomeration and that bodily, sensory experience is an important aspect of how, when, and why children use language and other communication strategies.

This chapter expands this understanding of language as relational-material, by focusing more specifically on how more-than-human soundscapes are involved in the emergence of young children's languaging practices. Attending to a more-than-human soundscape involves thinking about how human, non-human, and environmental sounds mingle and interact with each other and what this means for speaking and listening. Taking greater account of the more-than-human soundscape could include attending to:

- How sounds (including human vocalisations) are produced and sensed differently in indoor or outdoor spaces.
- How human utterances are produced in response to sounds generated by non-human life (a dog, a tree) or non-living objects (a stone, a raindrop).
- How "back-and-forth interactions" (Department for Education, 2024, p. 10) might spring up not just between a human adult and a human child but also with stray cats, bicycle bells, and footsteps.
- Utterances that children make that are not recognisable as words.

Sounds, including the vocalisations and words uttered by children and their grown-ups, are all entangled with place. Following this line of thinking, we propose that *new encounters with different kinds of spaces and soundscapes* are an important factor for considering young children's experiences of museums and their languaging as part of these experiences.

Introducing the study

We were interested in what young children's experiences of museums, galleries, and outside space might have to teach us about the emergence of young children's language and its relationship with place. To explore this, we carried out collaborative research with families and young children in the diverse spaces across HMP. We included a mix of indoor and outdoor spaces:

- A walled garden behind Wilberforce House museum, Hull (a session for babies and toddlers)

- The grounds and zoo at Sewerby Hall and Gardens, Bridlington (unstructured visits with families)
- The Medieval Gallery at Hull and East Riding Museum, Hull (staff-led visit for early years groups)
- North Lincolnshire Museum, Scunthorpe (dedicated under-5s session)

Sessions were organised by HMP staff in collaboration with their existing partner organisations and families. Researchers made repeated visits with participating families to these places, collecting field notes and continuous audio data via small wearable audio-recorders (mainly worn by the researcher or the child's grown-up, and carried around during the visit). The methodology involved analysing the written observations and audio recordings of young children and families as they experienced and explored HMP sites, with a focus on the children's language, vocalisations, and meaning-making. Below, we discuss four vignettes from this study in order to explore four themes: soundscapes, vocalisations, rituals and feeling, and creating comfortable spaces.

Language sits in a wider soundscape

We collected audio recordings and written observations of young children and their grown-ups exploring, moving, and playing in a range of indoor and outdoor museum sites. We expected that words would be only part of the children's communication, used in combination with gestures, gaze, objects, movements, and sounds. Listening back to the audio, in particular, emphasised how the children's words were tangled up with other vocalisations they made, the words and vocalisations of others, and a wider soundscape of all kinds of more-than-human noises such as the sounds made by toys or water splashing in the water tray. In addition, our observations and field notes showed us the importance of gesture, movement, touch, and gaze to how children and families communicated.

Often, in traditional transcriptions, audio recordings are 'neatened up' to foreground words (or other noises and gestures that are easily articulated as words). We wanted to avoid this approach because privileging certain aspects of language over others (MacLure, 2013) limits the kinds of stories we can tell about what happens with young children, place, and language. As we have argued elsewhere:

> gestures, words and sounds produced by the children and by the place are inseparable and difficult to transcribe. This however is not a methodological inconvenience, but an important insight into the more-than-human nature of literacy and language practices.
>
> *(Hackett, 2021, p. 77)*

As an illustration of this, in vignette 1 below, the sounds of Henry and his 婆婆 (paternal grandmother) get caught up with and transformed by the sounds of his toy as they play in an indoor space in the North Lincolnshire Museum.

VIGNETTE 1   North Lincolnshire Museum: Henry and the dinging ball game

Henry plays with a toy consisting of a piece of wood, with a rail coiling through, down which rolls a metal ball. As the ball rolls down the rails, Henry flaps his arms and jiggles his legs, his whole body undulating with glee. At the end of the rails, the ball strikes a tiny metal bell. Frequently, Henry says "ding" (or sometimes "bing"), slightly before or after the bell sounds. Henry's 婆婆 (paternal grandmother) watches as he plays. At first, she encourages Henry to describe the colours of the balls or count them. However, as the game progresses, 婆婆 begins to join in with Henry's dinging, cackling wildly each time she does.

This episode provides an account of a museum soundscape and illustrates how words and vocalisations sit within it. Sometimes early years educators are given the advice that quiet spaces are more 'communication friendly' (Jarman, 2013). However, we found the situation to be more complex than that, and it was difficult to predict what kinds of words, vocalisations, and gestures children were likely to make in different kinds of places and soundscapes. Whilst quiet spaces might be more convenient for adults to hear a child clearly, they can often create feelings of being surveilled and sometimes put pressure on children to perform the right kinds of talk and on parents to performatively talk to children in very particular ways. For example, in the vignette above, Henry's 婆婆 seems to approach the activity as an opportunity for rehearsing the kinds of language we associate with small children and early learning goals: specifically, numbers and colours. However, as the ding of the bell and Henry's playful 'ding' get the better of her, she starts dinging merrily along with him. Consequently, instead of seeking to develop generalisable rules for the 'right' kinds of spaces and soundscapes for children's communication, we found ourselves thinking about:

- The potential to provide a range of place and soundscape experiences for children and families.
- How to create atmospheres where different kinds of sound and movement feel welcome and comfortable.

- How to frame the spatial experience expansively: the journey to the museum, as well as the moving around the museum, including its corridors, entry spaces, and views from windows, can all matter.

Questions for reflection

- How do spaces invite movement and possibility?
- What makes a space inviting?

The significance of vocalisations

As we wrote field notes and played back the audio recordings, we found it extremely challenging to put into words both the general soundscape and the utterances produced by children. For example, we might write 'ding' for the sound a bell makes, but the word falls short of how it sounded. Equally, when children vocalised, we became aware of our tendency to try to listen for words, or to sometimes think we had heard a word, but after repeated listening realised it was either not recognisable as a word or a very different word to what we had thought it was. In this way, it was difficult to 'extract' discrete words from the wider soundscape and from place. Meaning was rarely embedded within the individual words or utterances of one child. Rather, it emerged collectively, not only between the humans involved but also between the space, context, and movement of bodies in that space.

In Vignette 2 below, we provide an example of how vocalisations, gestures, and single words bounced back and forth between two children and place, with connection and meaning emerging as part of this process.

VIGNETTE 2   Wilberforce House Museum: Tree Babies – vocalising on the move

The Tree Babies sessions took place in a very special walled garden space. The enclosed outdoor space, centred around an ancient lime tree, invited children to move, without the usual adult anxiety about safety. Two children, who had not met each other before, became magnetised to each other, moving in tandem as if attached by an invisible thread. Both children had been identified as reluctant to talk in playgroup/nursery environments. In the garden setting, the children used some single words with each other – but more often they vocalised single yells or sometimes repeated whoops that were rhythmically punctuated. Although it was hard to describe the sounds they made, they seemed to 'mirror' each other's sounds. This mirroring also characterised the way they moved in tandem with each other, holding the same objects and repeating each other's gestures to each other. The sounds they produced emerged with the rhythms and pace of their movements and in response to the encounters that momentarily stopped them in their tracks.

A large portion of young children's vocalisations during the study were not easily recognisable as words. Often, dominant accounts of child development emphasise words, and this is reflected in recent anxieties about the impact of the COVID-19 pandemic on early childhood, including a worry that children have reduced vocabulary. Importantly, in our research, it did not seem like the children's vocalisations were always trying to be words. Rather, the vocalisations did something in their own right, as part of a wider assemblage of bodies moving through space and the sociality of being and moving together. Therefore, it is important to rethink the assumption that children's vocalisations are all attempts at words (with an accompanying rationale that adults need to correct or improve children's pronunciation) and instead consider what vocalisations achieve in their own right.

Viewing the vocalisations as part of a soundscape, where they combine with movements, words, and other sounds in the environment, showed how meaning was collective and entangled with place. It seemed it was often in the gaps, silences, under the breath, and whispered into the wind, that new kinds of language emerged.

In order to value vocalisations just as much as words, we thought about:

- Creating welcoming spaces that invite and value all kinds of vocalisations, as far as possible.
- Offering activities and structures that have flexibility and space for different kinds of unplanned and unpredictable sounds.
- Asking "how much space can be left for noise?".

Questions for reflection

- What would happen if adults initiated less spoken language?
- How can we expand our view of communication to include more-than-words?

Language rituals and feeling connected

Previous research on young children in museums has identified how children participate in or create 'rituals' or repeated, shared ways of exploring or being in a particular location (e.g., MacRae et al., 2018; Wallis &

Noble, 2022). In this study, we noted the role of language and sound in diverse, newly invented rituals, which were characterised by the playful and relational language used by children and families. Rather than language being functional or concerned only with information exchange, these verbal exchanges were often about feeling connected to each other in the moment, about pleasurable actions and the anticipation of a shared moment.

In Vignette 3 below, Sasha and her mother call and return the phrase "waddle waddle" to each other, as they look for the penguins in the zoo at Sewerby Hall and Gardens.

VIGNETTE 3   Sewerby Zoo: Penguins that go "waddle waddle"

As Sasha and her mum search for their favourite penguin, Sasha's mum asks "and what do the penguins do?" in a confident and firm voice, and Sasha answers immediately "waddle waddle", in a loud voice with a slight sing-song inflection. Her mother responds immediately, emphasising the sing-song element "waddle waddle". Speaking at a slightly higher pitch, her mum's response sounds like singing and includes a slight laugh at the beginning of the utterance. Sasha immediately responds again "waddle waddle", this time in a flatter, less song-y voice, and her mum instantly repeats "ah…waddle waddle" in a deeper voice which seems to mark the end of the exchange.

Sasha and her mum's call and response of the phrase "waddle waddle" was not functional language or information exchange but an intimate ritual that references their frequent previous visits to the zoo and their shared love of the penguins. Playfulness and rituals can emerge when we least expect it, often led by children, with a liveliness that is difficult to pin down. We see this in different ways in each of the vignettes provided in this chapter: as Henry and his grandmother repeatedly ding the ball and laugh (Vignette 1) and as two toddlers mirrored each other's bodies and sounds (Vignette 2). Often during the research, the moments when families were relaxed, or when there was enough time for lingering, experimenting, or making space to notice children's interpretations and experiments, were when beautiful examples of personal language rituals emerged.

In order to better value language play and rituals that spring up spontaneously between children and their grown-ups, we considered:

- The nature and balance of activities on offer; are the activities outcome-focused or are there opportunities for freedom of expression and creativity?

- Grown-ups' awareness of how rituals tend to emerge and change through repetition and over time.
- Striking a balance between building in predictability and cultivating openness. Families and children often appreciate structure and predictability for helping to create a sense of safety. So how can we create opportunities for spontaneity without losing the safety of structure?

Questions for reflection

- What are the best conditions for playfully being together in spaces?
- How can we plan for unpredictability?

Creating comfortable spaces for early language

Early childhood language is impossible to separate from the strong messages educators and families receive constantly about the 'best' kinds of talk, appropriate pace of language development, 'quality' interactions, and the necessity of these things for children's future well-being and success. In many public spaces, parenting is policed and grown-ups can feel pressured (both implicitly and explicitly) to perform certain kinds of parenting and to encourage children to participate in this performance. Likewise, when early years educators bring groups of children from their settings to the museum, they are likely to feel a performative pressure in slightly different ways, as they use the visit to connect to the areas of learning specified by the early years curriculum.

In Vignette 4 below, Finn asserts and re-asserts his refusal to engage in the activities his Daddy would prefer him to do, while playing in an indoor space at the museum.

VIGNETTE 4   North Lincolnshire Museum: Finn's Escape!

Finn escapes from the Dudley's Den. He runs around a small island exhibit, making sure to keep it between himself and his Daddy, while laughing, non-stop. If his Daddy gets too close, he squeals in protest. The other children start singing "Wind the bobbin up". "We're not going to do wind the bobbin up?" asks Daddy. "Drawings!" Finn demands, followed by a howl of protest as Daddy tries to pick him up. "Oh dear", says Daddy, glancing at me from the corner of his eye. Eventually, the background singing transforms into the Bye-Bye Song. Finn flops down firmly on his bottom: "I sit down!". Finally, the Bye-Bye Song is over, Daddy expressing that we've "missed it". He tries to ease Finn up, who shrieks and flops backwards, almost hitting his head.

Here, Finn refuses Daddy's request and the lure of the Bye-Bye Song, not by saying 'no' but by using his whole body: he flops down, declares that he is sitting down, requests "drawings!", and shrieks in protest. Whilst the current climate for families with young children is characterised by anxieties about the 'proper' language and development of young children, it needs to be recognised that correcting or praising children for using words or playing in a certain kind of way has effects and produces certain kinds of atmospheres. Attending here to Finn's bodily refusal of the group singing activity shows the communicative value of transgressive, mobile, and emotive forms of communication that exist outside of narrow confines of 'proper' development.

Museum-based groups and spaces may have a particularly important role to play here. Families at several sites told us they preferred the museum sessions to other local playgroups because they viewed it as "less cliquey" or "not judgemental" and because they felt "comfortable". Whilst this may seem like a pleasing aside to the emergence of language in these spaces, our research points to the centrality of how people feel, how bodies move, and how people and bodies are able to relate to each other, to the emergence of language. In spaces where families and children spend time together, shifting power dynamics and atmospheres shape what kinds of movement, talk, and vocalisations feel possible or welcome in the space. Rubbing up alongside this potential are feelings and (sometimes) myths about the performance of proper kinds of parenting or 'being an educator' in public spaces. It is important to be conscious of and work to deconstruct or reframe these feelings and myths with families.

In thinking about how to create unpressurised spaces of welcome to families, we considered:

- Weaving hospitality into the atmosphere and physical design of the place, for example through relaxed blocks of time, thoughtfully arranged spaces, and trusting relationships.
- Creating conditions for children to experiment with movement and sound, which welcome vocalisations and noisiness and invite playful language for connection and belonging.
- Prioritising meaningful relationships between children, their grown-ups, staff, and spaces, instead of privileging word production between adults and children.

Questions for reflection

- How can we prepare and plan to build a sense of hospitality in the spaces where we work?

- In what ways can configurations of space and time offer unique forms of hospitality?

Conclusion

Our research shows how young children's language is bound up with place, body, movement, and collectivity when visiting museums. Viewing language as relational-material was useful for identifying the ways in which different museum spaces were relevant and beneficial to how young children used and experimented with language. The opportunity to experiment with different kinds of vocalisations, in different kinds of soundscapes, to playfully use language to create connection and a sense of belonging, and to do these things in an atmosphere that felt comfortable and hospitable were all important themes coming out of the study. By emphasising the role of place in how, when, and why children used language, our research highlighted important implications for the role museums have and could play in the everyday lives and language practices of children and families. Public, free spaces that welcome moving, sounding children and families are valuable in their own right, and the afterlives of the COVID-19 pandemic have foregrounded this even more.

References

BBC (2021, April 4). Covid: Young child development worrying, says Ofsted boss. *BBC News*. https://www.bbc.co.uk/news/education-60981450

Department for Education (2021). *Development Matters - Non-statutory Curriculum Guidance for the Early Years Foundation Stage*. https://www.gov.uk/government/publications/development-matters--2

Department for Education (2024). *Early Years Foundation Stage Statutory Framework for Group and School-Based Providers*. https://assets.publishing.service.gov.uk/media/65aa5e42ed27ca001327b2c7/EYFS_statutory_framework_for_group_and_school_based_providers.pdf

Hackett, A. (2021), *More-Than-Human Literacies in Early Childhood*. Bloomsbury.

Hackett, A., MacLure, M., & McMahon, S. (2021). Reconceptualising early language development: Matter, sensation and the more-than-human. *Discourse: Studies in the Cultural Politics of Education*, 42(6), 913–929. https://doi.org/10.1080/01596306.2020.1767350

Hackett, A., Procter, L., & Kummerfeld, R. (2018). Exploring abstract, physical, social and embodied space: Developing an approach for analysing museum spaces for young children. *Children's Geographies*, 16(5), 489–502. https://doi.org/10.1080/14733285.2018.1425372

Jarman, E. (2013, June 25). Communication friendly spaces – Early years. *Teaching Expertise*. https://www.teachingexpertise.com/articles/communication-friendly-spaces-early-years/

Jeffreys, B. (2021, April 27). Lockdowns hurt child speech and language skills – Report. *BBC News*. https://www.bbc.co.uk/news/education-56889035

MacLure, M. (2013). Researching without representation? Language and materiality in post-qualitative methodology. *Qualitative Studies in Education*, 26(6), 658–667. https://doi.org/10.1080/09518398.2013.788755

MacRae, C., Hackett, A., Holmes, R., & Jones, L. (2018). Vibrancy, repetition, movement: Posthuman theories for reconceptualising young children in museums. *Children's Geographies*, 16(5), 503–115. https://doi.org/10.1080/14733285.2017.1409884

Wallis, N., & Noble, K. (2022). Leave only footprints: How children communicate a sense of ownership and belonging in an art gallery. *European Early Childhood Education Research*, 30(3), 344–359. https://doi.org/10.1080/1350293X.2022.2055100

3d

SPACES OF REPRIEVE

An emancipatory practice centring Black and Brown children labelled with communication difficulties

Warda Farah and Vishnu KK Nair

Spaces of Reprieve

In this chapter, we, Warda and Vishnu, who are trained as speech and language therapists, invite you into the world of Maya. Though 'Maya' is a pseudonym, her story is all too familiar to the many children navigating the complexities of our schools today. Maya's journey mirrors the experiences of countless Black and Brown children whose lives are shaped by systemic racism and ableism. Therefore, Maya's story is woven into the narrative here as a recurring thread to interrogate the linguistic and communicative ideologies imposed on children within the profession of Speech and Language Therapy.

We believe that Maya's experience, and those like it, should push us to reconsider how we, as educators, speech and language therapists, carers, and society, can create spaces of refuge and empowerment – spaces where children are not labelled but seen in their fullness, their complexity, their brilliance. This chapter is not just a recount of Maya's story – it is a call to action, an invitation to radically shift our thinking about what it means to nurture a child's potential.

Maya

As I step into the playground, my eyes fall on Maya, standing alone in her neatly ironed dress. Her Hello Kitty bag hangs off her small shoulders, and her hair is meticulously styled in cornrows. Her wide eyes dart back and forth, brimming with wonder as she scans the area, clearly searching for someone. I assume she's looking for a friend, so I approach her gently and ask, "Hey Maya, who are you looking for?".

She turns her gaze to me, her familiar silence speaking volumes as she simply stares. Maya always stares at me like this. She extends her small, soft hand, placing it in mine, creating a brief, precious connection in the chaos around us.

Maya is autistic, and the staff often describe her as a "difficult child" who is "failing at everything". She is a constant subject of concern, with meetings frequently centred on her lack of progress. Questions about strategies to improve her language, communication, and academic performance are regularly discussed by the adults working with her, including me. During my time with Maya, I served as the school's dedicated speech and language therapist. My role was multifaceted, involving assessment of students, providing targeted interventions, and training staff to ensure the best support for our students' communication needs.

The struggles and challenges faced by Maya are not unique; they imbue the lives of so many children in schools everywhere. In this sense, the story of Maya becomes symbolic, representing narratives of children who bear the weight of existing in a world that fundamentally misunderstands their developmental trajectories. They are children who do not conform to the box of what is considered to be normal: they are labelled as atypical and described as not meeting developmental milestones and lagging behind their peers. Their language and communication are pathologised, viewed as deviating from the norm and in need of therapeutic intervention.

In this chapter, we do not aim to engage in a theoretical discussion or a tutorial on critical and decolonial praxis in Speech and Language Therapy, as these have been achieved elsewhere (e.g., Brea-Spahn & Bauler, 2023; Nair et al., 2023; Nair et al., 2024; Pillay & Kathard, 2015; Privette, 2023; Yu et al., 2022). Instead, we focus on deconstructing Maya's experiences and our own clinical experiences and practices anchored in a dominant Speech and Language Therapy philosophy – standardised testing and 'catching up' with developmental norms.

As minoritised scholars, our own journeys to break away from these dominant discourses have been complex and challenging. With 'Spaces of Reprieve', we imagined a route within our practice to free the children and ourselves, a means to diverge from and reject rigid Speech and Language Therapy interventions and methodologies, and to embrace a more fluid, humanising approach. Spaces of Reprieve is a physical space and a metaphysical embodied practice. Physically, it exists within the colonial structures of education and clinical practice, as a particular spatial location where Speech and Language Therapies and children can reinvent themselves, creating moments of genuine connection and understanding. In this space, children are not considered merely to be subjects of intervention or participants in a randomised controlled experiment but creative beings who are active in their own growth and well-being. Therefore, Spaces of

Reprieve calls for a deeper reflection into one's own ideologies of language and disability, including the ideological lens through which labelling takes place. It calls for critical interrogation of what that labelling does to the child in terms of linguistic remediation. Metaphysically, we expand the scope of Spaces of Reprieve as an embodied practice that any Speech and Language Therapy can adopt within their own context: it is a move to reject the harms of racist, colonial, heteronormative, and ableist ideologies, in favour of one with potential to support creative languaging, to centre local language practices, and to foster the citizenship of marginalised children.

Maya: childhood conceptualised as unmet milestones

We come back to Maya, as she represents the countless children that are labelled by the education and healthcare system. Maya symbolises the local and the global; a childhood characterised by the too-familiar feeling of not meeting the expectations set by a Eurocentric curriculum. We ponder these childhood(s) and often wonder what it must be like to be so small and impressionable and under the constant scrutiny of professionals. Every interaction, motor skill, behaviour, and piece of language that Maya produces is analysed, surveilled, documented, and used to inform the next annual reviews and progress meetings in educational settings. Childhoods chronicled in countless pages of documentation – notes from paediatricians, neurodevelopmental assessments, and case histories – stretching back to when children were just three years old, sometimes two or even one year.

As therapists, it can feel overwhelming to witness and be complicit in characterising children by their failures to achieve targets set by professionals. The unmet milestones of Maya's childhood presented in feedback and progress reports raise multiple questions regarding the yardsticks we rigidly adhere to. Where do they come from? Why do we always seek out what is 'lacking' instead of celebrating what is abundant within a child? It is quite clear that the milestones and the catching-up narratives are fundamentally rooted in the ideology of deficit, yet Speech and Language Therapydoes not engage in this conversation. This is illustrated by a recent debate. In 2023, the US Centre for Disease Control (CDC) changed the specifications for developmental milestones for language and communication development (ASHA, 2023). There was a perception among many professionals that CDC had lowered the standards for language milestones to conceal the negative impact of the COVID-19 pandemic on child development (Reuters, 2022). Whilst Reuters (2022) reported that this allegation had no evidence, there was considerable discussion on the issue within the Speech and Language Therapy profession, particularly in the USA, often stemming from fear-based assumptions that CDC's new milestones could further delay identification of language and communication disabilities (ASHA, 2023) or that they lacked evidence (Roberts et al., 2023). Although CDC's stance and the response within the Speech and Language Therapy community may seem to be in opposition (i.e., CDC changing the milestones and Speech and Language Therapies challenging it), they are rooted in the same ideologies of deficit and lack. The CDC perpetuates a uniform standard for every child to achieve, and the Speech and Language Therapy profession upholds such standards but goes beyond to label children who do not meet the milestones (and it fears that any changes to standards may delay the labelling, as in the case of the CDC debate).

The ideologies that underpin these debates are crucial here. Speech and Language Therapy conceptualises speech, language, communication, and social interaction as sets of skills, often narrowly specified, to determine what a child lacks rather than what they possess or embody. Deficit terms such as "delayed receptive and expressive language", "difficulties with attention and listening", and "echolalic speech" dominate reports. Newly constructed terms such as Developmental Language Disorder (DLD) obtain global influence without critical examination of the geographical (parochial) location of the construction (e.g., the UK or the USA) or the ideological lens (e.g., medicalisation) through which the construction emerged. Every mode of processing, understanding, and engagement of the child and their meaning-making with the world are subject to being labelled as delayed or disordered if they do not fit neatly into the box of standards, norms, and milestones that have been imposed. Maya becomes a child with DLD or a child with social communication disorder or a child who is apraxic or echolalic, or a combination of these categories – a child who is disordered or delayed at multiple levels.

The emergence of Spaces of Reprieve

Whilst from an early stage in our practice we realised the need to reject ideologies of deficit, it was not an easy endeavour. For context, Speech and Language Therapy is noted as one of the Whitest professions in both the USA and the UK (Nkomo et al., 2023; Yu et al., 2022). As marginalised scholars operating within a medicalised White academy, first we had to *unlearn*. A crucial part of our own unlearning was *unbecoming*. Unbecoming is complex because it is the reverse of what the academy wants us to be. It is to be wary of orthodoxy, to exist at the opposite pole as a critical thinker, questioning a body of knowledge and established practices. As marginalised clinicians and scholars located in the Global North, we also recognised that unbecoming is not just unlearning. It is a conscious and unconscious change that happens within our beings, a move away from the behaviours, manners, and languaging that Whiteness has imposed on us. We both had to constantly ask: What does it mean to exist within one of the Whitest professions with our multiple intersectional identities of race, sexuality, gender, and ability?

The emergence of Spaces of Reprieve is rooted in our own unbecoming – both Warda and Vishnu recognising that they have more convergence with Maya than the academy they are identified with. We recognise that readers may find this statement quite surprising or amusing, so we will explain. Both Warda and Vishnu have worked as Speech and Language Therapy clinicians. In Warda's case, her identity as a Black neurodivergent Speech and Language Therapy positioned her at odds with her experiences of the rich linguistic and multilingual familial and social environment she grew up in. She knew that the instruments used to diagnose, label, and remediate children will never capture the creative potential of their languaging. This insight was seeded in her journey from childhood where the languages she spoke, and the intersectional knowledge she embodied, were never valued by the wider system. She recognised that she had more in common with the children than the system, and her awareness of this convergence was a crucial way for her to deconstruct her own positionality. The difference between Maya and Warda became narrower, yet Warda held a licence to label Maya, a crucial power that exposes the problematic role of Speech and Language Therapy in dis-othering children within the current educational system. This quest to deconstruct and dismantle the power between her own self and the children within her interactive space inspired Warda to imagine Spaces of Reprieve.

Vishnu's identity as a queer neurodivergent man afforded him a deep understanding of what marginalisation meant, at an embodied and experiential level. Growing up in Kerala, the convergence of his queerness and neurodivergence meant that his own ways of being did not fit within the expected behaviour or communication standards of a heteronormative patriarchal society. Despite having intersectional caste and education privilege in the society where he grew up, he knew that his own embodiment diverged from the societal norms and he needed to create a space that would help him escape from the expected standards. As a Speech and Language Therapy student who sat in a classroom in the Southern Indian city of Mangalore, he was acutely aware of the inadequacy of the Eurocentric curriculum in the clinical training. The first stage of Vishnu's unlearning and unbecoming was to continually question his own clinical practice and the pressures on him to comply with a system that demanded lesson plans for interventions and measurable progress reports. He recognised the problematic nature of using assessment tools and materials developed in the UK or USA and of adapting those assessments for Indian children but retaining the same colonial ideologies of language and communication. Vishnu was mindful that post-colonial societies seeking to achieve the Indigenisation and decolonisation of power structures end up reinforcing and implementing the oppressive ideologies that colonised them. When Vishnu and Warda met, they quickly recognised their own convergences. They began to imagine Maya both as a child from the Global South facing multiple injustices and as a child excluded from Global Northern conversations (Nair et al., 2024). Within a Southern educational system, for example in India, Maya faces multiple marginalisations because of her class, caste, and language. Additionally, the Speech and Language Therapy profession requires her to behave like a child of the Global North through a set of expected socio-pragmatic norms developed in the USA or the UK – norms that are superficially adapted to the Indian context without critical examination of how coloniality is entrenched in the whole process.

As we deconstruct our own positionalities and our past and present clinical experiences from two different, historically connected locations in the South and North, we often come back to critical reflection on our own impulsive but constructive urges to react to injustices, often putting ourselves at great professional and personal risk. This was us birthing into our own new reckoning – a thread of our own experience and embodiment that was unspoken, unwritten (at least up until now), or even unpleasant yet so crucial to our imagination. We therefore come back to the matter of our convergence with Maya, which may have surprised or amused our readers, and we pose a question:

Is Maya (at least in part) an extension of our own childhoods?

We do not answer this question in the affirmative. This is because our convergence with Maya cannot be captured in a categorical yes or no response. We imagine Maya as a global child, an embodiment of self that is always evolving with full creative potential, rather than as a childhood framed by deterministic principles of progress and measured through language milestones and communicative predictability. For this imagining to occur, we created a space – a space that is not just a physical location – to collectively imagine possibilities beyond the pressures of hegemonic systems that we are operating under.

Who needs a Space of Reprieve? Is this a space imagined only for Maya? Or, as critical and marginalised Speech and Language Therapy clinicians, do we need this space as desperately as Maya? Once again, we come back to where we started, a place we often turn to in this chapter (and in our own daily lives), to remind ourselves and our readers that it is impossible to provide a yes or no response to these questions. Instead, the answers can only emerge through our own collective reflections, such as the ones below.

> We desperately needed a space to breathe, a sanctuary away from the relentless pressures, a refuge from practising in ways that unintentionally perpetuated harm. These thoughts haunted our lives, pushing us to seek a different reality. We knew we had to reframe our perspective, but first we needed to understand and accept our own self-making.
>
> Understanding and self-making are no easy feat; they demand patience, deep conversations, reflection, and moments of being engulfed by doubt, challenge, confusion. But crucially they are about unlearning and learning, unbecoming and becoming and to be all embodying self, and to recognise the tapestries of our own embodied knowledge that we have suppressed, to rediscover that knowledge and to oscillate within the beauty and the imaginative power of it – to co-create, build, and celebrate the languaging of little lights that have to come to us.

Spaces of Reprieve: the birth of a collective space

When the practice of Spaces of Reprieve is discussed, Speech and Language Therapies and other professionals often respond with, "That sounds great, but how do you actually do it?". They seek a magic recipe, a formula to follow, and quickly you learn that people crave a manual, a guiding document, or a list of dos and don'ts. However, Spaces of Reprieve is not about uniformity and nor is it a tool kit for practitioners to tick all boxes. Each space created is unique to those who co-create it with others, tailored to their specific needs and circumstances.

However, we offer two fundamental guidelines: (1) let the children lead and (2) choose the location together. This location must be a safe space where the expectations of the classroom and wider society are left behind. It is a sanctuary where children can shed the burdens of imposed norms and simply exist as they are. Creating Spaces of Reprieve is an organic process. It involves listening deeply to the children, understanding their world, and allowing them to guide the way. It is about finding that special place – a corner of the playground, a quiet room, a cosy nook – where they feel safe and free. This approach defies the conventional need for structure and certainty. It requires trust in the children's instincts and a willingness to step back and let them take the lead. It is about crafting a space that reflects children's individuality, where they can breathe freely and express themselves without fear of judgement.

Other common questions that get asked regarding Spaces of Reprieve are: How do we decide on the activities? What tasks are utilised? What linguistic or communication skills are targeted? In answer, we say, a practice that is rooted in an ethos of emancipation seeks not to remedy but to learn, not to target skills but to co-create, and not to measure progress using reductive instruments but to let joyous communication emerge moment to moment. Whilst we do not uphold any particular technique(s), we operate with a set of critical, decolonial, culturally sustaining, and neurodiversity-affirming perspectives. It is not our aim to explain these perspectives here, but readers are encouraged to refer to Yu and Sterponi (2023), Henner and Robinson (2023), and Nair et al. (2024) as a starting point if they are interested in specific lenses.

We envision Spaces of Reprieve as creating opportunities for therapeutic healing and meaning-making, enabling children to excavate the deep impacts of marginalisation. We argue that these spaces serve as a means to reject abyssal thinking that rests on colonial and fossilised ideologies of language, in favour of one that recognises hybridity and variability in communication (Henner & Robinson, 2023). We reiterate that a Space of Reprieve is not merely a physical location. It is a space for children and Speech and Language Therapies, a place that not only exists in the present but is also an imaginative space within each of us – a space for questions and critiques, opening oneself to learning and unlearning, to unbecoming and becoming. This is a space within us and outside of our being, a space to enjoy the profound power of simply existing, to discover your own local language practices and be grounded in them, and to connect to global practices. The evidence for the value of Spaces of Reprieve is not only in the joy and enthusiasm you see in children as they demand to co-share this space with you but also in the joy that you feel within yourselves in your own imaginative space, knowing that the children you work with are existing authentically for a moment in a world beyond confinements, categorisation, and catching-up narratives.

Conclusion

Warda conceived and envisioned Spaces of Reprieve but she did not do so in isolation, for its essence was never hers alone to possess. Vishnu's imagining of the Global Southern child looked beyond the importance of physical settings in Spaces of Reprieve, to consider the space as an embodied practice resisting colonial power relations within Speech and Language Therapy. Collectively, Spaces of Reprieve emerged from the quiet stirrings of a shared consciousness, guided by an unwavering commitment to the children who lay at its heart. It was the embodiment of a deep yearning – not to control or mould, but to create a space where these young minds could reveal their own power, where their freedom was not something bestowed, but something inherent.

Children like Maya are not mere participants; they are leaders. They do not passively absorb; they co-create, weaving their voices into the fabric of thought and action. Together, they shape an imaginary landscape where possibility and agency are intertwined, where creativity is stretched beyond its usual bounds, and where their presence breathes life into what might otherwise have remained abstract.

Far too often, these children have moved unnoticed through the pages of theory and practice, their hands shaping what scholars claim, yet their fingerprints unseen. Their ideas, their movements, their very being have quietly transformed the spaces they inhabit, yet seldom are they recognised as the true architects of these transformations.

To those children, in the past and present, we extend our deepest gratitude – not as a formality, but with true reverence. You have dismantled the certainties we clung to and unravelled the assumptions we mistook for truths. You have uneducated us, stripping away our pretensions and teaching us what it truly means to listen, to learn. Most of all, you have trusted us to bear witness to your unfolding, to be beside you in this ever-evolving journey of becoming.

It is in your trust, your willingness to engage with the world on your own terms, that the deepest wisdom lies. The pulse of Spaces of Reprieve has always been, and will always be, yours.

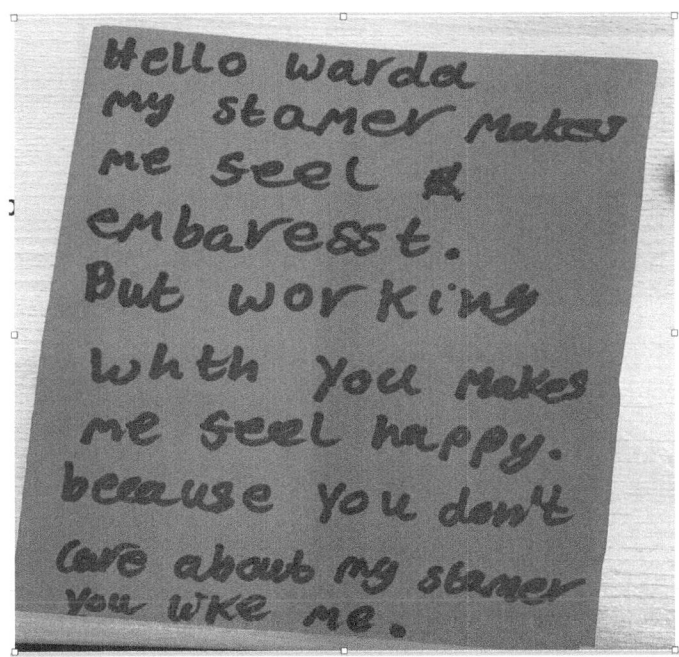

My Stammer

I am Creative

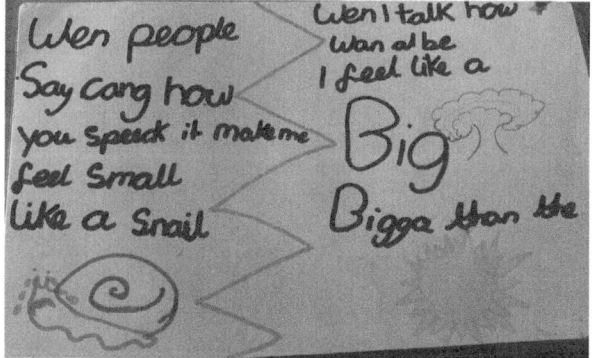

Bigga than the Sun

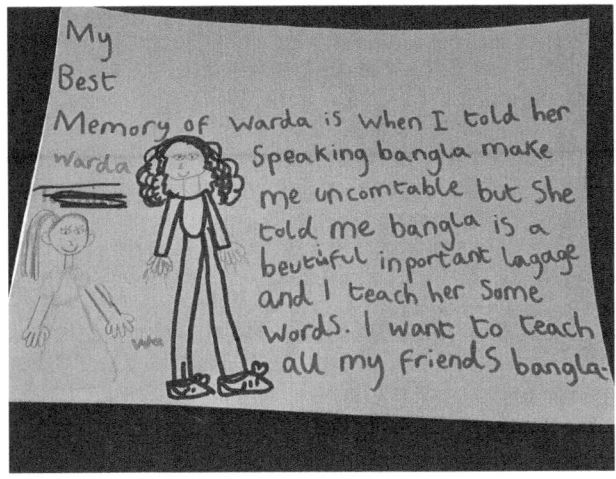

I want to teach all my friends Bangla

Acknowledgements

Warda would like to thank her grandmother Saffi Xaji Dhogor for being her first teacher, encouraging her love of languages, and keeping her connected to her roots. She would also like to acknowledge and thank Chance Bleu-Montgomery aka Neli Rankin for helping her navigate alternate modes of being. Most importantly she would like to thank all the children who have inspired her work. Vishnu would like to thank all the children and families he has worked with in India and the knowledge he gained out of it, without which the writing of this chapter would not have been possible. He is also grateful to his mentor and spiritual teacher Isis Bethany whose gift of wisdom gave deep insights into language and disability and gave him confidence to ground into non-Western knowledges as his true state of self-empowerment.

References

ASHA (2023, August 16). Study raises concerns that new CDC milestones may delay identification. *The ASHA Leader*. https://leader.pubs.asha.org/do/10.1044/2023-0816-cdc-milestones-slp/full/

Brea-Spahn, M. R., & Bauler, C. V. (2023). Where do you anchor your beliefs? An invitation to interrogate dominant ideologies of language and languaging in speech-language pathology. *Language, Speech, and Hearing Services in Schools*, 54(3), 675–687. https://doi.org/10.1044/2023_LSHSS-22-00135

Henner, J., & Robinson, O. (2023). Unsettling languages, unruly bodyminds: A crip linguistics manifesto. *Journal of Critical Study of Communication and Disability*, 1(1), 7–37. https://doi.org/10.48516/jcscd_2023vol1iss1.4

Nair, V. K, Brea-Spahn, M. R., & Yu, B. (2024). Decolonizing speech language "Pathology": critical foundational concepts for research, pedagogy and praxis. *Journal of Critical Study of Communication and Disability*, 2(2), 71–94. https://doi.org/10.48516/jcscd_2024vol2iss2.28

Nair, V. K., Farah, W., & Boveda, M. (2024). Is neurodiversity a Global Northern White paradigm? *Autism*. https://doi.org/10.1177/13623613241280835

Nair, V. K., Farah, W., & Cushing, I. (2023). A critical analysis of standardized testing in speech and language therapy. *Language, Speech, and Hearing Services in Schools*, 54(3), 781–793. https://doi.org/10.1044/2023_LSHSS-22-00141

Nkomo, C., Pagnamenta, E., Nair, V., Chadd, K., and the Royal College of Speech and Language Therapists. (2022). Analysing diversity, equity and inclusion in speech and language therapy. Royal College of Speech and Language Therapists. https://www.rcslt.org/learning/diversity-inclusion-and-anti-racism/

Pillay, M., & Kathard, H. (2015). Decolonizing health professionals' education: Audiology & speech therapy in South Africa. *African Journal of Rhetoric*, 7(1), 193–227.

Privette, C. (2023). Embracing theory as liberatory practice: Journeying toward a critical praxis of speech, language, and hearing. *Language, Speech, and Hearing Services in Schools*, 54(3), 688–706. https://doi.org/10.1044/2023_LSHSS-22-00134

Reuters (2022, March 1). Fact check: CDC and AAP review of childhood development milestones predated the COVID-19 pandemic. *Reuters*. https://www.google.com/search?q=Fact+Check%3A+CDC+and+AAP+review+of+childhood+development+milestones+predated+the+COVID-19+pandemic+%7C+Reuters&oq=Fact+Check%3A+CDC+and+AAP+review+of+childhood+development+milestones+predated+the+COVID-19+pandemic+%7C+Reuters&gs_lcrp=EgZjaHJvbWUyBggAEEUYOdIBBzg0MWowajmoAgCwAgE&sourceid=chrome&ie=UTF-8

Roberts, M. Y., Sone, B. J., Jones, M. K., Standley, M., Conner, T., Lee, E. D., Norton, E. S., Roman, J., Speights, M., Yoing, R., & Weisleder, A. (2023). What the evidence does (and does not) show for the Centers for Disease Control and Prevention child development milestones: An illustrative example using expressive vocabulary. *Journal of Speech, Language, and Hearing Research*, 66(9), 3622–3632. https://doi.org/10.1044/2023_JSLHR-23-00020

Yu, B., Horton, R., Munson, B., Newkirk-Turner, B. L., Johnson, V. E., Khamis-Dakwar, R., Munoz, M., & Hyter, Y. D. (2022). Making race visible in the speech, language, and hearing sciences: A critical discourse analysis. *American Journal of Speech-Language Pathology*, 31(2), 578–600. https://doi.org/10.1044/2021_AJSLP-20-00384

Yu, B., & Sterponi, L. (2023). Toward neurodiversity: How conversation analysis can contribute to a new approach to social communication assessment. *Language, Speech, and Hearing Services in Schools*, 54(1), 27–41. https://doi.org/10.1044/2022_LSHSS-22-00041

3e

THE ENTANGLEMENT BETWEEN SIGNED LANGUAGE, EMBODIMENT, AND PLACE

Leala Holcomb

This chapter explores the interconnectedness of signed language, embodiment, and place through several key dimensions. As a deaf individual, signed language is inherently the most accessible mode of communication for me, establishing a direct link between language and my embodiment. My deafness and use of signed language naturally draw me to environments where people communicate through signed language. Therefore, deafness, signed language, embodiment, and place are deeply intertwined.

My multi-generational deaf family in the United States includes a mix of deaf, hard of hearing, and hearing members. On my father's side, my deaf father was born to deaf parents (my deaf grandparents). His father, my deaf grandfather, was also born to deaf parents (my deaf great-grandparents), and these deaf great-grandparents were born to hearing parents. I am a fourth-generation deaf individual on my father's side. I have a hearing stepmother, two deaf siblings, and one hard-of-hearing sibling.

On my mother's side, my deaf mother was born to hearing parents, and all of her grandparents and great-grandparents were hearing.

I am married to a hearing individual and have one deaf stepchild and one hearing stepchild.

Everyone in my immediate family has equal access to signed and written language, but we do not have equal access to sound. As a result, we prioritise signed language and written communication at home, purposefully excluding spoken language to maximise and equalise communication access. However, this inclusive environment was not always the reality for the deaf members of my family born to hearing parents. In the following sections, I offer an insider's view of a family's life, with numerous examples of how language, body, and place manifest within the contexts of home, school, and community.

Language barriers at home

The hearing parents, such as my hearing great-great-grandparents on my deaf father's side and my hearing grandparents on my deaf mother's side, were initially unprepared for the birth of deaf children. They perceived deafness negatively, as a tragedy. Adhering to professional advice, they believed that sign language was bad and that their deaf children could learn to hear and speak through intensive speech therapy. This approach transformed home into a place of frustration, struggle, and exclusion. Both my deaf great-grandfather (on my father's side) and my deaf mother exerted tremendous effort to speak with their hearing parents and use listening devices around the clock, but they continued to face communication barriers.

As they reached adulthood, my deaf great-grandfather and mother began to explore deaf communities, where they eventually learned American Sign Language (ASL). Upon meeting other intelligent, successful, and literate individuals who were deaf and used ASL, my deaf great-grandfather and mother became angry about the ideologies of their own parents, validated by hearing professionals, in discouraging the use of ASL. They felt they had endured unnecessary suffering due to restricted language access and communication barriers throughout their childhood. Discovering ASL and experiencing ease in communication for the first time was both profound and emotional for them. Consequently, they sought partners who were deaf and used ASL, yearning for the accessible family experiences they had missed in their own non-signing, hearing homes.

The profound connection between signed language and deafness (language and body entanglement) has been a pivotal aspect of our home life across five generations. When deaf identity and signed language are embraced, our homes transform into sanctuaries. Conversely, when these aspects are rejected or devalued, homes can become places of trauma. This dichotomy is particularly relevant considering that 95% of deaf children are born to hearing families who often do not sign and who advocate for oralism, leading to widespread collective trauma within this demographic. My mother's decision to raise her deaf children differently has transformed our lives, and also influenced how we are raising our own kids, ensuring they grow up in environments where deaf identity and signed language are celebrated.

Question to ponder

- Why do some hearing people remain resistant to adding signed language to a child's life, despite deaf individuals repeatedly emphasising its importance?

Language access at home

My life, along with the lives of my siblings and those of our children and stepchildren, represents a significant departure from the experiences of my deaf great-grandfather and my deaf mother. They encountered barriers to communication at home with their non-signing parents, but we have enjoyed an environment rich in accessible language. In this section, I explore how signed language has enabled our homes to feel liberating.

In our family, the language development of deaf children in signed language mirrors the natural acquisition of spoken language by hearing children. For instance, just as hearing infants begin with vocal babbling, deaf infants in our family engaged in what is known as hand babbling. This early manual expression laid the foundation for our language and literacy skills.

My siblings and our children and stepchildren started signing their first words between the ages of six to nine months – slightly earlier than hearing children typically speak their first words. This precocity is attributed to the earlier development of hand motor skills compared to vocal abilities. Interestingly, this advantage is one reason some hearing parents introduce signed language to their infants, citing cognitive benefits. I was told that my first signed word was "ball", and I observed both deaf and hearing children and stepchildren in our family signing their first words, such as "dog", "fan", and "mom".

By age two, my siblings and our children began combining signs into simple sentences. By our third year, we were using grammatical patterns akin to those of adult sign language users, and our language fluency rapidly increased. We created signed rhyme and rhythm and told imaginary stories. By the time we reached kindergarten age, we were proficient in signed language. Additionally, between the ages of 3 and 5, we started engaging with written language, learning to fingerspell, recognising printed letters, and writing simple words like "mom", "dad", or "dog". When we entered kindergarten, we were starting to write simple sentences, such as "I love mom".

As a family, we relish playing with language. Our dinner chats might turn into a signed rhyme competition, or we might invent our own amusing fictional stories. We are always in awe seeing our children and stepchildren become creative and expressive with their ASL and English, often crafting stories far more intriguing than any we could imagine. We even started learning Spanish through a learning app, fingerspelling or writing Spanish words to each other for fun. When visiting Latin America, my stepchildren, both deaf and hearing, enjoyed communicating in basic Spanish through writing back and forth with locals.

Question to ponder

- How can the educational system be better equipped to support deaf children and their families throughout their signed language acquisition journey?

Our home as a mobile sanctuary

In my current home, it is me, my partner Damon (who is hearing), and my two stepchildren. Despite half of us being able to hear, spoken language is not our mode of communication. Instead, we consistently use ASL, maintaining this practice even when only hearing members are present in the room. Even when Damon and my hearing stepchild are alone in the house, they continue to use ASL. This norm shows that they value ASL for communication and are not using it just for the sake of the deaf person in our family. In this way, our home is transformed into a true sanctuary of belonging where all members are equally included.

Our approach extends beyond the confines of our home. When interacting in public, such as at restaurants, Damon and my hearing stepchild choose to write their orders instead of speaking. This decision prompts the waiter to also respond in writing, thereby maintaining equitable access to communication for everyone at the table. If Damon or my hearing stepchild were to speak, the waiter would likely respond in kind, which leaves out the deaf individuals from the conversation and placing Damon in the difficult position of deciding whether to interpret. Relying on Damon to interpret, rather than having everyone use the most accessible and equitable communication method – writing – reinforces power imbalance, making accessibility and inclusivity in the conversation with the waiter dependent on burdening Damon with the responsibility of interpreting. By communicating through written language, we level the playing field, avoiding placing additional responsibility on any family member. We also demonstrate to others how to engage inclusively with us.

This conscious choice to communicate without sound, even among those of us who can hear or speak, is a powerful approach to inclusivity. We reject modality chauvinism, the belief that spoken language is the only or best way to communicate. This approach makes interactions accessible to everyone involved, including external parties like waiters. Therefore, our home is not just a physical space but a model of inclusiveness that we carry with us, teaching others how to interact with us respectfully and thoughtfully. This ongoing, mobile sphere of inclusion is what truly defines home for us, ensuring that every family member feels connected and valued.

As a family, we frequently interact with non-signing hearing individuals during community events, at family gatherings, and through organisations. In these situations, we often use interpreters or our phones to facilitate communication. We particularly value connecting with those who are curious about and open to multimodal communication. These interactions feel fulfilling because there is a mutual willingness and investment in exploring different ways of communicating that go beyond conventional spoken or signed language. For example, we might use a mix of gestures, fingerspelling, written messages, and/or visual aids. This approach accommodates our family members and also invites non-signing individuals into our communicative world, fostering a shared experience and connection. By navigating these exchanges together, we invite people into our mobile sanctuary and make it even bigger.

Question to ponder

- How comfortable are you engaging in multimodal communication that does not rely on sound?

Deaf schools as a sanctuary

For deaf families like ours, finding a sanctuary in education is essential. High-quality bilingual deaf schools, characterised by a high proportion of deaf administrators, teachers, and staff and hearing colleagues who sign, offer more than just education – they provide a safe haven where deaf children are fully included and can thrive. Unfortunately, these schools are rare, often viewed as a last resort rather than a primary choice for deaf students, and typically considered only after academic failures in mainstream school settings.

Understanding the impact that different education environments have on deaf children's learning and well-being, my parents decided to move to a different state where a reputable bilingual deaf school was located. At this school, my siblings and I were fully included, around the clock, inside and outside the classroom, because we had complete access to communication through signed language and written language. Similarly, Damon and I prioritise the proximity of a high-quality bilingual deaf school when deciding where to live and work. We understand that being one of the only, or few, deaf children in a predominately hearing school where sound is the primary mode of communication can severely limit a deaf child's access to learning and well-being. Thus, bilingual deaf schools serve as sanctuaries, ensuring that our deaf children thrive academically and socially.

In these educational sanctuaries, my deaf stepchild is surrounded not only by peers who are deaf or hard of hearing but also by those diverse in race, gender, sexuality, and linguistic identities. This diversity serves to enrich both educational and social experiences. The curriculum, delivered through both ASL and written English, is tailored to optimise deaf students' comprehension and access to appropriately stimulating (i.e., grade-level) subject matter across disciplines such as science, social studies, mathematics, and language arts. Teachers facilitate a range of interactive learning activities, from producing essays in ASL or English, to translating between languages and analysing distinct grammatical structures; all these activities are designed to forge a deep connection between ASL and written language through methods like fingerspelling, viewing signed language, signing, reading, and writing. This bilingual approach supports deaf students in learning English as a second language.

By interacting with deaf role models such as school administrators, leaders, or other staff, and learning from their experiences, deaf students gain the tools and confidence needed to navigate predominantly hearing, non-signing spaces outside school walls. My deaf mother often reflects on the stark contrast between my experience attending a deaf school and her own experience of mainstream schooling. In her school, as one of the few deaf individuals among hearing peers and adults, she lacked access to deaf role models. This absence made it difficult for her to feel confident about her place in society, as hearing teachers and peers could not provide the unique perspectives or skills necessary for navigating life as a deaf person. My mother emphasised the importance of giving me access to diverse deaf role models, highlighting their role in fostering independence and success for deaf students like me. Learning from these deaf role models empowers deaf students to advocate for themselves when facing barriers or discrimination.

Most importantly, the visual orientation of bilingual deaf education means that deaf students are not at the mercy of their auditory capabilities to access learning and socialisation. While some deaf students, like my deaf niece, may choose to take speech classes to practise spoken English, others, like my deaf stepchild, may find them unnecessary or unhelpful. Deaf students are supported in their decisions regarding speech therapy without pressure. Success is never measured by a deaf student's ability to hear or speak. This inclusive philosophy helps shield students from audism and linguicism, making deaf schools a sanctuary where they are free to embrace their deaf identities in any forms.

Question to ponder

- How can schools ensure that deaf students have access to an abundance of deaf role models?

Maintaining sanctuary across communities

Our society is made up of multiple intersecting communities. Just as deaf people are part of hearing communities, hearing individuals are also part of deaf communities. The perceived dichotomy between deaf and hearing communities is misleading, and it is high time our societal narratives evolved to reflect this reality more accurately. Too often, policies, educational practices, research focuses, and medical advice perpetuate negative narratives about what it means to be deaf, influencing the beliefs and attitudes of hearing parents who raise deaf children. This results in deaf children being brought up without access to signed language, and often struggling to find their place in both home and school environments. For deaf people, the interplay between language, the physical embodiment of being deaf, and their environments can either restrict or enrich their experiences of access and inclusion, and their sense of belonging. My family's story, rich in languages, cultural practices, and social engagement, challenges the often grim portrayal of signing deaf people as tragically limited or insular. Understanding deaf people's lived experiences is important in order for homes, schools, and communities to become attuned to the needs of deaf individuals. By embracing and celebrating deafness and signed language to the fullest, we are capable of transforming spaces into inclusive environments where reliance on sound is not required for connection, socialising, and learning.

3f

COMING TOGETHER

Roundtable discussion on place and language

Warda Farah, Abigail Hackett, Leala Holcomb, Vishnu KK Nair, and David Ben Shannon

This section of this book focused on the entanglement of place with children's early language. The following roundtable conversation brings together authors from each chapter in this section (Warda, Vishnu, Leala, David, and Abi) to discuss the relationships, overlaps, synergies, and tensions between each of our practices. We framed the discussion around the following questions (which we first introduced in Chapter 1).

- What *else* (in terms of objects, spaces, atmospheres, and so on) might be important to children and their language practices in our contexts?
- What might 'joining in with place' look like in our contexts?
- How might we create irresistible opportunities for joining in, which are welcoming and relevant for all children?

Finally, we reflect on what we hope other practitioners and researchers might take away from this chapter to use in their own work.

What *else* (in terms of objects, spaces, atmospheres, and so on) might be important to children and their language practices in our contexts?

David: All of the chapters in this section pay attention to how children are active in carving out or transforming place in some way: the "ongoing, mobile sphere of inclusion" that Leala describes in their chapter, the Spaces of Reprieve that Warda and Vishnu advocate for, or the studies in Abi's and my literature review chapter (for instance, how Björk-Willén describes parents and children using their multilingualism to create linguistic barriers that exclude professionals from private spaces). So, I think, paying attention not just to 'where' as a backdrop to children's talk, or even 'where' as something that constitutes children and their talk, but also 'where' as in where is *created* by and with talk.

Abi: I am fascinated by atmosphere and the role it plays in all of this. It brings a wild element into what might unfold or be possible in any given place, because it is difficult to control or pin down. One of the things I appreciated about the Humber Museums Partnership research we did was being able to research across such a wide range of indoor and outdoor spaces. There is always something in the back of my mind about how seductive it would be to be able to draw some generalisable conclusions – 'outdoor spaces are usually best for this', 'stately homes instigate this kind of language' – but the way language and place come together is never that neat or predictable.

Vishnu: I think also, when we discuss spaces or atmosphere like this, we tend to externalise them. However, I also think of spaces that are held within, how children negotiate that space of creative language-making within themselves, and with the demands imposed on them by the outside world. I am curious about this internal-external relationship, what is compromised and created in this process, and how this process in itself teaches us that the internal and external are not as separate as we might initially think. They are tied together as a collective process in creative languaging, which is too often trivialised and overlooked in the traditional developmental psychology and psycholinguistics literature. This is beautifully captured in David and Abi's chapter as they discuss how certain 'things' are unmeasurable.

Warda: Just thinking more on that idea of the internal and external and their relationship being partially unmeasurable, I believe the 'vibe' of an environment is often overlooked, particularly when it comes to language and communication in children. By 'vibe' I mean the essence of a place – the energy it exudes and the feeling it evokes. A space with the right vibe is one that pulses with energy, brimming with potential, hope, joy, love, and even challenge. It's a place where both adults and children feel safe, connected, and naturally drawn to be. On the flip side, an environment with the wrong vibe can make people feel uneasy, disconnected, or even compelled to stay away.

Abi: Absolutely. Lucy Cooke and I presented the Humber Museums project at a conference last week – on historic houses in public ownership. Often these kinds of museums sit in parks or parklands, and sometimes they are free to enter. Yet, a common theme that people were talking about is how busy their outside spaces are, but how difficult it is to get visitors to cross that boundary into the indoor space, no matter how accessible, free, and welcoming you try to make it! I think this comes down to atmosphere, or vibe as you describe it Warda, and how bodies (and thus capacities for moving and sounding) feel and change as you step through the door into a space like that.

Warda: The atmosphere of a space can profoundly shape an experience, either uplifting or undermining it in ways we often don't notice. This idea is essential to all of the chapters in this section, I think.

What might 'joining in with place' look like in our contexts?

Abi: I wrote a blog post for Early Childhood Outdoors (Hackett, 2020) where I developed this idea of 'joining in with place as a conversational partner' – it draws from Abram's work in *The Spell of the Sensuous*, where he talks about vocal gesticulation. Abram writes about learning language as a bodily act which begins with experimental vocal sounding joining in with a surrounding soundscape. To learn, "it is necessary simply to begin speaking, to enter the language within one's body, to begin to move with it" (Abram, 1996, p. 83). Abram writes:

> by actively making sounds – by crying in pain or laughing in joy, by squealing and babbling and playfully mimicking the surrounding soundscape, gradually entering through such mimicry into the specific melodies of the local language, our resonant bodies slowly coming to echo the inflections and accents common to our locale and community.
>
> *(Abram, 1996, p. 75)*

Leala: In our chapters, we have all looked at how children's language develops in different places, and my focus is on making sure that environments are accessible to deaf children too. Most places rely on sound for communication, but for deaf kids, it is vital to have sign language around. When schools, museums, and even homes include sign language, they really help deaf children develop a strong sense of their deaf identity and connection to their community. When we talk about 'joining in with place', for me, it means creating spaces where deaf children can fully access information, actively participate, and be meaningfully involved without needing interpreters. This can be as simple as having people who sign be a regular part of these environments.

Warda: Similarly, Spaces of Reprieve, for me, is about the importance of creating spaces where every child can engage in their own way, reflecting the diversity of communication and interaction styles. As Leala pointed out, in order for children to 'join in with place', the place in question must be accessible to fit their needs. It also means recognising that there are many valid ways to participate, and children should have the autonomy to choose how they connect or join in with a space, or be supported in building the agency to do so. Participation is a deeply personal choice and varies for each child. While we may assume that children on the periphery of an activity are not involved, it is vital to understand that their contributions might take less visible, but equally meaningful, forms.

How might we create irresistible opportunities for joining in which are welcoming and relevant for all children?

Abi: Feeling comfortable and gaining experience of a wide range of different kinds of spaces is, in itself, a good starting point. The chance to experience how a body feels and what it can do in wide open rural spaces, and busy urban spaces, different kinds of public buildings, places where there is music and movement, long corridors and grand halls, animals and wildlife, expanses of water and the shoreline. There is a push for younger and younger children to spend a lot of time in early years classrooms at the moment (because it is associated with better school-readiness outcomes), but how can we value place-based experiences beyond classrooms?

Vishnu: Top-down structural changes are really needed. For example, access to sign language in multiple spaces, or decentring speech and language monomodality in speech and language therapy. From this perspective, Leala's chapter is so crucial because monomodal linguistic ideologies are imposed top-down.

Leala: The government could ensure that there are fundings to support sign language accessibility across public spaces, like town halls, doctor appointments, or play groups. By making it a default,

	deaf children can grow up in an inclusive society where sign language is normalised and celebrated. But also, museums could have special days where everything is communicated in sign language, with docents and staff who are fluent signers. This shows intentionality and commitment to changing the environment to make it meaningfully accessible to deaf visitors.
Vishnu:	Yes, I think we also need a bottom-up process that recognises the multiplicities of the local contexts, where 'creating irresistible opportunities' is a situated process of individual reflective practice. Spaces of Reprieve is envisioned through this lens: we do not use a tool kit or a prescriptive list of activities for joining in or welcoming children. The biggest question I have always asked when working with a child is: How can I disrupt my own patterns and perceptions that may not recognise the infinite potential of a child? When I say I'd like to create genuine, moment-to-moment connection in communication, I am not really talking about a uniform activity for all children. Rather, I am perceptive of my own differences and the differences that a child may bring in a given space, recognising that who each of us shows up as is perfectly perfect in every way.
David:	Just building from this, and it's not a particularly novel answer, but I think tuning into children's interests in individual contexts and leaving things open enough to bring their own interests in, but also building new things together. My chapter with Willow and Jess in section 4 speaks to this a little bit: there's an example they brought of a café space that the adults created but then the children continued to modify and add to with and without permission. I guess that also resonates a little with the chapter on the Humber Museums work in this section (3c). Henry and his 婆婆 created this new ritual together, around the dinging bell on the toy: something that he led on creating, but that they refined together through play.

What key messages and recommendations do we hope others take away from this book section?

Vishnu:	This section is an invitation to acknowledge and appreciate the pluralities of being and languaging. The lenses utilised in this section also question the narrow construction of evidence in and evidence-based practice in mainstream models of language development. It shows that multiple possibilities emerge when we think of language beyond linearity and milestones, and such

possibilities are present regardless of locations. It offers a reflection of how we can move beyond a brain-based, cognitive understanding of language towards an understanding that embraces the complexity and beauty of the seen and the unseen, the spoken and the unspoken, and the unmeasurable and the embodied.

Abi: Yes, I would love for people to let go a little of a key tenet of how we currently think about young children's language – that we can measure or assess it in one place and then the result of that assessment is relevant for describing that child's capacities as a whole. We see time and again, throughout these chapters, how dramatically children's language practices shift and change depending on place, context, how they feel, and how they are positioned by those around them. The child who seemingly 'never spoke', the child who could speak multiple languages outside of school, the child leading the action with gestures and vocalisations when they seemed too reticent before. We swap these stories with each other, often with a misplaced sense of surprise and amazement. It shouldn't be a surprise, considering the experiences we have had and the number of stories that accumulate. But there is still a shock in these moments, which rub up against the ways we are supposed to understand children's language and how it is acquired.

David: I think, related to Abi's point, I hope readers might walk away with a sense of how children's language is being framed everywhere through *lack*, but there is also a renewed popularity in highly stringent behaviour measures that deliberately close down where, when, and how language can happen: don't talk in the corridor, don't talk while you're working, make sure you only speak English, and so on. Years ago, we had this young man who didn't use any spoken language at all when he came to us. We worked really hard all the way through Key Stage 1 supporting his spoken language. Then, one time, I saw him on the stairs and he said "Hi Mr Shannon!" And I said, "Ooo, make sure you walk quietly on the stairs." Can you imagine? So, I hope we are emboldening practitioners to attend to these tensions in practice: the school rule is *this* regarding the where, when, and how of talk, but we also know *these* things about children's practices.

Warda: Yes, my hope is that this chapter inspires practitioners to step forward with confidence. This book weaves together multiple themes and practices, but at its heart lies a powerful reminder: regardless of our profession, experience, or focus, our work ultimately centres on the whole child. It calls for a shift in how we perceive communication and language, encouraging us to embrace their fluid, dynamic nature and move beyond rigid, traditional frameworks. More broadly, it highlights an exciting and overdue change in what is regarded as professional wisdom: a tide that is turning towards a deeper, more inclusive understanding of children's languaging and how we engage with it. So, my hope is that practitioners feel they can try out approaches that affirm and truly honour children's unique ways of expressing themselves.

References

Abram, D. (1996). *The Spell of the Sensuous*. Pantheon Books.

Hackett, A. (2020, October 23). Joining in: Place as a conversational partner in your children's talk. *Early Childhood Outdoors*. https://www.earlychildhoodoutdoors.org/joining-in-place-as-a-conversational-partner-in-young-childrens-talk/

SECTION IV
Language beyond meaning

4a

LANGUAGE BEYOND MEANING

Khawla Badwan, Ruth Churchill Dower, and Abigail Hackett

This chapter introduces theory and scholarship that helps us to think about language as more than merely the exchange of information or meaning. We begin by reconnecting with the ideas introduced in Chapters 2a and 3a, that language is material – it emerges from bodies in places, and it affects and is affected by bodies and places (Canagarajah, 2020; de Freitas & Curinga, 2015; MacLure, 2013; Martin-Bylund, 2018). As we discussed in Chapter 1, Western education systems tend to over-emphasise the process of transferring information from one person to another when it comes to learning and communication. This heavy focus on information transfer reduces language to a cognitive skill located in the brain and conceives of communication as the mere exchange of ideas between minds (Badwan et al., 2024; Pennycook, 2018) rather than between entire bodies, entangled with matter. One of the premises of this book is that this perspective does a disservice to what children often do with and bring to language, which is creative, unpredictable, bodily, and deeply connected to their home identities. Therefore, language does not simply *represent* things (e.g., a dog, a tree) and convey 'stable' meanings or messages. It goes beyond representation and includes "all the tears, sneers, sighs, silences, sniffs, laughter, snot, twitches or coughs that are part of utterances" (MacLure, 2013, p. 664). Indeed, language seems to evade attempts at tight definition, as it corresponds to and seeps across many different categories of being: language as something in our heads, as something exchanged between people, as something governed by rules and norms, as something used to internalise meanings, as something used to externalise thoughts, as something used to socialise, as something idealised that no one speaks perfectly

DOI: 10.4324/9781032677927-18

(Hall, 2020). Language refers to all these categories and more, leading some scholars to argue for using it as a verb, rather than normatively as a noun. For example, Badwan (2021, p. 7) defines language as "a verb with no boundaries: open, dynamic, overlapping, creative, responsive, proactive, human, post-human, and always in the making". As these different conceptual contributions shake the confidence that this thing we call 'language' can be pinned down, it might be more productive to pay attention not so much to what children's language is or what it *means*, but to what it *does*. What does language open up, close down, put into motion? What connections or relations does it seem to build in any given context?

In Chapter 1, we invited readers to consider these questions:

- How can we plan for the unpredictable?
- How can we make space for things we have not yet imagined?
- How can we resist demanding fixed meanings and clear logics?

The chapters in this section of this book help us explore some possible responses to these questions. We affirm that bodily expressions – the gestures, vocalisations, "tears, sneers and sighs" – are all absolutely part of language, and should be valued and acknowledged as such. This stands in contrast to what Blum (2015) has called 'wordism', that is, an approach to thinking about language that privileges distinct words and their clear unequivocal meanings above all other aspects of language. This is the kind of perspective of language that underpins the problematic notion of the 'word gap', which we discussed in more detail in our introductory chapter.

We find Badwan's (2021) use of 'languaging' helpful, as a single word that encompasses body and sound, meaning and non-meaning. Moving from language to languaging emphasises language as a *doing* rather than a *thing* – a doing that is constantly in motion and lively in the world. This section of this book, then, helps us explore the complexity within that definition of 'language' when it comes to childhood, place, and body. What are the moments when words are important, *and* when words are not needed or wanted? What are the moments when language seeks urgently to pass on a fixed meaning, *and* when language is about the kind of connection that does not rely on fixed, definite meanings? How do we value, acknowledge, and welcome all of this in our work with children?

These wonderments are linked to our commitment to challenge "the partiality of the linguistic tale" (Finnegan, 2015, p. 14) in order to open up a merciful and expansive space for language education. The focus on mercy is deliberate here, especially when children are positioned in a neoliberal education system that exclusively centres knowledge and skills.

We add mercy as a moral value that needs to underpin our work with children. Through a merciful lens and a merciful ethic, we pay attention to what is missing from the gaze of the adult as they make judgments or assessments for labelling children as 'competent' or 'incompetent' in linguistic and communicative abilities.

This means that our work is not just about expanding conceptualisations of language, or providing avenues for methodological and pedagogical innovations, but is also (and perhaps more importantly) about adding an ethical dimension to our work with children's language, creating a space for wondering about what ethical encounters might mean in children's education. Such a question is inspired by the ethics turn in applied linguistics (Kubanyiova & Creese, 2024) which challenges us to ask *how can we exist for each other ethically and aesthetically?* That is, beyond what language means, how is it experienced? We attempt to respond to this challenging question by emphasising the need for merciful arrangements that are expanding, accommodating, acknowledging, respecting, recognising, and indeed challenging (Bhabha, 1994).

In the following sections, we introduce some key ideas from theory that we have found helpful when thinking about children's language beyond meaning.

Expression and improvisation

Thinking about language as something that emerges in relation to others and to the world and through improvised flows of moving bodies experiencing places together, helps us reframe what we mean by 'expression'. Children use language to express themselves. However, there is often a sense that this expression should be the neat and clear articulation of ideas and desires that sit inside individual brains. Instead, we could think about expression as something that happens through the body, not necessarily through words. It does not start from somewhere 'inside' each of us, but is an ongoing response to/with different forces and flows of the world as they work through human and non-human bodies. Since all children experience the world differently, depending on their historical, cultural, social, and economic situations, their expressions of the world will be unique and situated and therefore multivarious and, often, beyond our understanding. In fact, we like to argue that understanding is always partial at best (Badwan et al., 2024).

Expression happens constantly, with millions of tiny movements of bodies, whether we can observe them or not. Expressions manifest in sounds, movements, gestures, humming, ticks and clicks, winks, smiles, tears, shrugs, signs, silences, and silliness – sometimes all at once. These might be a response to a material object, a surfacing of a partial memory, a felt sensation, an attempt to connect with another person, an unusual way of moving. How can we, as grown-ups, make space for and encourage expressive flows (which include ideas, actions, and embodied responses) between children and place and grown-ups, flows that unfold in the moment rather than being neatly mapped out from the start? In Chapter 1, we proposed Arculus and MacRae's (2022) notion of pedagogies of improvisation as an approach to working with children that makes space for the unexpected or illegible. Improvising with children is a skill, rather than merely a stance of 'anything goes', and it takes experience to extend a child's line of inquiry, to respond to their cues. For Churchill Dower (Chapter 4c), this kind of practice begins with listening with and to the body. This starting point encourages expression by "curating welcoming, relaxing conditions (with no expectations to speak) in creative places that are interesting to children" (Churchill Dower, this volume).

Louise Klarnett's approach to listening (Chapter 4e) is grounded in dance practice and polyvagal theory. Asking readers "have you ever had an eye dance?" she explores in exquisite detail how small flickers and responses form the heart of how we connect with others and the world. This work provides an example of how grown-ups might begin to tune into these expressions better, by starting with the body rather than with meaning. Spencer, Clarke and Shannon (Chapter 4b) argue for the importance of children's bodily autonomy – squatting on the carpet or stimming on the grass, for example. They make the important point that when bodies move, it can be meaningful *or* meaningless (or both, or something in between!), and our job as adults is to value *both* and remain open to both possibilities. Valuing and making space for children to squat instead of sit on the carpet, or to stim on the grass, is important and it is not necessary to ask what it means or demand a rationale first. However, Spencer et al. also give us the example of a child stimming in the sand area as a meaningful action that expressed his joy, which they describe as "communicative even though it's not specifically intended to communicate". This is a good example of expression as we have described it above: emerging in the moment and in between human and non-human bodies, it communicates something, but also does more than this. Not all this communication has clear meanings, but we can certainly emphasise that it matters to the being and becoming of the child, and it is our job as educators working with children to adjust our lenses and gazes with mercy, to see children beyond our assessment of their words.

Worlding

> Again and again, we tell children not to be so silly. What if, instead, we recognised the capaciousness of the "multiform and rebel speech of children"?
>
> *(Leal, 2005, p. 119)*

'Worlding' is a term that Donna Haraway (2016) often uses and defines as making worlds together or the co-making of worlds. Words are not the only way of knowing the world. Children know with their senses, they form intense attachments to things, and they respond to the world with motion, (e)motion, and (co)motion. "Children turn into animals, plants, stones and toys", writes Leal (2005, p. 121); this description of playful co-making of the world may be familiar to many readers. We could, perhaps, imagine such bodily, playful co-making as world-making conversations, ones that highlight the affective, the sensory, and the non-representational within language (Canagarajah, 2023). This kind of knowing and responding to the world, through bodies as well as language, is what we mean when we talk about worlding or world-making.

Henner and Robinson (2023) and Canagarajah (2023) propose a critical disability studies frame as a route to understanding language more expansively as an expression of the interconnected relationship between mind and body. Henner and Robinson name this centring of disabled perspectives, practices, and scholarship in conceptualisations of language as 'a cripping of linguistics' which disrupts assumptions about language hierarchies, including the privileging of mind, representation, and individual meaning, over body, mutual understanding, and interdependency.

Recognising worlding means we must take a more capacious approach to language. Instead of thinking of words as simply naming the world, we could think about the lively-ness of language and how it emerges and mutates through play and curious inquiry. In making these shifts, we recognise that oftentimes children are better placed than grown-ups to perceive their connectedness to the world around them. In this respect, adults might themselves be moved to pay attention to the world in new ways when in the company of children. What can we learn from children's world-making practices?

Language as worlding comes into sharp relief in Lee's Chapter (4d) where she describes the struggles and problematics of adults choosing and designing Augmentative and Alternative Communication (AAC) technology for users. Her collaborator Jamie Preece's question "who chooses my words?" points to the importance of language as more than communication and asks how to incorporate sarcasm, humour, irreverence, nonsense, and intimacy into AAC. Spencer et al. (4b) write about the joy of newly invented words, connecting this approach with Biklen and Burke's writing on 'presuming competence'. This also links to Lee's discussion of sound and word play and familect (invented words or phrases that are meaningful within a family) in AAC and how to value this better in the design of AAC devices.

Opacity

The assumption of, and desire for, a knowable child is central to early childhood education (Cannella & Viruru, 2004). There is often an assumption, for example, that educators should be able to predict how children will respond, be able to adapt activities accordingly to elicit the desired responses, and then be able to explain 'why' and 'what next'. Whilst it is often the case that grown-ups who work with children do know them deeply and build important trusting and loving relationships, Glissant's (1997) work on opacity, which we introduced in Chapter 1, helps us to think about what and who can be fully knowable or totally transparent.

For Glissant (1997), every single being is rich, complex, interconnected, and brings their own history and stories (conscious and unconscious) that sit in their bodies, minds, and souls. Therefore, we can create an illusion of 'fully knowing' another being only if we flatten and simplify them – that is, we create a less rich and complex version of that person for our own purposes. Glissant describes this happening in colonialism, while Canagarajah (2023) writes about the implications for linguistics, and Viruru (2001) discusses this process in relation to young children.

This important idea of the 'right to opacity' disrupts many of education's assumptions about what language is for and how it is experienced in childhood. It disrupts the idea that clear, easily understood spoken language is preferable or superior, pointing instead to all the potential and power that can emerge from the kinds of less-transparent bodily expression we described above. We draw on Glissant's (1997) theory of opacity to ask what happens when certain kinds of language are imposed too quickly onto young children – what that might *do* in terms of children's sense of identity and their potential for creative bodily experimentation (Shannon & Hackett, 2024; Viruru, 2001).

The contributors to this book demonstrate how powerful the experience of coming alongside, not talking, feeling comfortable, and valuing time just being together, can be for building deep connections between children and the grown-ups working with them. For example, Spencer et al. (Chapter 4b) show how leaning into a child's fascination for a bee, even if you do not fully understand it, can be a way of honouring and building on a child's funds of identity without demanding transparency or legibility first. Lee (Chapter 4d) advocates for child-led and collaborative approaches to assisted communication, even when these are less clear or less convenient in the classroom. And for Klarnett (Chapter 4e), the fleeting nature of dance is part of its power, resulting in practices and connections that are rarely described or recorded.

We acknowledge there is a tension between normalising and valuing children's not-speaking, or the times when what is being communicated is not clear, and ensuring we are prepared to listen to and take children's expressions seriously. What is named often becomes what is valued. Taking stimming as an example, in her Chapter (4d) 'Who chooses my words?', Lee points out that there is no AAC sign for stimming, and that gestures, squeals, and stims are often deemed less acceptable as children get older. For us, the balance comes in the stance of presuming competence, and respecting the complexity, contradictoriness, and texture of every individual (child or adult), without requiring evidence of that competence first.

Hierarchies of language in educational settings

We turn our attention now to the question of power and, in particular, the tendency of formal education settings to require certain kinds of language from children, the kinds of language that do foreground meaning and representation (Arculus & MacRae, 2022; Olsson, 2009). The importance and potential of dismantling these hierarchies shows up in different ways across the chapters in this section. For example, Churchill Dower (Chapter 4c) describes how her work pushed back some of the dominant approaches for working with non-lingual children, which are often exclusively or mostly focused on getting children to talk. Spencer et al. (Chapter 4b) appeal for joyful practice in the context of a teacher retention crisis and working in classrooms and communities that do not fit the white, middle-class, able-bodied, monolingual mould around which our educational system is currently constructed. Lee (Chapter 4d) describes how the demands of school-based communication tend to dominate the design of AAC communication aids and suggests approaches that might counter this or offer a more personal approach.

We often hear the argument that children need to acquire as much language as quickly as possible for the benefit of their learning, or that children who cannot perform standardised English on demand will struggle in the future. These concerns are real in the sense that within our current structures it can be more difficult for children to thrive in some contexts without as-many-words-as-possible in the dominant language (English in our context), spoken clearly and confidently in full sentences. However, our point is that we should not place the communicative 'burden' on the children: we should avoid the typical neoliberal logic that places responsibility on disadvantaged individuals, rather than on systems, structures, policies, and ideological gazes. Instead, we need to reimagine a more merciful, generous, and inclusive educational system and society.

As the contributors in this book demonstrate, if the process of accelerating and shaping children's 'language gain' is approached in the wrong way, there can be many drawbacks. We risk the non-linguistic being considered less valuable (Churchill Dower, Chapter 4c), bodily trauma and emotional wellbeing being overlooked or sidelined (Klarnett, Chapter 4e), and sucking the joy out of working with young children (Spencer et al., Chapter 4b). When hierarchies of language are created, and clear meanings sit at the top – meanings that are in a language and from a perspective the adult can easily understand – children no longer feel that their home identities and multiple languages are valued, and they no longer feel they can bring their whole selves into every space (Baker-Bell, 2020). We pose a question first asked by Viruru (2001): what is lost when language is gained? This is an unsettling question in our current educational context, where gaining language is usually assumed to be a beneficial process with no drawbacks. Indeed, there are multiple interpretations of the loss and gain framed in this question, including losing community languages when school language is gained (and reinforced as the only valued and legitimate means of communication), losing the effectiveness of embodied language when verbal language is gained (and reinforced as the only valued and acceptable means of communication), losing the messiness and unpredictability of children's language when pre-engineered language is gained (and reinforced as the only correct and accurate means of communication). Through the lens of merciful ethics and aesthetics, we need to work collectively to challenge the too-many losses that children incur in education as a result of the imposition of an industrialised notion of language that is often "false, linguaphobic, racist, half-baked, or, at best, partial" (Gramling, 2021, p.7).

References

Arculus, C., & MacRae, C. (2022). Clowns, fools and the more-than-Adult toddler. *Global Studies of Childhood*, 12(3), 209–233. https://doi.org/10.1177/20436106221117569

Badwan, K. (2021). *Language in a Globalised World. Social Justice Perspectives on Mobility and Contact*. Palgrave Macmillan.

Badwan, K., Nunn, C., & Pahl, K. (2024). Working with/beyond 'language': Insights from a listening walk with young men from asylum-seeking backgrounds in a rural treescape. *Language and Intercultural Communication*, 1–14. https://doi.org/10.1080/14708477.2024.2373156

Baker-Bell, A. (2020). Dismantling anti-black linguistic racism in English language arts classrooms: Toward an anti-racist black language pedagogy. *Theory into Practice*, 59(1), 8–21. https://doi.org/10.1080/00405841.2019.1665415

Bhabha, H. (1994). *The Location of Culture*. Routledge

Blum, S. (2015). "Wordism": Is there a teacher in the house? *Journal of Linguistic Anthropology*, 25(1), 74–75.

Canagarajah, S. (2020). English as a resource in a communicative assemblage. In C. Hall & R. Wicaksono (Eds.), *Ontologies of English: Conceptualising the Language for Learning, Teaching, and Assessment* (pp. 295–314). Cambridge University Press.

Canagarajah, S. (2023). A decolonial crip linguistics. *Applied Linguistics*, 44(1), 1–21. https://doi.org/10.1093/applin/amac042

Cannella, G. S., & Viruru, R. (2004). *Childhood and Postcolonization. Power, Education and Contemporary Practice*. Routledge.

De Freitas, E., & Curinga, M. X. (2015). New materialist approaches to the study of language and identity: Assembling the posthuman subject. *Curriculum Inquiry*, 45(3), 249–265. https://doi.org/10.1080/03626784.2015.1031059

Finnegan, R. (2015). *Where Is Language? An Anthropologist's Questions on Language, Literacy and Performance*. Bloomsbury Academic.

Glissant, E. (1997). *Poetics of Relation*. University of Michigan Press.

Gramling, D. (2021). *The Invention of Multilingualism*. Cambridge University Press.

Hall, C. (2020). An ontological framework for English. In C. Hall & R. Wicaksono (Eds.), *Ontologies of English: Conceptualising the Language for Learning, Teaching and Assessment* (pp. 13–36). Cambridge University Press.

Haraway, D. (2016). *Staying with the Trouble*. Duke University Press.

Henner, J., & Robinson, O. (2023). Unsettling languages, unruly bodyminds: A crip linguistics manifesto. *Journal of Critical Study of Communication and Disability*, 1(1). https://doi.org/10.48516/jcscd_2023vol1iss1.4

Kubanyiova, M., & Creese, A. (2024). Introduction: Applied linguistics, ethics and aesthetics of encountering the other. *Applied Linguistics Review*. https://doi.org/10.1515/applirev-2024-0083

Leal, B. (2005). Childhood between literature and philosophy: Readings of childhood in Manoel de Barros' poetry. *Childhood & Philosophy*, 1(1), 111–124.

MacLure, M. (2013). Researching without representation? Language and materiality in post-qualitative methodology. *International Journal of Qualitative Studies in Education*, 26(6), 658–667. https://doi.org/10.1080/09518398.2013.788755

Martin-Bylund, A. (2018). Minor (il)literate artworks: Inventive processes of biliteracy and the role of expertise in early childhood bilingual education. *Global Studies of Childhood*, 8(1), 23–37. https://doi.org/10.1177/2043610618758424

Pennycook, A. (2018). *Posthumanist Applied Linguistics*. Routledge.

Olsson, L. M. (2009). *Movement and Experimentation in Young Children's Learning: Deleuze and Guattari in Early Childhood Education*. Routledge.

Shannon, D., & Hackett, A. (2024). Opaque reciprocity: Or theorising Glissant's 'right to opacity' as a communication and language praxis in early childhood education. *Discourse: Studies in the Cultural Politics of Education*, 45(1), 118–130. https://doi.org/10.1080/01596306.2023.2273336

Viruru, R. (2001). Colonized through language: the case of early childhood education. *Contemporary Issues in Early Childhood*, 2(1), 31–47. https://doi.org/10.2304/ciec.2001.2.1.7

4b

BEYOND 'DEFICIT' OR 'LACK'

Enjoying the richness of language and meaning-making in a complex early childhood classroom

Willow Spencer, Jess Clarke, and David Ben Shannon

This chapter is animated by two questions: How can we 'find the joy' as teachers in England's early childhood education system? And how can we use that joy to dismantle deficit perspectives on children's meaning-making and meaning-sharing practices? As has been argued elsewhere in this book, deficit perspectives on children's communication practices are rife in England. At the same time, schools in England are in the midst of a sustained recruitment and retention crisis: in the academic year 2022–2023, 9.7% of the workforce quit, while a quarter of new teachers only stay in the profession for three years (Department for Education, 2023; McLean et al., 2023). In these bleak times, it seems more important than ever to find the joy in the classroom.

That said, joy is a tricky concept. What one person finds joyful, another might not. While someone else is experiencing joy, you might be experiencing something quite different! Early childhood education scholar Liselott Marinetti Olsson (2009) links the feeling of joy to a body's increased capacity to act. Olsson is inspired by 17th-century philosopher Baruch Spinoza, who argues that *what* and *how* a body feels is tied to that body's increasing or decreasing capacity to act. Olsson gives the example of swimming, where new capacities – such as floating, splashing, and diving – might be experienced as joy, while feeling restricted – trapped beneath the water, struggling to draw breath – might elicit fear. Importantly, for Spinoza, these feelings are shared between bodies in complex ways: the joy felt by a child is also felt by the adult, possibly as more joy, but possibly also reluctantly, with one eye on the clock, or even as downright irritation. For instance, a child's joy at expanding their capacities upon returning to

DOI: 10.4324/9781032677927-19

the playground will definitely be experienced by the adult, but perhaps as escalating panic over how that child had managed to jimmy the playground door open part-way through a maths lesson!

This chapter is written by three teachers who all worked together for a time at 'Sparrows Academy' (not its real name): Willow and Jess, the Early Years Foundation Stage (EYFS) teachers, and David, the school's former Special Educational Needs teacher (and one of the editors of this book). Sparrows Academy is a primary school that serves a richly diverse but economically deprived community in northern England. Over 70% of the children speak one of 42 home languages other than English, and most students are new to English when arriving at the school. The proportion of children who have special educational needs is double the national average. Additionally, the school's rate of mobility is 25%, which means that a quarter of the cohort leaves the school every academic year and is replaced by new students (who are typically also new to English): this has implications for how effective the school can be at establishing long-term speech, language, and communication (SLC) plans for students, as well as their English language learning provision. In this complex and challenging environment, in which children are subjected to multiple overlapping patterns of marginalisation, it would be easy to sink into deficit narratives of the communication practices of children who speak English as an additional language and children with special educational need: narratives that emphasise what they *can't* do rather than the exciting ways they explore talk and gesture that go beyond simply transmitting and receiving information. In this chapter, we share some anecdotes from our practice that illustrate our children's experimentation with language, communication, meaning-making, and the body. Their shared senses of joy in these experimentations push back on narrations of our children as deficient or lacking. We offer a series of questions that have emerged over the years when reflecting on our own practice.

Is it a speech and language disability? (Or are people just not listening properly?)

It has long been a part of educational policy in England that children should not be classed as having an SLC disability just because they speak English as an additional language (Department for Education and Science, 1978). However, it often feels too easy to lump children with any kinds of linguistic differences together, regardless of whether these are caused by a disability or by speaking more than one language. We think it's important to ask ourselves: Do they *really* have an SLC disability? (Or are people just not listening properly?)

This question is further complicated because speech and language assessments are usually conducted in English, by professionals who are not so familiar with that child, and without considering the perspectives of their parents. The practice anecdote below illustrates how we deliver more customised speech and language assessments and supports, by making use of a staff member's home language.

> **PRACTICE ANECDOTE: CULTURALLY SPECIFIC ASSESSMENT**
>
> One thing that can help differentiate between SLC needs and EAL (English as an Additional Language) is having good relationships with families and caregivers. For instance, we had a little boy who spoke Urdu at home and was new to English. Our teaching assistant spoke Urdu, so we asked her to support the speech and language assessment and trained her to deliver the therapy plan each week in Urdu. This meant she could recognise the difference between a gap in his English language skills and areas where he needed support in his language development more generally. Importantly, though, she could also speak to his mum in Urdu. His mum would tell us, "We're working on this with him at home", and we could say, "Great, we can look at that in school too!" and vice versa. That said, we may not have picked up on that unless we had staff from the Urdu-speaking community.

When children get assessed or when they're doing these speech and language interventions, it is instilled that they're doing things wrong because the focus is always on English. By contrast, this anecdote illustrates how we were able to deliver communication and language programmes in ways that were more tailored and de-emphasised English slightly. In so doing, the capacities of those involved are increased in some small way: both the child and the staff member got to enjoy using their own home languages in school.

Questions for reflection
- Are you listening to your children?
- Are you building relationships with families?
- Are the ways you listen to children adding to their capacities to act (i.e., making space for joy)? Or reducing them?

Is it the 'wrong' word? Or just a new word?

In our complex, multilingual setting, many of the kids speak a home language other than English and many others have diagnoses of SLC needs. From time to time, new words emerge in our practice. In the practice anecdote below, we describe the emergence of a new word and how we made space for it to become part of our class vocabulary.

> **PRACTICE ANECDOTE: SNICKERS AND STICKERS**
>
> One of our children had difficulty pronouncing certain consonants: for instance, she would swap the sound 't' with the sound 'n'. So, when asking for a sticker, she'd say 'snicker'. But then this started spreading throughout the class so that now, whenever anybody wants a sticker, they ask: "Can I have a snicker?" But they also didn't know that a Snickers is a chocolate bar. So, I showed them and said: "This is actually what you're saying: This is a chocolate bar but, if you want, we can carry on calling a sticker a 'snicker' in our class?" And they said yes, so that's what we did.

In this anecdote, we describe how the 'mispronunciation' of the word sticker led to the creation of a new meaning for the word Snicker in our classroom. Often, our instincts when working with young children are to correct errors in pronunciation, or else to interpret the word as referring to a 'real' word. For instance, young children often say the word yellow as 'yeyow'. Adults hear this word and then interpret it as a placeholder for the word (and colour) yellow. These perspectives emphasise words as vehicles for transmitting and receiving meaning, rather than something that should be enjoyed in and of themselves. However, in the anecdote above, the mispronunciation of the word sticker as snicker takes on its own life as a new, community-created word.

Michael Davidson, in his book *Distressing Language: Disability and the Poetics of* Error (2022), describes the ways that mishearing spoken words can sometimes be interesting, generative, and humorous. Such mishearings are called mondegreens. Famous song lyrics often make for delightful mondegreens: for instance, "Ah, ah, ah, ah, stay in the lab, stay in the lab" or "Somewhere over the rainbow, weigh a pie" (Goldsmith, 2002, as cited in Davidson, 2022, p. 36). Davidson (2022) writes that "Children trying to decode adult language live in a world of mondegreens" (p. 35). However, in our practice anecdote, the mondegreen is an equally delightful error in speech rather than hearing: the mispronunciation of the word sticker as the word snicker generated a new, shared word for the stickers used in the classroom. Rather than correct the mondegreen, we let the children share in our delight of it. This reminds us of Christina Tatham's (Tatham-Fashanu, 2023) research, which describes how words sometimes pick up new, shared meanings in multilingual classrooms: she offers the example of the Urdu word *shaadi*, which means 'wedding', and describes how it acquired the new meaning 'party' in her research classroom, through children's play with orange felt. What is important for both Tatham's work and our own practice anecdote is that the new word is illustrative of the new culture being created in the classroom, which goes far beyond the simple meanings of words. Tatham (Tatham-Fashanu, 2023) uses Homi Bhabha's notion of the Third Space, which captures how encounters between people mix together aspects of each individual's culture to create a new, shared culture. As with snicker, Tatham argues that shaadi comes to stand in for an entirely new culture created specifically in that classroom.

In our practice, we make sure to distinguish between the traditional words (sticker and Snickers) and the new word (snicker). But, within the four walls of our classroom, rather than point out the new word's inaccuracies and correct more and more children as they began to take it into their own vocabularies, we decided to enjoy it: to allow 'snicker' to take on a life of its own as both a new shared word and *world* that exist only in the third space of our classroom.

Questions for reflection

- Respecting children's emergent language practices might sometimes also mean respecting emergent vocabulary! What new words are springing up in your practice? How can you nurture them?
- (When) Do you need to close new words back down?

Are you teaching for your children's whole bodies? Are you respecting their bodily autonomy?

There is pressure on early years practitioners from curriculum and policy documents to introduce increasingly formalised learning. This requires that children in EYFS must increasingly learn at desks, write in books, or sit on the carpet with their legs crossed, listening to teachers while studying systematic synthetic phonics or maths (e.g., see Ofsted, 2017). While it's important to prepare children for Year 1, we also feel that it's important to teach for their whole bodies, rather than against those bodies by making them be still, without fidgeting, staying silent, and so on. In the anecdote below, we think about sitting, squatting, and carpets.

> **PRACTICE ANECDOTE: PICK YOUR BATTLES**
>
> Some children, no matter what you do, just won't sit on their bottoms on the carpet. For instance, some children prefer to squat. However, if they're joining in, participating, listening, and learning, then squat if you want to. Shuffle on your knees if it helps. We think we kind of have to pick our battles: if they're joining in and we're getting something from them, then sitting on bottoms really isn't the point.

In this anecdote, we illustrate how important it can be to acknowledge children's understanding of their own bodies: if they don't seem to be able to sit 'nicely' for extended periods of time, it might be because they know that they can't, or because the movement helps them concentrate. This acknowledging of children's bodily autonomy is particularly important for children who don't use spoken language. Some autistic children, for instance, might use a range of embodied practices. They might *stim* (self-stimulate), engaging in a repeated motion or gesture such as rocking back and forth for sustained periods of time. It's important to give children space to do this, as illustrated in the practice anecdote below.

> **PRACTICE ANECDOTE: STIMMING ON THE GRASS**
>
> During a recent Ofsted inspection, one of our children was on the grass, rocking back and forth. Later, the inspector commented: "I'm really pleased to see that you just let him do that because that's what he needed at that time." Sometimes visitors come in and don't know how important stimming is for some children, so the Ofsted inspectors giving their approval felt like it was giving us licence to keep advocating for those children.

As we can see from this anecdote, it's important to let children stim. As the inspector commented, "that's what he needed at that time". In this way, it's important to recognise children's knowledge of their own bodies. In Chapter 2b of this book, Yvonne Williams and David Shannon argue that there is a need to distinguish between *communication* behaviours, which are intended to communicate something to another person, and *communicative* behaviours, which can communicate something even though they're not expressly intended to. Self-stimulatory behaviours are not typically *communication*, in that they're not for or about transmitting something to somebody else. However, they can sometimes be *communicative*, in that those familiar with that person's movement patterns can sometimes discern something from them. The following practice anecdote gives an example of this communicative-ness. We describe how we began to notice that a young person's stims were illustrative of their enjoyment of an activity, even if they seemingly weren't involved with it.

> **PRACTICE ANECDOTE: STIMS IN THE SAND AREA**
>
> Some children, when they first come in, won't engage with anything: they might just walk around, or rock backwards and forwards to calm themselves. But, with one young person, we began to realise that he would flick his hands a little when he was happy in an area. For instance, in the sand area, he would flick his hands to the side. He wasn't touching anything, but we began to realise that this flicking meant he was getting something out of that activity, even though he wasn't physically touching the sand.

In this practice anecdote, we illustrate how a young person stimmed in different ways when feeling nervous or unsettled and when happy or content. There can sometimes be an assumption by neurotypical people that autistic people only self-stimulate in order to soothe themselves. However, as the example above shows, sometimes children might rock or move or stim because that gives them everything that they need: the rocking or stimming meets their sensory needs and so, when they're doing that, we know that they feel safe, they're having a good time, and they're getting what they need. Conversely, sometimes these movements have nothing to do with sensory needs and instead are about opening up the body to learning in ways we may not always fully understand (Manning, 2020). Biklen and Burke (2006) encourage us to 'presume competence'. By this, they mean that neurodivergent service users – such as autistic children in a classroom – know their own bodies and make requests or take steps that are reasonable for them. This viewpoint contrasts with perceptions of neurodivergent and autistic people as not capable of making reasonable choices. In the anecdotes discussed here, presuming competence means respecting children's bodily autonomy: presuming their competence in their capacity both to seek their own enjoyment and to express that enjoyment to us.

Eunjung Kim (2015) goes further, urging us to move beyond easy notions of competence. Kim argues that competence and reason are neurotypical ideals – something that we only need because neurotypical people always-already understand neurodivergent people as incompetent and unreasonable. In this way, the idea of presuming competence is compensatory. Instead, Kim argues that we should make competence irrelevant to our work with others. In the classroom, this might include enabling ostensibly neurotypical children to jump, rock, shake, and flap if they need to: stimming isn't just for autists! But it also might involve us adjusting our understanding of the value of stimming. Rather than understand stimming as valuable *because* we presume a child is regulating their own needs, or *because* it enables them to access their learning, what if we instead came to understand stimming as inherently valuable? – to enjoy the physical excess of the stim without trying to register it as meaningful.

Questions for reflection

- What is stimming communicative of? Does it mean that you need to intervene, or is it a sign of contentment? Does it mean that a child is enjoying an activity, when previously you might have thought they weren't?
- More importantly, do you need to presume it means anything?

How are you building on children's funds of knowledge (and acknowledging their funds of identity)?

Early years educators often notice trends in their children's interests and build activities around them to make learning more engaging. For instance, in the practice anecdote below, we describe how we built from the children's interests to add a café to the outdoors area.

PRACTICE ANECDOTE: THE SPARROWS CAFÉ

We were talking about different places, and the kids were saying one of their favourite things around the school is that there's loads of cafes. And I was like, "Sick, we'll put one outside!" It started off really small, but they keep growing it. For instance, I had these things in the drawer that looked like table numbers, and one morning they'd just made their way onto the café tables. The kids started saying things like: "Right, you're at Table 1!" Open Table 2!" Or they're saying, "Can I book a table for half-five?" "No, sorry. It's closed." And they'll even look at the menus and say "Oh, I want the chicken pizza" and they're like, "Sorry, hun, we're out of chicken" and they're like, "Fine, I'm not paying! This place is a scam!" and they run off: they just run away! Honestly, when I'm outside, I'm just in that cafe now. It's great.

In this practice anecdote, we have described how we built from children's interests to design a very popular outdoors space: the Sparrows Café. This had obvious implications for children's enjoyment of and engagement in the learning. Moreover, it illustrates that actively supporting children's interests has advantages for language development. Richardson and Murray (2017) identify how unplanned activities outdoors impact the kinds of words that children use: they found that children tend to use more verbs, exclamations, and adjectives in child-led outdoor learning. Similarly, we can see that, by giving them space to lead their own learning and build their own capacities, children used a range of language that they might not have used otherwise. However, we also think that activities like the café help to activate anti-racist, anti-deficit perspectives on children's knowledge and identities.

As we mentioned at the start of this chapter, our school community is linguistically and ethnically diverse but economically deprived. Consequently, it would be easy to stumble into deficit perspectives on our children, whereby they are understood as lacking knowledge, lacking money, and even lacking language. The above anecdote illustrates how we reverse this perspective in our classroom, by building activities that acknowledge the wealth of information that our children have. This reminds us of the ideas of 'funds of knowledge' (Moll et al., 1992; Vélez-Ibañez & Greenberg, 1992) and 'funds of identity' (Esteban-Guitart & Moll, 2014). The concept of funds of knowledge was developed to counter racist and deficit narratives of the Mexican-American community in Tucson, Arizona. It refers to the idea that children and young people have a wealth of knowledge that is useful and important at home, even where it might not map easily onto school curricula. Later, drawing from Vygostky's idea of *perezhivanie* (lived or emotional experience), Esteban-Guitart & Moll (2014) argued that funds of knowledge are part of an individual's sense of personhood, which they called funds of identity. The children's use of the café imagery in this anecdote illustrates how these funds of knowledge and identity can be accommodated in the classroom.

Moreover, by following children's interests, drawing from their funds of knowledge, and acknowledging their funds of identity, we found that the number of challenging behaviours reduced. Since the pandemic, we've noticed an increase in challenging behaviours at school. These can be difficult for teachers, but also for the children: for instance, if it's a behaviour that's quite upsetting, such as spitting, people can tend to avoid that child and that can be really sad for them. However, we've noticed that following children's interests tends to reduce the number of challenging behaviours. Our experiences here resonate with those at Eagleby South State School in

Australia, where principal Andrew Barnes noted how staff morale improved and the need for punitive behaviour management decreased because of a 'loose parts' approach to play that allowed children to respond to their own interests (coincidentally, also involving a café: Australian Institute of Play, 2024). As in our anecdote, supporting children to follow their own interests seems to be associated with improved behaviour.

The café anecdote illustrates how we can create opportunities for joy in the classroom by building activities related to children's interests, drawing from their funds of knowledge, and acknowledging their funds of identity. These opportunities expand the children's capacities (and those of adults) while also supporting language development and improving behaviour. However, funds of knowledge and identity don't need to do these things to be worth making space for in the classroom. Indeed, sometimes, try as we might, we can't build children's interests into classroom activity because we simply don't understand them! In the anecdote below, we highlight the joy that one child experiences on exploring their interest in bees, and our failure to capitalise upon it.

> **PRACTICE ANECDOTE: PICKING UP THE BEES**
>
> One of our children was obsessed with the garden but they would not stop trying to pick up the bees. And I'm like, "Please don't get stung." And they're like, "Hi, bee." And then they'll see another one. "Hi, bee." And they'll just carry on like this. "Hi, bee. Hi bee." And everyone's like, "Please, just please be careful." So, now we've tried to bring it out into the provision, cut flowers and stuff for them to look at, and stuffy toy bees. But they're just desperate, so desperate, to hold the real thing.

In this practice anecdote, we tried to build this young person's interest in bees into the provision. However, something eludes us. The joy upon encountering a real bee – "Hi, bee." – is not evident in their engagement with the artificial bee provision we designed. In other words, we sometimes think we've captured what a child is interested in only to find that we've missed the point. Caribbean poet and philosopher Éduoard Glissant argues that there is something in each of us that can never be understood from the outside, and that keeping this "fundamentally unknowable kernel of difference" (Simek, 2015, p. 369) indecipherable is an important political commitment: Glissant (1997) calls this the 'right to opacity'. We want to advocate here for valuing this opacity.

Questions for reflection

- How can you make space for children's interests, and build upon their funds of identity and knowledge, when designing provision?
- How can you make space for yourselves to not understand those interests?

Final reflections

In this chapter, we've tried to trace some of the approaches we use to make space for enjoyment of children's rich, diverse communication and meaning-making strategies in our EYFS classrooms. In these final reflections we want to emphasise the importance of sharing and reflecting on this enjoyment as a whole team, as illustrated in our final practice anecdote below.

PRACTICE ANECDOTE: LAUGHING WHEN LISTENING

Sometimes children, when they're listening to something, they won't just sit quietly. Instead, they might laugh or make some other kind of vocalisation. At first, that insecurity bites a little bit: Are you laughing or vocalising because someone is messing around? Or because somebody is doing something they shouldn't? So we make sure to communicate that to our team and to staff that come in so that they don't think this is just 'poor behaviour' but rather that it is communicative of the fact they're listening and attending.

As we've illustrated in this practice anecdote and argued across this chapter, children will often engage in practices that are communicative even though they're not specifically intending to communicate. We make sure to discuss our realisations around these practices with our team, but also with any ancillary and supply staff that come in, and school leadership.

We want to finish with questions for reflection:

- The increasingly challenging nature of the Key Stage 1 curriculum means that the kinds of realisations and practices we've shared here can get forgotten in the transition. How can you support children and colleagues to carry on these enjoyments into Year 1?
- Whether it's been a really good day or a really terrible day, we remind ourselves that ultimately this is somebody's child. How can you create space for colleagues to reflect on this with each other?

- As early years teachers, we often find ourselves needing to advocate for children in our classes, especially if they have special educational needs and especially if their grown-ups don't speak a lot of English. How can you create a culture of advocacy?

References

Australian Institute of Play (2024, February 22). *Principal Andrew Barnes Adopting Loose Parts Play Now a Life Long Advocate* [Video]. YouTube. https://www.youtube.com/watch?v=zevlk57r8n0

Biklen, D., & Burke, J. (2006). Presuming competence. *Equity and Excellence in Education*, 39(2), 166–175. https://doi.org/10.1080/10665680500540376

Davidson, M. (2022). *Distressing Language: Disability and the Poetics of Error.* New York University Press.

Department for Education (2023). *Reporting Year 2022: School Workforce in England.* https://explore-education-statistics.service.gov.uk/find-statistics/school-workforce-in-england

Department of Education and Science (1978). *Special Educational Needs: Report of the Committee of Enquiry into the Education of Handicapped Children and Young People (The Warnock Report).* HMSO.

Esteban-Guitart, M., & Moll, L. C. (2014). Funds of Identity: A new concept based on the Funds of Knowledge Approach. *Culture & Psychology*, 20(1), 31–48. https://doi.org/10.1177/1354067X13515934

Glissant, E. (1997). *Poetics of Relation.* (B. Wing, trans.). University of Michigan Press. (1990).

Kim, E. (2015). Unbecoming human: An ethics of objects. *GLQ: A Journal of Lesbian and Gay Studies*, 21(2–3), 295–320. https://doi.org/10.1215/10642684-2843359

Manning, E. (2020). *For a Pragmatics of the Useless.* Duke University Press.

McLean, D., Worth J., & Faulkner-Ellis, H. (2023). Teacher labour market in England: Annual report 2023. *NFER.* https://www.nfer.ac.uk/publications/teacher-labour-market-in-england-annual-report-2023/

Moll, L. C., Amanti, C., Neff, D., & Gonzalez, N. (1992). Funds of knowledge for teaching: Using a qualitative approach to connect homes and classrooms. *Theory into Practice*, 31(2), 132–141. https://doi.org/10.1080/00405849209543534

Ofsted. (2017). Bold beginnings: The Reception curriculum in a sample of good and outstanding primary schools. www.gov.uk/government/publications/reception-curriculum-in-good-and-outstanding-primary-schools-bold-beginnings

Olsson, L. M. (2009). *Movement and Experimentation in Young Children's Learning: Deleuze and Guattari in Early Childhood Education.* Routledge.

Richardson, T., & Murray, J. (2017). Are young children's utterances affected by characteristics of their learning environments? A multiple case study. *Early Child Development and Care*, 187(3–4), 457–468. https://doi.org/10.1080/03004430.2016.1211116

Simek, N. (2015). Stubborn Shadows. *Symploke*, 23(1–2), 363–373. https://muse.jhu.edu/article/605678

Tatham-Fashanu, C. (2023). A third space pedagogy: Embracing complexity in a super-diverse, early childhood education setting. *Pedagogy, Culture & Society*, *31*(4), 863–881. https://doi.org/10.1080/14681366.2021.1952295

Vélez-Ibañez, C. G., & Greenberg, J. B. (1992). *Schooling Processes among US Mexicans, Puerto Ricans, and Cubans: A Comparative, Distributive, and Case Study Approach* (ED347022). ERIC. https://files.eric.ed.gov/fulltext/ED347022.pdf.

4c

HOW MIGHT BODY-LISTENING OPEN UP SPACE FOR BODY-LANGUAGING?

Ruth Churchill Dower

Introduction

Question: How easy is it to *not talk* to our youngest children? I mean, to share the same spaces with them, playing, moving, digging, building, perhaps even singing or making funny sounds together, enjoying sharing the space, but *not* talking? Even if you are an excellent listener, if you are also a talker, it is actually quite hard to resist! I wonder where those spaces are for being, reflecting, thinking, creating, and doing together, without the need for continual talk? Where is the space to watch, take in, sense, listen to, feel, be touched by, and interact with (what I call 'body-listening') each other's funny little ways of expressing our likes and dislikes, our curiosities and emotions, our thoughts and ideas about the world, in head-tilts, tongue-twists, hand-dances, foot-taps, guttural-utterances, and unplanned actions that our bodies can't help but release (what I call 'body-languaging')? In this chapter I will explore how *body-listening* to children's *body-languaging* can broaden adults' experiences of young children's capabilities beyond the usual definitions of language and communication goals. I will discuss how educational definitions of 'progress' in speech can be oppressive for children who experience and express their worlds differently. I also offer some examples and ideas of how sensory practices can open valuable routes to attuning with nonlingual children in highly generative and productive ways for both children and adults.

DOI: 10.4324/9781032677927-20

Researching nonlingual ways of being through movement

Practices that attune to children's multimodal languages are not always easy, especially when body-languages – often considered insignificant – are the predominant way a child expresses themselves. Although it may not be obvious, sensory attunement is often nurtured by reciprocating small expressions of body-languages, and this attunement can open up relationships with children to their creative potential beyond simply meeting basic communication needs. This practice needs *practice*, which is what I tried to do as a curious learner with my PhD research participants. These were all families with a child under the age of five years who often does not speak outside of their homes, even to close relatives and friends. The families attended six weeks of research sessions (one a week) over Zoom during the COVID-19 lockdown in the UK, followed by two months of weekly face-to-face sessions in an art gallery. They came with a slightly hesitant curiosity about my research into moving-not-talking, and a willingness to play-with, think-with, move-with, and enjoy these spaces for *nonlingual* expression. I am a doctoral researcher at Manchester Metropolitan University with an interest in neurodivergent ways of moving, relating, not talking, and still feeling capable and creative. I say 'still' because there are lots of ways of being and knowing that are valued in young children's lives, but not-talking is usually *not* one of them. I come to this research with a long history of arts education practice, as a former drama teacher, a musician, a physical theatre practitioner (often combining mime with dance), and as the founder of Earlyarts – a research and training consultancy for arts and early education professionals.

Research with nonlingual children (such as children diagnosed with selective mutism or autism) often advocates strategies and therapies that encourage nonlingual children to talk (e.g., Fernandez et al., 2014; Jones & Odell-Miller, 2022; Kovac & Furr, 2019). However, the increasing over-focus on literacy, language, and social communication targets in educational settings, combined with vocalising treatments designed with the best of intentions for a child's social integration, can sometimes be counter-productive to a child's sense of confidence, capability, and well-being. My research proposes an alternative approach that broadens how children's expressions are defined, and the creative ways of tuning in to them. It focuses on how we can listen differently to children's many languages and ways of being in the world, some of which are, frankly, much more exciting than talk. Turning normative expectations on their head means considering what it would take for *adults* to become confident and competent in *not-talking*. There's a challenge! Therefore, in this chapter I draw from my research to ask two key questions: How might we attune to children's (and adults') body-languages? And could (adult) practices of body-listening help amplify the value of (children's) body-languaging in early education and care?

To explore these questions further, I describe how two non-speaking four-year-olds from different families were invited to experiment with sensory, collaborative movements, whilst their significant adults practised listening-with their and their child's body-languages. Spontaneous and surprising movements become co-produced as a result of moving in ways and spaces that welcome different ways of becoming, and knowing, *with* the world. In this space, moving together seems to offer physical and sensory challenges that these children – often made to feel in some ways incapable with speech – are only too delighted to try out and play-around-with using their finely honed expertise. By curating conditions that are welcoming and relaxing (with no expectations to speak) in places of creativity that are interesting to children (such as an art gallery), perhaps these opportunities for deeper engagement with touch, sensory, proprioceptive, and kinetic languages might be enough for children to feel supported in communicating without words. After all, children appear to have little problem with nonlingual expression.

FIGURE 4C.1 Preparing the art gallery setting for nonlingual movement research

The following images and vignettes animate key moments of sensory attunement that left their mark on my bodymind during the research and have resonated with me since.

VIGNETTE 1

I am about to do some movement improvisation with six children and their parents in an art gallery space. It has large windows across the width of the sloped ceiling, letting in strong beams of light that reveal the dust particles fizzing and dancing amongst us. As I am setting up the space before the families arrive, I enjoy a few moments of standing within the beams and dancing-with the particles. My hands chase these elusive dust particles, disrupting their flow, trying to order them into circular motions, but they are always faster than me, moving out of the way before I can even touch them. Their ability to always outwit me makes me laugh out loud.

Around the walls are 20 contemporary paintings by a local artist, full of colours, shapes, textures, objects, and figures that also seem to be moving within their own, curious stories. This is the venue for two months of fieldwork sessions during the COVID-19 pandemic in 2020, where we are permitted to meet whilst observing social distancing rules. I dance with a large teddy bear, whilst each parent and child dance together within their 'family bubble'. Each bubble has a small pop-up tent to hide in or explore as they wish, and several blankets, duvets and cushions around their tent to make the gallery floor a little more inviting of collaborations. All adults are masked and required to sanitise hands on entry. I wear a full-face transparent visor to ensure my lips can be read even if my words are blurred.

As big and little bodies enter the space and choose a 'den', I notice the space being filled with adult voices greeting each other, getting comfy on their cushions, helping their child remove shoes and coats, rearranging jumpers and brushing hair. There are no child voices. There are, however, lots of body-languages being exchanged as children look around at the windows, their dens, the dancing dust columns and the art works, sometimes sneaking a glance at me or each other. They often look carefully at their parent, drawing them close with their hands or feet and listening intently with their bodies to the conversations being had. Parental voice seems to draw out reassurance and one or two children smile or nod as parents bring them into the chatter. The atmosphere is full of wonder and anticipation as

I welcome the families and invite them to spend some time enjoying movement explorations together (based on some provocations I offer with unusual materials). I gently reiterate that I have no expectations for children to speak, even if I might chat with them as we move.

What's the problem with talking?

Spoken language is increasingly considered an important measure of competence in young children, with many curricula emphasising the importance of gaining 'proper' communication skills from the early years. By implication, this suggests that a child who does not speak is incompetent or, worse, not a 'proper' child, and there is often an emphasis on potential failure in later life (e.g., Mroz, 2012; Nuffield Foundation Education Limited, 2021; Pro Bono Economics, 2024). Several scholars have critiqued this pathologisation of not-speaking (e.g., Goodley & Runswick-Cole, 2016; MacLure, 2016; MacLure et al., 2010; Murris, 2016). Indeed, Murris (2016) asserts that these orthodox approaches create injustices that constrain children's sensory knowing. I use the term 'injustices' because these approaches increase the risk that nonlingual ways of being are considered less valuable, less trustworthy, and less important than lingual knowledge with all its traits, prejudices, sleights of hand and twists of tongue.

Through my fieldwork sessions, I introduced practices that treat language not as a disembodied, solely cognitive process that arises with the so-called 'natural' growth and development of the child through age-appropriate norms (Murris, 2016), but as an expression of how the body, mind, and senses engage with the world together, all the time, through body-languaging. Just as thoughts are not created in some kind of cognitive vacuum, a person's actions, movements, and being are all created in relational and dynamic processes (Sheets-Johnstone, 2011). Yet, because they don't quite register as solid, demonstrable, cognitive 'skills', young children's nonlingual languages can prove challenging to recognise and learn-with in spaces that are not conducive to their more-than-bodily expressions. The textures, soft textiles, hidey-holes, light windows, fizzing atmospheres, and generous spaces (with slidey floors) in which we moved during the research sessions were an attempt to invite and acknowledge the legitimacy of nonlingual practices through bodies rather than words.

In the same vein, Olsson (2009) nurtures an ambition for educators to become open to children's many expressions. She encourages teachers to question the "predetermined map" of competences (2009, p. 13) designed to regulate children's behaviours according to the normalising theories of developmental psychology and cognitive science. To resist these theories, which largely underpin education frameworks in the West, Olsson urges us to focus on "the idea of the child as perpetually becoming and not being defined once and for all" (2009, p. 14). To put this ambition into practice, she suggests focusing less on what an individual child can or can't do and more on the relationships, encounters, and preoccupations that happen between children's bodies and their environments. This is what we did in our sessions.

VIGNETTE 2

During the first session at the gallery, parents and children are engaging in a gentle, sensory exploration of hands using brushes, pouring jugs and water. The atmosphere is relaxed and calm with an undercurrent of humming (from me) and giggling (from families) as their skins experience tickles, splashes and rubs. But this stillness does not correspond with the jumping forces in the body of **Jumper** (not her real name) which call out with vim and vigour to map out circuits of the whole gallery space. Jumper begins to run around the gallery space in between tents and around the outside of the tent circle. Her sister follows her, apparently quite excited by the possibilities of space, bodies, slidey feet, and fast legs. Mum has already pulled sheepskin sock-slippers onto their feet, which make a fabulous slapping, splatting sound on the gallery floor as they run. Slap-splat-slap-splat-slappity-splat, interspersed with jumps and squeals of delight.

At the end of each circuit, they jump onto the sofas in the far corner of the gallery, rolling about on their plush leather seats. Jumper's squeals of unbridled excitement encourage her sister to join-in-with the game. Jumper climbs higher onto the back of the sofa and walks gingerly along the back, arms out for balance, jumping from one sofa to the next and back again. Having navigated these slippery, knobbly leather trails, Jumper then jumps backwards into the seat, flipping her body horizontally, trusting in the softness of its leathery sponge to catch her landing. Her little sister seems content to slap the sides and arms of the sofa as she, too, squeals with delight at each of her sister's crash landings. Then off they go again running round and round the gallery, big sister followed by little sister, little matching dress dancing to the tune of big matching dress.

Meanwhile, mum and dad's bodies are crouching tensely in front of their tent, sitting back on their haunches like coiled springs, perhaps feeling a little exposed. Glances are exchanged, senses on high alert to the squeals and shrieks of entangled dress-slipper-sofa-dances going on behind them. An anxious face calls to the girls and a finger lifts to the lips, making a 'shush' sound. Their bodies seem disturbed by the possible disturbances of other bodies. Dad brings the girls back to their tent twice, before they jump back into action and fly off again. Mum offers me a look of apology across the tent-circle and I respond with relaxed smiles and invitations not to worry. There are no expectations for 'regulated' behaviours in this space.

But, of course, there are. The atmosphere is thick with the wider social pressures to be considered more or less 'normal'. All the research families are caught up in a struggle of 'being' and 'becoming', of accepting the different ways their child might explore and express themselves in the world, and of wondering if there are other 'right', 'correct', or more 'normal' ways to be. Even in this light, comfortable gallery where we care for each other and make space for doing things differently, parents nonetheless talk of their hopes for deeper understanding and possible relief from this struggle. But this is not a space for meaning-making; there are no solutions, resolutions, or revolutions here. Just a space to experiment with what might be.

FIGURE 4C.2   Jumping, running, fizzing, and flying around the art gallery

Working with sense rather than meaning

Olsson (2009) discusses how the meanings generated through children's movements are often a far cry from how adults interpret them, as if a truth exists about how a child 'should' move or be in control of their body, regardless of the forces interacting with them. Rather than searching for a *meaning*, which can only ever be understood through individual bodies, Olsson encourages educators to discover *sense*. Sense is continually and collectively produced through the relations children make with other bodies, materials, and spaces. By attending to the general sense rather than the specific meanings that children produce through their sounds, speech, and actions, Olsson suggests, educators can become skilled at noticing what kind of sense (including nonsense) or problems children are making, even when language is not spoken or when children's actions might appear to diverge from the norm. Olsson explains further: "When looking at it from the point of view of not already given, but continuously produced sense, even children's oddest expressions are never random. It has become clear to many teachers that children produce sense all the time" (2009, p. 102). In other words, sense is not about fitting into a given meaning but about feeling well with the world. Seen from the perspective of the forces arising as a small body experiences the world in a large space, Jumper's jumping makes perfect sense.

VIGNETTE 3

Every time Jumper is picked up by adult hands, she lifts both feet as high as possible, as if trying to make the most of an assisted jump. It doesn't matter whether she is being lifted onto a lap, into a cuddle, off the sofa, or onto a chair, both feet go up as high as humanly possible, as if it's a reflex. These feet simply do not want to be on the ground, carrying weight, or marking time and space. Jumper's deceptively small body hides a million, huge jumps just straining to be let out wherever the environment urges her to do so. Her legs, arms and torso seem drawn to the sensations of swinging and flying – forces so great, that maybe her body could get airborne if it could only overcome gravity.

When children climb onto their adult to have a piggyback, Jumper takes a running jump and flies onto her dad's back. When children stand on their parent's feet to be walked around, to feel how their parent's body feels with wide legs and long strides, Jumper's legs simply won't stay straight. She jumps up, pushing her weight down into her mum's hands, to propel her legs upwards once again. This body seems to thrive on taking flight, its jumping-flying-swinging actions taking up twice the space of the still body. It is a tremendous achievement, a skill honed over many vertical and horizontal jumping experiments. It is an incredible way to make sense of this space, using the lightness of this small body so creatively to express the strong forces pulling her into orbit. Even if words were available to Jumper, it is possible they would not be enough to articulate the intense expression of entangled physical, emotional, and sensorial satisfaction that this flying body appears to enjoy.

I consider Viruru's question, "what is lost when language is gained?" (2001, p. 31). In Jumper's case, her body might lose the opportunity to dance, the ability to fly, the skills to navigate space in three dimensions, to express the strong forces without and within, and to release the squeals

FIGURE 4C.3 Jumping, swinging, flying bodies propelling themselves into different orbits

and sounds of these forces as they satisfy her desires. It seems to me that these are all important competences that are neither measured nor valued in any national curriculum. What is more, such vital sensory expressions are often misunderstood and pathologised in the education system, putting them out of reach of being valued.

Most curricula are largely divided into outcomes for cognitive, physical, emotional, and social development. Although unable to answer the question 'what does it mean?' when a small body is compelled to fly through the air at great heights, educators can feel duty-bound to measure the more generic outcomes for Physical Development (as a prime area of learning in the curriculum) in ways which are disconnected from a body's other faculties. Nonlingual bodies frequently excel in the technical skill of jumping, rolling, running, skipping, and doing fiddly things with buttons, zips, and laces, as the forces arising make a bid to express physically what cannot be said verbally. But the progress of these bodies often comes at a cost of having to regulate this liveliness in accordance with requirements for meaning-making in normative ways. These are meanings made to satisfy adult understandings about what is being learned, but they can have the effect of constraining children's own ways of body-languaging, of making sense (not meaning). Jumper's parents regularly provided the musculoskeletal scaffolding, strength, and balance for her smaller body to make sense of its need to learn and express in a certain way. Far from considering Jumper incapable or lacking, her parents' body-listening (even when it felt awkward) helped them engage with Jumper's important, intelligent, alternative ways of being and knowing in the world.

Sensory attunements offering new perspectives

When body-languaging makes sense across more than one body, we might say we are 'touched by' or 'in touch with' the other, meaning we share the same understanding. This happens continually, almost intuitively for some, through our senses. Like spiders feeling for the vibrations of a fly, our sensing of each other's emotional or physical vibrations is how our bodies navigate the tangled webs of social and physical interaction (Sheets-Johnstone, 2011). For nonlingual or divergent bodies whose senses might operate on different frequencies, tuning in takes practice. Body-listening means developing a sensory attunement to the different vibrations of body-languaging. It goes both/many ways: listening to the embodied expressions of others enables a more attuned reciprocity, drawing in a closer listening from the other(s), and becoming open to new perspectives on expression, potentiality, and relationality (Olsson, 2009). This practice is not necessarily about being still to listen or observe, but about being open and actively involved with the other without interpretation, expectation, or restriction, just as another of my research families demonstrates.

VIGNETTE 4

Dynamite (not his real name) is a dynamic force in the shape of a blurred body. He seems perfectly calm, happy, and relaxed when preparing for our movement improvisation sessions. His mum says he wants to tell me how much he enjoys them, as he offers me a tiny smile from behind her back. But the minute we begin exploring the space with a long, silk scarf, he is off. It is like he unzips his whole skin and out jumps a force of movement so great that his mum wonders if she will ever get it back inside again. Dynamite runs with the scarf around every inch and corner of the room, exploring its waves, circles, twists and textures. He runs with it wrapped around his head, his torso and his legs, often tripping and rolling over with peals of silent laughter. He is deeply in cahoots with this scarf, experimenting with its potentialities and trying to overcome their limitations. He runs so fast to make it fly above his head, climbing the cushions, chairs, and even tables in surrender to the mighty scarf. Whooshing-legs-silk-dancing-air-molecules become alive, enmeshed, speaking volumes without words until their forces are exhausted and come to settle in stillness again.

In another session, we wonder how hands can dance together. Mum, Dynamite and little brother play with patting, slapping, clapping, tapping, mirroring, and folding each other's hands within their own. Different sizes, shapes, textures, stickinesses, and smoothnesses are explored in these motions, bringing attention to the many differences in each hand. The dances draw us into an intimate looking, feeling, touching and sensing the haptic and animate nature of each palm, digit, nail, and knuckle. It seems there are so many worlds to explore in the lines, creases, flexibility and stiffness of each hand. But more than what can be observed is what can be felt. It seems almost imperceptible in the familiarity of touch between the boys and mum, but there is a sense of deep knowing between them, of love and trust, of care-full-ness and care-free-ness. These feel like happy hands. How this can be sensed from experiencing three hands dancing together in a brief, wordless encounter, I do not know. But these are the words that emerge in my body from witnessing this encounter.

In this encounter there are vibrations, frequencies, intensities, and sensations that I cannot put into words, despite that my body is able to feel them.

FIGURE 4C.4   Happy hands

The closest I come is in having a sense of joy in their 'happy hands' from the registers I experience in their faces and how these resonate deep within my body. How often must our bodies attune to the offerings of other bodies in the world, either present, virtual, or in our memories, and register sensations that are as strong as words (perhaps stronger) but without an articulable meaning? Dance scholar and philosopher, Maxine Sheets-Johnstone (2011), considers body-languages as highly important and calls for greater legitimacy to be afforded them in education. Reminding us that body-language emerges *prior* to spoken language, Sheets-Johnson refers to movement as the "mother tongue" and "the foundation of our conceptual life" (2011, p. xxiii) and suggests that "rather than speak of the period before language as the pre-linguistic, we should speak of the advent of language as post kinetic" (2011, p. xxxi).

However, rather than think of body-languages as separate, labelled entities (e.g., sensory or kinetic; verbal or nonverbal), I support Badwan's (2021) emphasis on the singular form of 'language', particularly the use of the verb 'languaging'. This use enhances the notion of language as a fluid process, a complex multitude of expressions that includes the histories, cultures, and environments that come with each body. In other words, body-languaging (as opposed to body-languages) signals multimodal, multisensory practices and meanings which are not divorced from *who* a body is and *what* a body brings into the world. This is especially useful for considering nonlingual bodies not as lacking or incapable, but as overflowing with rich possibilities. Dynamite did not speak a word during these sessions, but his languaging was alive with the depth and breadth of knowledges he has and continues to acquire/create in his experiments with materials, movement, and dancing. As Olsson reminds us, "rather than working with trivial universals, [this way of working] harbours a more complex, deep and creative approach to learning" (2009, p.18).

Ethical and educational possibilities

To engage in practices of body-listening and body-languaging is both a political and an ethical move that counters the oppressions of linear, developmental projects. Olsson (2009) invites us to think of this as an ethics of "uncertainty" where a practice of "collective, intense, and unpredictable experimentation" (2009, p. 83) challenges the universalised ethics that are often reduced to technical skills-based measures which mark a child as incompetent. For adults working with children who do not always speak, this might mean reducing questions, curbing the need to understand better, improvising more, allowing curiosity to grow, and making time and space to play and learn alongside. In other words, it means listening together for children's different ways of languaging.

Jumper and Dynamite invited their parents to collaborate with the forces in their bodies by feeling and responding to their different rhythms, vibrations, sounds, and affects. These are how their bodies sense, make sense, and become open to more of their potentiality as they explore their worlds. Their body-languages are unpredictable, intense, and immeasurable, and yet generative of intelligent and highly capable knowing and being. It is easier for these children to generate greater potential when the space is unregulated and open to affective, embodied, and sensorial expressions. Over only a few weeks, the research parents became more confident to move with their children in improvised ways, to value and

FIGURE 4C.5 Families listening with their bodies and attuning to nonlingual expressions

extend their body-languaging and become open to sensory expressions. They sat with the discomforts of listening-through-moving with adult bodies to witness many moments of joy, humour, and openly verbalised language, whilst entangled in their children's evolving dances. The learning, skills, and confidence gained by the adults seemed to open up both ethical and educational possibilities for recognising and valuing children's nonlingual ways of being that are still being practised in homes and classrooms.

I propose that these practices can create a space that allows expression through listening and listening through expression – neither seems enough on its own. Listening signals to a nonlingual child that their languages, no matter how silent, are seen/heard/felt/sensed and valued. Listening encourages trust, motivates ideas, and inspires expression. Listening says, "I am not going to 'fill in' your voice; I will hold the space for you to experiment with different ways of being, as capable and creative, with or without words." Listening also creates space for adult bodies to find new ways of learning, teaching, being capable and creative with children. The movements of body-listening and body-languaging are so entangled that there is no beginning or end, just many possibilities from which emerge new productivities, experimentations, inklings, ideas, and languages.

This kind of body-listening helps to shift the centrifugal forces away from the notion of 'child' as a predetermined being, away from a normative approach to development, and away from socially constructed identities of having or not having, of being or not being, of progressing or lacking, of speaking or not speaking. Spaces that replace simplistic binaries with divergent complexity are important because, as Olsson highlights, "the only thing one can do is to create more space for desiring bodies to expand their capacities; [because] we do not know what a child [...] can do" (2009, p. 187).

Photo credits: Ruth Churchill Dower.

References

Badwan, K. (2021). *Language in a Globalised World Social Justice Perspectives on Mobility and Contact*. Springer International Publishing. https://doi.org/10.1007/978-3-030-77087-7

Fernandez, K. T. G., Serrano, K. C. M., & Tongson, M. C. C. (2014). An intervention in treating selective mutism using the expressive therapies continuum framework. *Journal of Creativity in Mental Health*, 9(1), 19–32. https://doi.org/10.1080/15401383.2013.873706

Goodley, D., & Runswick-Cole, K. (2016). Becoming dishuman: Thinking about the human through dis/ability. *Discourse: Studies in the Cultural Politics of Education*, 37(1), 1–15. https://doi.org/10.1080/01596306.2014.930021

Jones, K., & Odell-Miller, H. (2022). A theoretical framework for the use of music therapy in the treatment of selective mutism in young children: Multiple case study research. *Nordic Journal of Music Therapy*, 1–25. https://doi.org/10.1080/08098131.2022.2028886

Kovac, L. M., & Furr, J. M. (2019). What teachers should know about selective mutism in early childhood. *Early Childhood Education Journal*, 47(1), 107–114. https://doi.org/10.1007/s10643-018-0905-y

MacLure, M. (2016). The refrain of the a-grammatical child. *Cultural Studies, Critical Methodologies*, 16(2), 173. https://doi.org/10.1177/1532708616639333

MacLure, M., Holmes, R., Jones, L., & MacRae, C. (2010). Silence as resistance to analysis: Or, on not opening one's mouth properly. *Qualitative Inquiry*, 16(6), 492–500. https://doi.org/10.1177/1077800410364349

Mroz, M. (2012). Meeting the recommendations of the Bercow Report: The challenges and the potential within initial teacher education. *Child Language Teaching and Therapy*, 28(3), 309–324. https://doi.org/10.1177/0265659012450896

Murris, K. (2016). *The Posthuman Child: Educational Transformation through Philosophy with Picturebooks*. Routledge. https://doi.org/10.4324/9781315718002

Nuffield Foundation Education Limited (2021). *Nuffield Early Language Intervention* (NELI). https://www.teachneli.org/

Olsson, L. M. (2009). *Movement and Experimentation in Young Children's Learning: Deleuze and Guattari in Early Childhood Education*. Routledge. https://doi.org/10.4324/9780203881231

Pro Bono Economics (2024). *Early Literacy Matters: Economic Impact and Regional Disparities in England.* https://www.probonoeconomics.com/early-literacy-matters

Sheets-Johnstone, M. (2011). *The Primacy of Movement* (Expand 2nd ed., Vol. 82). John Benjamins Pub. Co. https://doi.org/10.1075/aicr.82

Viruru, R. (2001). Colonized through Language: The Case of Early Childhood Education. *Contemporary Issues in Early Childhood*, 2(1), 31–47. https://doi.org/10.2304/ciec.2001.2.1.7

4d

WHO CHOOSES MY WORDS?

Andrea Lee

Introduction

Most of us give very little thought to how we choose our words. We are blissfully unaware of the complex decisions going on behind the scenes until the occasional dilemma suddenly brings this into our consciousness. Thoughts such as "Am I ok to swear in front of this person?", "Did that sound offensive?", or "I'm not sure this word means what I think it means?" alert us to decision-making and may cause us to change track. It is often only when we sense discomfort, or maybe humour, that we become aware of a faux pas such as an unintended innuendo, an older person attempting teenspeak, or a mis-remembered idiom. The effect can be offensive, such as when a swear word is spoken in a non-swearing context, or someone is misgendered. Or it can be comedic, such as verbal faux pas scripted in sitcoms or naturally occurring in TV bloopers. Conversation happens so quickly that we usually only reflect on our word choice retrospectively; most of us can relate to midnight introspections where we replay conversations hoping that we didn't offend or give the wrong impression, or we pray that those listening could see the intended funny side.

Understanding the delicate and complex process of how we choose our words is key to supporting non-speaking people to communicate. People who can speak and write can choose their own words from their lexicon using the building blocks of sounds or letters to form them. Those who cannot speak or write are reliant on others selecting words on their behalf and teaching these words in a format accessible to them. Their word bank may be learnt as manual signs or as images (photos or graphic symbols) from which they can then select the one(s) they want to communicate. It is my role, as a specialist speech and language therapist supporting children and young people on their communication journey, to provide non-speaking or semi-speaking children with the tools they need to develop their word and message banks.

This chapter will explore some of the tensions and dilemmas inherent in the use of symbols as a communication method for children and young people, from three perspectives. First, I will explore how the nature of child-led communication interplays with the challenges of introducing alternative communication methods. The second section will discuss observations from practice relating to the control by others of a non-speaker's or semi-speaker's communication and the systemic restrictions impacting on that communication. The final section will view these discussions and observations through the lens of ableism and normativism and ground them in Crip Linguistics theory.

This chapter is underpinned by my positionality as a practitioner who embraces and advocates personalised, multimodal communication and values the richness of spontaneous and creative self-expression and peer interaction. Whilst the focus of this chapter is the use of symbol communication strategies and disability languaging, the points expressed can be applied to language more broadly, helping us reflect on our assumptions about what language is and does and how we support young people's communication skills.

What is AAC?

AAC (Augmentative and Alternative Communication) is the umbrella term for person-based strategies and paper or electronic communication aids which are used by adults and children who are non-speaking or semi-speaking to communicate their messages. Person-based AAC includes strategies that speaking people may use, such as body language, facial expression, finger pointing, gesture, and vocalisations, and strategies created more specifically by and for non-speaking communicators such as eye pointing, sign languages, and particular actions for yes/no responses. Paper and electronic communication aids use symbols to represent words or messages, which may be spoken out by the communication partner or by electronic voice output. Symbols can have a single meaning such as a banana symbol representing 'banana', or they may have multiple, related meanings, for example a rainbow symbol representing 'rainbow', 'LGBTQIA+', 'multicoloured', or the category of 'colours'.

AAC users often combine strategies and develop ingenious ways of compensating for items missing from their word and message banks.

The following examples are all taken from practice and demonstrate the creativity, spontaneity, and individualism that are often seen in children and young people determined to get their messages across.

- Making windscreen-wiper side-to-side eye movements to communicate 'clean my glasses'.
- Using the symbol on a planets page for 'Mars' to request a Mars chocolate bar.
- Looking repeatedly between their partner's ear and mouth to ask to phone someone.
- Looking at their partner's mouth and then at coloured items on a picture to request food, e.g., the grass for 'peas' and the beach for 'chips'.
- Combining the Makaton sign for 'airplane' with pointing to their nose to mean 'Manchester airport' because that was the airport where they had a nosebleed.
- Kicking legs for 'yes' and staying still for 'no' and using degrees of movement for nuances of yes and no, ranging from big kicks for 'most definitely yes' to frozen posture for 'absolutely not'.
- Pointing to their eye and their incontinence pad to request their iPad.
- Squeaking their wheelchair to mean 'my turn / include me' or 'I'm excited'.
- A single gesture, sign, or symbol combined with a giggle and a knowing look to a parent to ask them to recount a funny anecdote.

Child-led communication

Prior to the introduction of symbol communication through therapy or education, non-speaking children have often devised sophisticated and complex person-based communication methods to interact with those around them. A key feature of communication with all young children is partner collaboration as often they do not have the language to create an unambiguous, fully formed message. This collaboration is amplified for non-speaking children and is often referred to as co-construction, where the child and their partners work together to form a shared message using 'clues' from the above methods, the context, and creative thinking.

There is a perception that using a voice output communication aid, where the user creates and speaks their message without partner involvement, supports independent communication, whereas co-constructive methods, such as symbol or alphabet charts which rely on a partner speaking the message, create co-dependency. This perception relates to the sender-receiver model of communication (Petersons & Khalimzoda, 2016) which is rarely seen in natural spoken conversations and would only really suit school-based situations like a 'show and tell' presentation or an assessment. This model is seldom seen amongst symbol communicators whose messages are often ambiguous and require interpreting in the context of their body movements, facial expressions, and environment. In opposition to the sender-receiver model is the reality of messy to-ing and fro-ing and overlapping conversation turns, and the shared creation of a narrative. Hackett et al. (2021) describe interactions in which "adults and children are moved by a more-than-human milieu, caught up in some-thing bigger than themselves" (p. 926, and refer to Gilles Deleuze's description of the "wild element in language – something mobile, lively and relational that resists definition and evades capture by representation" (Deleuze, 2004, as cited in Hackett et al., 2021, p. 915). This wild element can often be seen in natural, spontaneous AAC interactions and it demands, above all else, the time and engagement of dedicated and skilled communication partners – partners who can think holistically about the message in the context of the person, the activity, and the environment before suggesting interpretations.

It is challenging to simultaneously support several symbol communicators, for example in a classroom context, but the preference for systems with voice output must not stem from the need to reduce the 'burden' of the human resources needed for collaborative communication. If we imagine a busy classroom at circle time, it may be more convenient and efficient to have the children independently naming the day of the week and labelling the weather on a voice output communication aid, as opposed to each child requiring a conversation partner to turn the pages of a symbol book, interpret their hand or eye pointing, and speak their message. The benefits of collaborative communication are often traded for the assumed benefits of more independent methods, but for many children the co-constructive methods may be their preferred and most effective option. The question raised here is whether we need more communication partners to enable children to choose and develop their preferred methods or whether it is acceptable to insist on the less collaborative methods to create more convenient communicators in an already demanding classroom.

A multimodal communication approach gives equal value to the development of all communication methods and is the preferred trajectory for children using AAC, as this approach encourages them to be flexible and creative in their communication and to use the most effective or preferred method depending on the type of messages, their partners, or their environment. It is important that all AAC strategies continue to progress, are given equal value, and are supported by the communication partners.

Control and systemic restrictions

Personalisation – who chooses the words?

Symbol-based AAC strategies are pre-loaded with generic word banks and designed to be customised to meet the individual user's needs. In reality, the customisation is often limited to adding personal details such as names and favourite items or removing words deemed unnecessary. The effectiveness of symbol-based AAC is impacted by the inherent issue that they are designed **for** non-speaking, pre-literate, disabled children **by** speaking, literate, non-disabled adults. Their design uses predefined words and messages based on evidence around the words most frequently used by neurotypical, non-disabled speakers. Symbolised words and messages then need to be inserted, deleted, and organised by a different person to the user. More often than not, this is an adult professional from a different cultural, linguistic, social, or racial background to the user. In some cases, several people may be trained to customise the word bank. Each may have different language, age, or cultural biases which affect their word and message choices.

The AAC company, Assistiveware, recently collected data about customisation and reported that they:

> observed changes that did not align with AAC best practice and which undermined AAC users' ability to grow their language over time. Ideas like "my child is not ready for these words" or "my student will never need these words" drove many to make changes.
> *(Neimiejer & Sheldon, 2021)*

This need for personalisation is very clearly expressed by AAC user, disability activist and researcher, Jamie Preece. He describes how he supports young users to think about the importance of taking control of their own words, and discusses examples such as whether they would want their mum to choose the words they will use on their first date. Likewise, he asks the support team "would you want someone else to choose the words you can use when intimate with your partner?" (Preece & Lee, 2023). This point can be expanded to a fundamental question – can we ever really choose someone else's words? I think most would agree the answer would be a resounding no!

Another predicament of those supporting symbol communication users is that the users often don't have a way of communicating before using AAC. The catch-22 then unfolds – how can we know what someone wants to say when they don't have the experience of having a voice and don't have a way to tell us? The reality is that the best option we have for creating a system that meets an individual's needs is through a combination of strategies: applying evidence based on comparable communicators; gaining and respecting information from all those who know the individual best (including siblings and peers); and incorporating the features we can observe non-verbally, such as their humour, their sarcasm, their ruling-passion vocabulary, and their preferred phrases. It is essential that the individual is involved in the process of personalisation, to foster self-advocacy and ownership of their communication aid, and to embed the concept that this is not just a box of words but a tool to reflect their identities and grow with them.

Curriculum vocabulary

The educator influence in the design of communication aids is apparent in the strong bias towards curriculum vocabulary over social, emotional, or identity-based vocabulary. For example: words for school subjects will always be present but words to describe autistic behaviours such as 'stimming', 'meltdown', and 'sensory overload' are often not; words for shapes are often plentiful but words that may be required to discuss a safeguarding issue, such as 'penis', 'trusted adult', 'secret', and 'social worker', are often not. Such issues concerning the choice of words given to children and young people are rooted in the challenge of how we measure 'successful' communication. Currently, the focus is often the length of utterance, the range of word types, or the sentence structure, reflecting bias towards language and educational targets. If the measure of success was determined by the impact of the message or the reaction to the message then word choices may look very different. Differing communicative impacts are demonstrated in the examples in Figure 4d.1. The messages in green boxes may hit the academic targets of syntax, semantics, and well-formed sentence structures, whereas the messages in red boxes may get a more animated response from the partner or peer, which in turn provides a stronger sense of social communication success.

Symbol-based AAC strategies undoubtedly facilitate curriculum access, particularly for language and literacy, for non-speaking children. However, a shift in perspective is needed to recognise and value all aspects of communication and to understand the distinction between communicative impact and language and literacy development. Two very different examples – sound play and swearing – are used here to illustrate the need for a range of vocabulary.

FIGURE 4D.1   A comparison of symbolised messages showing the difference between messages with 'standard' language structure (left image) and messages with high communicative impact (right image)

Valuing different vocabulary

Being immersed in sound and word play is a central part of children's language and literacy practices. Children's songs and stories burst with rhyme and onomatopoeia and are full of humorous, novel, and imaginative words and names. Children use novel words and sounds to assert control over their environment, for example by regularly renaming their soft toys, by creating secret words with friends, or by deciding they are a dog and they're going to bark all day. Children using symbol communication systems are limited to the words that have been chosen for them, which are predominantly words that label things or have a curriculum focus. These children are mostly excluded from opportunities to play with words for improvisation, creativity, exploration, and control. In the farm example (Figure 4d.1), a child using symbol communication to sing 'Old MacDonald' may be able to participate by naming the cow but not by saying 'E-I-E-I-O' or spontaneously deciding that 'Peppa' lives on the farm.

The need to recognise communication as broader than the curriculum is often brought to life through emotive debates about swear words and words of a sexual nature. At what age should a child be allowed to access swear words or words for sexual relationships, anatomy, or identity? Whose decision should this be? Which words should they be given access to? And where is the line between functional, exploratory, and sometimes humorous words, and those which may cause offence or confusion? This dilemma may be unanswerable without the context of the individual AAC user but it illustrates the challenge of balancing adult-led preconceptions about communication needs with individual needs or peer-led social inclusion. Unfortunately, the reality is that it is not uncommon to see words relating to sexual anatomy or identity words or swear words provided by some supporting adults and then deleted by others (be they family members, support assistants, or health or educational professionals). The converse age-appropriacy argument is also seen – for example, a person's vocabulary around Peppa Pig may be discouraged or hidden because they are now a teenager.

The philosophy informing any debate around age or social appropriacy needs to be firmly rooted in the understanding that AAC is for all aspects of a child's or young person's communication, of which social and emotional development forms an integral part. The impact of providing, omitting, and withdrawing vocabulary from a person's word bank requires careful consideration, and the responsibility and power to do this must not be misused to control or mediate the person's expression. Omitting words and messages may appear harmless and may seem preferable to risking misuse of words or risking challenging conversations. However, the risk of omission is oppression: constraining a young person's personal, social, and emotional communication may inhibit their psychological development and increase vulnerability by limiting their ability to disclose health or safeguarding concerns.

Dialect, sociolect, and familect

Dialect and sociolect are an important part of an individual's identity and contribute to a sense of belonging. Children may want to use the same words or messages as those in their locality but also the same ones as their peers or others with similar interests or religious or cultural backgrounds. This can be a challenge for the person inputting words and messages if they are not part of the same social groups. Teen sociolect is known for its ever-changing and idiosyncratic nature as teens dissociate from the language of those around them and push boundaries with neologisms and adoption of new word meanings. Due to much of teen communication now taking place on social media platforms only used by that age group, teen sociolect is increasingly isolated from other social groups. The chasm between an AAC user's internalised dialect or sociolect and the words and messages they can express externally may leave the user feeling that their communication aid doesn't reflect their sense of self.

Family groups often develop their own words or phrases which then become embedded and can provide a subtle bond between 'those who know' whenever they are used. This is known as familect. It may be deliberate, such as deciding to call the family grandmas 'Granny J' and 'Granny P', or it can develop organically from a humorous, endearing, or sometimes embarrassing mispronunciation or misnomer which quickly becomes rooted within the family's communication and often continues into adulthood. 'Cow-horse', 'bouncealine', and 'tiramashite' are examples of my own familect: the 'cow-horse' derived from children unable to agree on whether a horse with patches was a cow or a horse so they settled on 'cow-horse'; no one can remember the origin of 'bouncealine' but it always seemed more apt than 'trampoline'; and the 'tiramashite' was how a friend described the dessert she had made which wasn't up to her usual gold standard. All terms were adopted to become part of the family's word bank.

Dialect, sociolect, and familect may not seem to be an essential feature of communication but they are important for a sense of self and sense of belonging. Henner and Robinson (2023) use the expression 'Dinner Table Syndrome' to describe the implications of being unable to use these aspects of language: "[it] is not about simple language deprivation, but being shut out of family dynamics, being ignored, and sometimes being subject to abuse because of a refusal to recognize the reality of a disability" (p. 6).

Being excluded from dialect, sociolect, or familect, or having access only to words and messages which are mismatched to their identity, may leave an individual feeling othered or marginalised, or alienated from their communication aid.

Crip Linguistics

Supporting AAC users to integrate different communication styles into a speaking world raises the philosophical question of whether AAC strategies should aim to create organic, unique interactions or whether they should aim to replicate spoken interaction. And, if it is the latter, then whose speech should they aim to replicate? Crip Linguistics (Henner & Robinson, 2023) offers us one route forwards for responding to these questions, from a strengths-based perspective that insists on valuing all language practices. Henner and Robinson write:

> The core tenet of Crip Linguistics is that no one language is wrong; however, the stigma of disability is such that first, people look for ways to center white abled ways of languaging (e.g., speech), and second, people tend to assume that disabled people are automatically unable to language well without some kind of intervention and support.
>
> *(2023, p. 5)*

Here, Henner and Robinson are highlighting the challenge of normativist and ableist attitudes to communication. There are several ways in which these attitudes can unconsciously seep into practice when supporting AAC. It is easy for those supporting young AAC users to lean towards attempting to replicate speech that the adults would like the children to use. In this case, their word bank may prioritise needs-based or educational curriculum-based messages, as opposed to the seemingly less important, nonsensical banter that might be taking place within their peer group. It is perfectly understandable that given the choice of teaching your child to say "something hurts" or "Alexa, can you fart?", most parents would choose the former as the more functional and purposeful. However, a child may wish to prioritise the latter in order to get them the desired response of laughing siblings and peers. Both have their part in developing a well-rounded communication profile.

The question here is whether the intention of the AAC strategy is to 'fix' the AAC user's speech deficit and enable them to communicate as similarly as possible to their speaking peers, or whether AAC is a unique disability language, akin to sign language, and consequently the intention is to have the differences embraced and their peers adapt accordingly. Using the definition of ableism as "a system that places value on people's bodies and minds based on societally constructed ideas of normality, intelligence, excellence, desirability and productivity" (Shew, 2023, p. 9), people who support AAC users need to be mindful of the risk of imposing ableist attitudes and need to ensure that support is driven by individualism and not over-assimilation.

Normativism

Those who support the AAC user may express preferences towards using a symbol book or an electronic voice output over the person's natural communication methods. For example, a child may be encouraged to use symbols to convey that they are excited as opposed to using their natural high-pitched squeals or animated hand flapping. Their natural methods may have been 'acceptable' at home or when younger but are deemed less 'acceptable' in older children or in public where they attract attention. Communication methods may be being selected due to external, societal pressures and as an attempt to subdue 'less desirable' methods, rather than centred on the AAC user's best interests of having the most effective method to get the message across. Normativist practices such as these require sensitive discussion with families and those supporting the user, to ensure natural communication methods are respected and validated.

Ableism

AAC is taught and supported in schools alongside other subjects. Access to symbols is a useful tool for language learning and literacy alongside communication, and symbol use is encouraged. However, the differences between the functions can sometimes lead to confusion and restrictive practices regarding communication. For example, a message being communicated may be formed of key words only, use homophones (e.g., 'bear' for 'bare'), have incorrect grammar or word order, lack punctuation, and be misspelt. The user may not be able to achieve the desired language or literacy accuracy, but if the message is successfully communicated, even if it required some clarification, then this message is unequivocally a communication triumph and should be recognised as such. The internalised pressure of having language and literacy perfection prioritised over communication success can lead to withdrawal and inhibit communication attempts. The relief in a child's or young person's face when I introduce myself as "not interested in spelling or grammar but interested in what they like talking about" is unmissable. Challenging ableism towards communication and disability is rooted in the core commitment to reconfiguring disability or a disabled person as *not* lacking or less-than, or something to be fixed.

Technodazzle/technoableism

There is potential for communication partners to have unconscious bias towards AAC methods that more closely assimilate non-disabled speech, and it is vital that this is recognised and challenged. 'Technodazzle' is a term used to describe the wow factor or overhyped presentation of new technology, and 'technoableism' is "a belief in the power of technology that considers the *elimination of disability* a good thing, something we should strive for" (Shew, 2023, p. 8). The concepts of technodazzle and technoableism need to be recognised to prevent situations where those supporting the AAC user impose strong preferences for a particular technology either through their personal curiosity and passion for technology, or their desire to 'fix' the person or 'correct' the perceived communication deficit. It is imperative that the drive to use technology comes from the individual AAC user and is grounded in their understanding of how it may enhance their communication without devaluing other methods. It should not come from a place where those supporting the AAC user are wanting to replace effective, atypical communication styles with other styles that may appear more typical. Effective and personally preferred methods of communication should always take precedence over normalcy. It is critical that the message conveyed is not the one critiqued by Ashley Shew, that "in the constant praise and promise of bodies-fixed-through-technology, we see that disabled is a bad state of being and that disabled people must be altered to be worthy" (Shew, 2023, p. 9).

Positive changes coming into practice

Over the past decade there has been increased consideration of cultural and linguistic diversity both from AAC developers and practitioners. Whilst there is still a long way to go, there have been significant steps towards facilitating multilingualism, developing culturally appropriate symbols, and recognising diverse vocabulary needs such as food, clothes, and identity words.

Alongside the growth of the neurodiversity movement, there has also been greater consideration of what constitutes typical or atypical communication and how this applies to symbol AAC use. Whereas vocabulary for talking in depth or repeatedly about a ruling passion or for info-dumping was often seen as unnecessary empty language or distracting, we are starting to see a shift towards prioritising this vocabulary. Stimming or self-talk on a communication aid was previously treated as something to be discouraged but is now recognised as valid use with communicative, emotional, or sensory purpose.

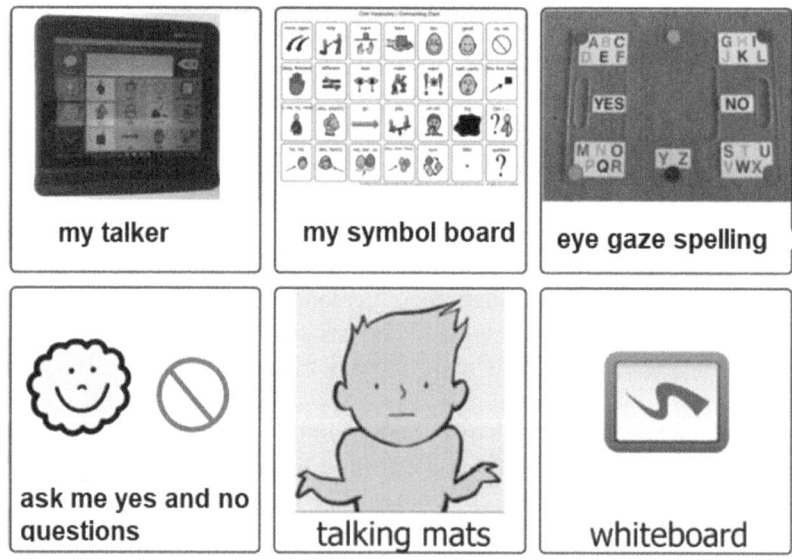

(Talking Mats Ltd, 2013)

FIGURE 4D.2   A choice board designed to empower the communicator by enabling them to have control over which communication mode they use (Talking Mats Ltd, 2013)

There has also been a shift in some aspects of speech and language therapy in its move away from the consultative model to greater emphasis on collaborative practice. Team support, client autonomy, and self-advocacy are becoming priorities and, consequently, AAC users are encouraged to have more ownership over their communication styles. This is demonstrated by this "my voice/my choice" card in Figure 4D.2 recently seen on a child's desk.

Conclusion

The challenge going forward is for those supporting AAC users to question the predetermined view of what 'quality talk' might look like and to shift the focus towards promoting enjoyable, meaningful, and impactful interactions. Conversation must be viewed as a means of expressing identity, belonging, and personality, and for developing thought, rather than purely as a tool for providing information or for academic performance. As communication aid user, Jamie Preece, stated in his recent article:

> I now think more in words. That may sound strange, but I didn't used to. Words are more than just talking tools: they are thinking tools. I didn't used to have an inner voice. I had ideas floating around, but without the words attached to them. I now have an inner dialogue and have the words I need to talk through situations in my head as well as out loud.
>
> *(Preece & Lee, n.d.)*

Despite the positive changes in approaches and attitudes to AAC described above, the subconscious bias towards normalcy over atypicality still underpins practice. There is a need to dissociate communication from academic success and social and economic mobility, and to move interventions away from the clinical desire to fix and 'correct'. As I have argued in this chapter, communication support needs a shift in attitude to embrace diverse methods and styles of communication and to facilitate authentic expression of self.

References

Hackett, A., MacLure, M., & McMahon, S. (2021). Reconceptualising Early Language Development: Matter, Sensation and the More-Than-Human. *Discourse, Studies in the Cultural Politics of Education, 42*(6), 913–929. https://doi.org/10.1080/01596306.2020.1767350

Henner, J., & Robinson, O. (2023). Crip Linguistics Goes to School. *Languages, 8*(1), 48. https://doi.org/10.3390/languages8010048

Neimiejer, D., & Sheldon, E. (2021, November 30). Why Can't I Change the Base Vocabulary of Proloquo? *AssistiveWare Blog*. https://www.assistiveware.com/blog/base-vocabulary-of-proloquo

Petersons, A., & Khalimzoda, I. (2016). Communication Models and Common Basis for Multicultural Communication in Latvia. *Society, Integration, Education. Proceedings of the International Scientific Conference*, 4, 423.

Preece, J., & Lee, A. (2023). Jamie: Who Chooses My Words? *The Journal of Communication Matters*, 37(3), 4–7. www.communicationmatters.org.uk

Shew, A. (2023). *Against Technoableism*. W. W. Norton & Company Ltd.

Talking Mats Ltd. (2013). https://www.talkingmats.com/ [Accessed 05 January 2024].

# 4e

LISTENING BODY

Louise Klarnett

Introduction

I see you. I listen, whole-bodied. Breathe, move, invite, without expectation. A dance unfolds. Sometimes invisible to others. A range of emotive expression, communication, through this somatic connection.

As a dance artist I listen, to connect, to relate, through presence and movement. This chapter shares windows into my practice with young children from two nurseries and a community organisation, The Magpie Project (https://themagpieproject.org), a charity for women and their children under five affected by homelessness (see also Klarnett & Underwood, 2020). All three venues are in Newham in East London, UK. My work is deeply embedded in these settings. Drawing on dance improvisation, listening touch, intensive interaction, developmental movement, and trauma-informed approaches, my work supports children's 'voices' to be unlocked.

To begin...

I recently learned about a technique used to support newly planted trees. Rather than connecting them to a vertical pole, they are supported by a stake at a 45-degree angle to allow movement as they grow, supporting them to adapt and strengthen in response to the weather and their general environment. This approach aligns with my work as a dance artist in health, education, and community contexts. My broader practice extends beyond the early years, but in the settings I write about here, I work with newborn babies, toddlers, and children under five years. At The Magpie Project, this includes their mothers. In these settings, through the breadth of my practice, I aim to see, support, hold space, create safety, invite, and encourage expression in its many forms.

The purpose of my role in these settings is to support children's communication, physical development, and emotional well-being through artistic and creative exploration and engagement. I am not a dance therapist although the work has many therapeutic benefits. I also do not refer to my work as play. My early-years practice is recognised by the dance sector and I have led training for many dance, art, and music organisations as well as for local authorities and organisations across London and the UK. I was a 'critical friend' for the Royal Opera House in 2018 for their 'Dots' early-years dance programme and have worked extensively with Scottish Dance Theatre supporting early-years participation, creation, training, and engagement. I am however happiest working on the ground in these Newham settings where I have built longstanding relationships and my work has been witnessed and recognised as beneficial to children's communication, health, well-being, and creativity. At times when dedicated funding cannot be obtained, each setting continues to employ me as an essential part of their ongoing work.

The word 'dance' can be intimidating. In the contexts of these settings, it encompasses movement of the whole body or *any* part of the body, as well as stillness, pause, rest. It involves subtle responses such as the flicker of an eyelid or a change in facial expression or muscular tone, a deep breath, a yawn, a smile, laughter, squeals, yelps, and other sounds. It also involves negotiated touch, mirroring, movement conversation techniques, intensive interaction, and a lot of improvisation. I sometimes use props and materials which include (but aren't limited to) chalk, coloured tape, thin elastics, koosh balls, feathers, and variously shaped pieces of fabric. Also frequently used are things in the environment such as twigs, leaves, water, sand, or random toys. A honeydew melon and a small pumpkin have been brought into the dances. Materials are sometimes a way into 'meeting'. Through soft observation in the moment, I see what a child might be playing with or curious about, or I make a considered choice from the things I have with me to offer as an invitation to the child. This, accompanied by a soft sideways step, can lead to deep explorations together. Sometimes these materials are naturally discarded during an interaction in favour of a more direct body-oriented connection, and sometimes they are integral. However, regardless of the materials, the work is primarily oriented around use of the body and the relational space between myself and a baby or child.

Listening body 213

FIGURE 4E.1 Stratford Circus Arts Centre. Image taken by Laura Zotova

The settings

All settings are in Newham, East London.

The Magpie Project is a charity working with mums and under-5s in temporary or insecure accommodation. They provide families with practical essentials, advice, and support from organisations and other professionals that include Shelter, London Black Women's Project, Health Visitors, and Children's Centre Family Support Workers. They offer a drop-in supported stay-and-play in a small community building. In a three-hour session, 45–60 mothers and many more children come and go and get their needs met – advice, advocacy, housing support, nappies, food, case work. The women accessing the project bear the physical and emotional effects of forced migration, homelessness, trafficking, Female Genital Mutilation (FGM), abuse, violence. They live with a low sense of safety and unaddressed trauma exacerbated by their continuing insecure housing and immigration status.

In our current space, I work inside, generally on mats in the back corner, but the work gently permeates the whole space. Sometimes, simply because there is carefully selected music playing, and because my attention and my dancing are often wide, I 'globally' hold an awareness of the feel of the space, the tone, and the movement and flow of the families as they come in and out to have their needs met. At the same time, my attention is 'local', with deep awareness of which baby or toddler I'm working with (Klarnett, 2023).

Kay Rowe Nursery School and Children's Centre is an inclusive setting where all children can follow their interests supported by enthusiastic and qualified staff. The setting is passionate about outdoor learning and has a large garden space, open all year round, where much of the children's play takes place. I have a list of children, mainly with SEND (special educational needs and disabilities), often with (often undiagnosed) language, communication, social, and emotional needs to target. I work with them at the time they are ready and wherever they might be in the setting, freely flowing. In addition, as I flow, I sometimes interact with children who aren't on my list. This commonly occurs at the beginning of the academic year, with new starters, where the children's friendship dynamics may need support, or new challenges in their lives are affecting mood, behaviour, and level of engagement at nursery. There are many staff members present. Staff do not necessarily witness all interactions unless the child has a specific one-to-one person, or they are being observed that morning, for example if it's their 'special week'. I spend a lot of time dancing outside in the large garden space as well as inside, not currently in a dedicated area. For a window into the pre-pandemic work in this setting, see the film 'The Acorn Project' (Klarnett & Tomos, 2018).

FIGURE 4E.2 The Magpie Project

Ronald Openshaw Nursery Education Centre (RONEC) is an inclusive setting integrating a maintained nursery school. It is a specialised provision for children with complex special needs. The facilities are built, staffed, and resourced to cater for wheelchairs/mobility needs, medical and personal care needs, as well as learning and play needs. I work with children one-to-one indoors, in a large space with mats, a swing, and other soft play equipment including a slide. There are dedicated staff present (each child has a one-to-one) who always witness the sessions. I generally work with the children with the most complex needs first, and then move on to a long list of children with varying SEND.

The work

Underpinning the improvisation work is a series of 'scores'. By this I mean I create a set of instructions, guidelines, or tasks that serve as the starting

216 Language, Place and the Body in Childhood Literacies

FIGURE 4E.3 Kay Rowe Nursery School

point for improvisation or as a communication tool for generating movement and action. Some scores relate to wider theories and approaches, most commonly Porges' polyvagal theory (1994) (discussed below), Winnicott's 'holding' (see Abram, 2015), principles of infant movement development (see IBMT, n.d.), the physical body and nervous system, as well as creative ideas both open-ended and specific. My scores are ever-growing and changing. Usually, the less complex, the better. Most scores ultimately are intended to lead to a dance of attunement, to 'meet' the children, who

FIGURE 4E.4 Ronald Openshaw Nursery Education Centre

and how they are in all their diversities. These scores are not generally shared explicitly with anyone; they discreetly hold me within the work. Each dance interaction is utterly unique.

Examples of scores:

'I see you' – hold in presence, body-witness, hold in wider attention, create safety to 'find' the eyes…

'Orient' – to the body, to others, the space/environment, through the window…

'Trace the face' – light touch, can promote facial expression/ muscular activation/ downregulation/ deeper breathing and social engagement (polyvagal)

'Map the body' - with different types of touch - pitter patter/ brush… (embodiment/sensation interoception)

Mirror

Question / Answer – body, eye, breath, object conversations…

Push pull, swing/rock, wrap, roll, spin, meet/match (proprioceptive/ vestibular)

Co-regulation – 'holds', 'breathe', 'roots from afar', 'see from the side'

'Where are you now? And now? And now?' (Inspired by dance artist Cai Tomos)

'Hand on heart' (interoception).

Some of these scores were used to inspire short films during the time of the pandemic, in 2020, for the families of The Magpie Project. These films continue to be used for wider CPD (continuing professional development) training for dance artists, non-dance early-years professionals, volunteers, students, and staff in organisations including Scottish Ballet, Suffolk County Council, Newham Early Years Conferences, and People Dancing (the foundation for community dance). Most importantly, they have been used in workshops for the families of The Magpie Project.

The science

The mind-body continuum has long been a topic of study and research. Neuroscientist Antonio Damasio's (2010) extensive exploration of the relationship between the brain and consciousness has led to the understanding that feelings are mental experiences of body states which arise from the interactions between the brain, body, and environment. There are many models and ideas for how to think about the brain: for neurophysiologist Charles Sherrington (1906), it is 'an enchanted loom'; neuroscientist and pharmacologist Candice Pert (1997) described the brain as 'a large bag of hormones'; physician and founder of osteopathic medicine, A.T. Still (1902), called the brain 'the body's pharmacy'; and so on…

In the triune model of the brain, it could be considered that each of the three parts – neocorticol, mammalian, and reptilian – speaks its own 'language':

> The human body has a triune brain, each part speaking its own 'language'. Together they form the body-brain connection. Neocortical speaks the language of words. Mammalian (mid-brain) speaks the language of feeling. Reptilian brain speaks the language of sensation (primitive response of sensory and motor systems that moves us out of danger; no words, just sensations).
>
> *(Adcock Doyle, 2017, p. 176)*

Whilst not all of my work is initiated from a perspective on trauma, approaches that are trauma-informed, psychologically informed, and somatically informed are part of my practice. Quillman (2013) writes: "much of the work of treating trauma is to help the patient [participant] move from dorsal vagal hypoarousal (dissociation) or sympathetic hyperarousal (terror/rage) to ventral vagal connection (social engagement)" (p. 385). Candice Pert (1997) has conducted extensive research into the mind-body continuum. She quotes Elmer Green, the Mayo Clinic physician who pioneered biofeedback treatment for disease:

> Every change in the physiological state is accompanied by an appropriate change in the mental emotional state, conscious or unconscious, and conversely, every change in the mental emotional state, conscious or unconscious, is accompanied by an appropriate change in the physiological state.
> (Green & Green, 1977, as cited in Pert, 1997, p. 137)

Pert writes about the role of the body in carrying emotional trauma: "Repressed traumas caused by overwhelming emotion can be stored in a body part, thereafter affecting our ability to feel that part or even move it" (1997, p. 141). This is a rapidly developing field of study, and Pert's research resonates in the ongoing work of many others including Peter Levine (1997), Bessel Van Der Kolk (2014), Stephen Porges (1994; 2011), and Daniel Siegel (2020). Polyvagal theory helps us understand how our body and brain work together to respond to stressors that are a part of everyday life, as well as experiences that are more significant, such as trauma (Porges, 1994). In my sessions, I use the principles of polyvagal theory, together with presence, connection, and attunement through engagement with dance/movement techniques such as mirroring, witnessing, breathing, body mapping, postural, and movement awareness. Through this approach, children can begin to find a sense of safety, build trust and relationships, and shift into a state of social engagement, however fleeting. This can lead to greater self-awareness, motor coordination, self-expression, social interaction, degrees of empathy, and emotional regulation.

The case studies

The exponential need for a polyvagal dance – part 1, and an epilogue...

At The Magpie Project, I observe an array of nervous system states in the participants. Dissociation is very common in the mums, as well as, tragically, toddlers and babies. Through the work, I endeavour to attune to and invite them into social engagement through polyvagal activity, creating a sense of safety, and I 'see' them.

For me, to 'see' is to body-witness. It is soft, it is whole and encompassing breaths. The eyes receive from behind me, looking without looking. It is vastly different to the regulatory adult gaze, or one which keenly observes measurable goals and achievements. Having said that, I appreciate the significance and importance of tracking children in order to identify next steps. Body-witnessing removes expectation. It emphasises acceptance and gives permission to be. It is warm and invites curiosity, as happens frequently when I am on the train, witnessed by one of my teenage sons. He says, "you're doing it again, aren't you?" We've discussed how I 'see' babies and toddlers; he's even tried it for himself!

A five-month-old baby is brought over by her mum. She has witnessed me working with other babies and toddlers. Today is their first time at the project. Through very little verbal language, mum communicates that she wants me to work with her baby and I invite them to the mats. At first, mum places the baby on the mat, away from her. Baby M almost holds her breath until she cries, a silent, single tear. Mum seems to want me to do something, but I place baby M back onto her lap, into her arms to soothe her. Less is so often more. I use very little language in much of this work. I hold space for them to simply be.

I begin to slowly, delicately move my fingers and hands, small dances exploring the air, close to them, imagining trails of golden light are visible to baby M. I don't seek her attention as I do this, though without looking, I am holding her in mine. Using the words of John Chitty (2016), a Polarity and Biodynamic Craniosacral Therapist, I say to her in my head: "I know who you are, I know where you came from, I know why you're here." Her face remains expressionless, but she turns to follow my finger dances, visually tracking, side to side, up and down. She takes a deep breath and turns back towards her mum. This repeats, slowly, several times, until her attention is with me for a little longer. We non-verbally negotiate that baby M is happy to lie on the floor, with mum close to her. The hand dances are now above and around her. My hands playfully land on her body – trunk, shoulders, outer legs and arms, then head – and fly away many times. I begin to trace her head and face lightly with my fingertips. This provokes tiny movements of the muscles of her face which I mirror. Mum is witnessing intently, urging the connection on. The eyes which were blank seem to ignite – and baby M's expression changes, it softens, her eyes seem clearer. Baby M appears to be seeing me and has come into connection through these actions. Mum is smiling. I gently bring in more touch, to the feet, showing them to baby M. She gazes with a little smile at me through them. We playfully rock, swinging her legs, holding the hips to encourage mobility through the spine and to lightly support infant movement development – patterning which is often missed due to trauma and living conditions.

Mum has seen me working with babies on their tummies, and through a gestural conversation, places baby M onto her front without distress.

I lower myself onto my front, to meet at floor level. Her face is seeking now, she lifts her head and watches my face, hands. She pushes her chest up and I mirror. She smiles at me, at her mum. I ask her "where is your voice?" not expecting a reply, and she responds with a sound! In my mind I hold the score, "Where are you now? And now? And now?" As she sounds a little more, she pushes up and mobilises her head and neck, reaches with her fingers to touch mine. And now she needs a nappy change. Something which sometimes happens. The dance is over, almost…

Epilogue

Stepping away from baby M, a beautiful movement trio unfolds between a baby who is not quite crawling, a toddler who is just walking, and myself. Crawling, falling, rolling, walking, reaching, looking, smiling. The toddler is modelling movement development for the baby, how to come into the upright from a squat (a model we often utilise at our termly Baby Labs, where babies and toddlers are the experts, 'showing off' their developmental stages and skills for one another and their mums). And next to the mats, now in a clean nappy, is baby M, lying across her mum's lap on her tummy, the pair of them witnessing this trio, both mum and baby M beaming joyfully. The cascade of the polyvagal work is powerful and infectious if it can be ignited.

A conversation in five minutes – have you ever had an eye dance…?

He stands by the door, holding a toy doll with a Spiderman costume under his arm.

He is sniffing and breathing through his mouth. N (staff member) is sitting next to where he is standing. I say "hello". He looks at me. He has what is referred to as a speech and language delay, a returner to the setting. I didn't meet him last academic year. He looks at me, without any head movement. He sniffs.

He stands tall, and seems, perhaps, a little unsure of me. I crouch near to him but not too close. He holds my gaze. I say "hello" with my eyes to his. I say with my eyes, "I see you. It's good to meet you". He seems to respond with a yes, through his eyes, holding my gaze, appearing to look deeper into mine. I maintain this open gaze, and move my right arm slowly as if it's unfurling, untwisting, becoming something else. I place the hand gently on the right side of his torso, holding all the possible cues of a no. The diaphragm feels a little tight, as if he's holding his breath. He keeps looking with ok-ness, steady eye contact, and no hint of a contraction in

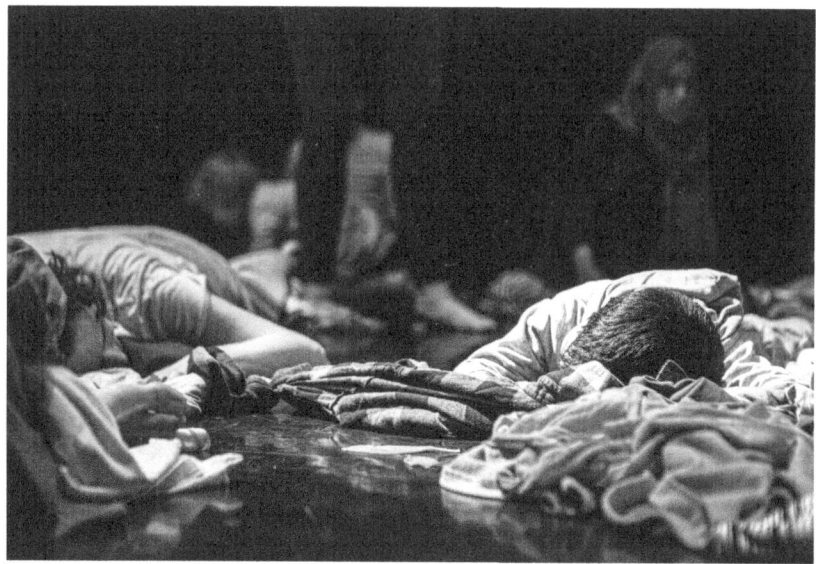

FIGURE 4E.5 Further Images of Stratford Circus Arts Centre. Image by Laura Zotova

the body away from the point of contact. A point of suspended contact, he isn't leaning in but there is a poised connection, as if something is ready, or about to happen. N (staff member) is witness. She is my clear measure of permission, a safe/known person to R. His body softens a little, and his eyes shine. He sits on the floor, removes his shoes, and indicates, with the toy, a reach, a direction or instruction. He places the Spiderman suit on a stool. I start to move, to turn, slowly, holding him lightly at the edge of my attention. He watches, then springs into motion. He runs, I run, he spins, I spin. He leaps and squeals joyfully, almost performing a barrel roll in the air….

A conversation over an academic year – a first meeting and the last…

A first meeting…

A little boy, B, standing, hood up, blank tear-stained face. I observe from the doorway to the conservatory. Trains, cars on the floor, two other boys in the space. The two boys leave, running towards the garden. I move slowly and sit near B. I wait, quietly, a soft piece of music plays. He doesn't react to my presence. I move closer and kneel alongside him, gently place a hand on his back between the shoulder blades. After a few moments, without looking at me, he silently hooks his arm under and around mine, holding onto my bicep through my sweatshirt. I bring another hand to his other hand, which is cold. I wait in stillness, holding him, the room, the noise from the setting, in my attention. Body listening. I slowly trace his hand with my fingertips, deeply aware of the impact of such listening touch. His three-year-old's fingers feel like huge expanses of land as I read the contours through the slow touch. He looks at me. He makes tiny movements of his head, tilting it side to side. The music continues to play from the speaker on the floor in the doorway. A subtle shift of his weight from foot to foot emerges. I observe this tiny movement through the connectedness of our arms. I am close to his side, next to him, zipping up the space between our bodies. We slowly begin a dance together, we rock and sway, a little; if we were witnessed, you might miss it in its size, yet it grows. It is unclear who started this shared motion, he leans into my body and I extend the rock, he lifts away from the floor, momentarily suspended in the air, and back. This movement pattern repeats several times. He wiggles onto my lap, hands and arms in contact. We rock some more from this new position. Side to side, forwards and back, a very small asymmetric dance unfolds. He takes a deep breath and yawns. I lift him from my lap, he stands upright, looking at me. He looks away and I know the dance for today is over. I sign and say that the dance is finished and goodbye. He drops to the floor and picks up a train.

The last meeting…

B arrives, as always, looking sad with tear-stained cheeks. This has never failed to sadden me. I am concluding an interaction with another child. Music plays in the indoor space. B sits at the table where there is clay. When I am ready, I crouch close to him with my hand on his back. We have worked together for many months, exploring a great deal of movement, bringing him from shutdown (shutdown, or freeze, occurs through the dorsal branch of the vagus nerve; it can move us into a state of immobility or dissociation) as well as distressed/activated states, to connection with glimpses of momentary joy. He has said very little verbally to me in all that time. However, sometimes, his eye contact can be sustained, his eyes light up and he smiles or laughs. Today I say "hello B". He says "sad". I ask why he's sad. He replies "home". I don't enquire further. I place my hands around his cold hands and rub them to warm and awaken them. To bring my attention fully to him (to any of the children in this setting) can sometimes be a little challenging, softly declining others' wants and attempts to interact with me, often utilising staff to steer them, kindly, away, to refocus their attention. Some continually orbit my work for a morning, coming and going into and out of the centre of my attention as

I move through my list. B is one of these children today. But first, I hold him solely in my attention. I gesture that we stand, he follows. We hold hands and turn, a 'ring of roses' for two without words. He lifts his gaze and looks at me. We are inside, in a busy space, the home corner, table of clay, painting area all buzzing with chatter and children. Still holding hands, with my bag on my back, I lead B into the garden for more space. My speaker, which plays from inside my backpack, is hooked onto a fence or apparatus. It often promotes curiosity, a bag that plays music...

Outside, a playful spinning dance morphs into a gentle pushing, pulling, balancing, falling, rolling dance. B's weight falls into my arms with such trust. I lift him, horizontally, facing the sky, and turn very slowly – he can see treetops, planes, cranes. I pause. He is held in safety and stillness within the noise and hubbub of the nursery and the city. I set him down and he wanders off. My attention turns to the next child.

A morning of dance unfolds in the nursery. B is close by, then disappears all morning. When alongside, he is witness to many other dances. Towards the end of the morning, he returns wearing his backpack. He sets it down next to mine which is now on the floor, still playing music. The head teacher is watching us. B is smiling. She says, "B has a backpack and Louise has a backpack." He smiles even more and we engage in a short, joyful, energetic dance together, leaping, running, falling, rolling, up and down from the ground, before the call for 'tidy-up time'.

In the case of B, visible trauma or distress in the body does not appear to be neatly resolved at the end of a year of these weekly encounters. These moments of connection do however offer some space, moments for the nervous system to feel into, or experience briefly, the possibility of safety, connection, moments of joy. In his case, he has also been supported through his regular attendance at the nursery. At The Magpie Project, frequently, encounters are brief and irregular; sometimes I work with a child only once. This is the painful truth of the state of the hidden homeless, the transience, the ongoing nature of the family's trauma. In these cases, supported by project staff, I have to trust that one interaction is better than none.

Last words...

Within these windows into my practice, one may need to look for the 'language'. I see every connection, whether of the eyes, breath, or whole body, as a dance. And I see these babies and children, though under five years, as my collaborators. The interactions are ultimately dances of communication. There have been hundreds of these dances over many years, with very few written about, filmed, or photographed, so there is nothing captured, no tangible trace. Yet, when an encounter is simply witnessed and experienced in the moment, it is my hope that it changes something somewhere, that an imprint remains in the nervous system... In the words of choreographer Crystal Pite:

> Dance disappears almost at the moment of its manifestation. It is an extreme expression of the present, a perfect metaphor for life. Dancers sculpt space in real time, working inside a form that is constantly in a state of vanishing.

References

Abram, J. (2015). Donald Woods Winnicott. *Institute of Psychoanalysis, British Psychoanalytical Society*. https://psychoanalysis.org.uk/our-authors-and-theorists/donald-woods-winnicott

Adcock Doyle, K. (2017). Laying the Foundations. In M. Tufnell, *When I Open My Eyes:* Dance, Health, Imagination. Dance Books Ltd, 165–183.

Chitty, J. (2016). *Working with Babies – A Five Part Therapy Method for Infants and Their Families*. Polarity Press.

Damasio, A. (2010). *Self Comes to Mind: Constructing the Conscious Brain*. Pantheon, Vintage.

IBMT (Institute for Integrative Bodywork and Movement Therapy). (n.d.) *Infant Movement Development*. https://ibmt.co.uk/infant-movement-development/

Klarnett, L. (2023). The Dance of Attunement. *Animated: Current Issues and Practice in Participatory Dance*. Winter 2023. https://www.communitydance.org.uk/DB/animated-editions/Winter-2023

Klarnett, L., & Tomos, C. (2018). *The Acorn Project*. https://www.youtube.com/watch?v=4VjJp9MtC28

Klarnett, L., & Underwood, A. (2020). *The Magpie Project*. https://themagpieproject.dance/

Levine, P. A. (1997). *Waking the Tiger*. North Atlantic Books. https://www.somaticexperiencing.com

Pert, C. (1997). *Molecules of Emotion: Why You Feel the Way You Feel*. Scribner.

Porges, S. (1994). First presentation of Polyvagal Theory in Presidential Address to the Society for Psychophysiological Research. Atlanta, GA. https://condor.depaul.edu/dallbrit/extra/psy588/Orienting%20in%20a%20Defensive%20World.pdf; https://www.stephenporges.com

Porges, S. (2011). *The Polyvagal Theory: Neurophysiological Foundations of Emotions, Attachment, Communication, and Self-regulation*. WW Norton.

Quillman, T. (2013). Treating Trauma through Three Interconnected Lenses: Body, Personality, and Intersubjective Field. *Clinical Social Work Journal*, 41(4), 356–365. https://doi.org/10.1007/s10615-012-0414-1

Sherrington, C. (1906). *The Integrative Action of the Nervous System*. Yale University Press.

Siegel, D. (2020). *The Developing Mind* (3rd ed.). Guildford Press. https://drdansiegel.com

Still, A. T. (1902). *The Philosophy and Mechanical Principles of Osteopathy*. Hudson-Kimberly Publishing Company.
Van Der Kolk, B. (2014). *The Body Keeps the Score*. Viking Penguin. https://www.besselvanderkolk.com

Further reading

Davies, M. (2003). *Movement and Dance in Early Childhood*. Sage.
Gerhardt, S. (2004). *Why Love Matters*. Routledge.
Goddard Blythe, S. (2004). *The Well Balanced Child*. Hawthorn Press.
Gopnik, A., Meltzoff, A., & Kuhl, P. (1999). *How Babies Think*. Weidenfeld & Nicolson.
Gray, E. A., & Porges, S. (2021). *Restoring Core Rhythmicity: Polyvagal-Informed Dance/Movement with Survivors of Collective Trauma* https://www.youtube.com/watch?v=01O_CEe8mKU
Haines, S. (2016). *Trauma Is Really Strange*. Singing Dragon.
Hartley, L. (1989 & 1995). *Wisdom of the Body*. North Atlantic Books.
Magsamen, S., & Ross, I. (2023). *Your Brain on Art: How the Arts Transform Us*. Random House.
Manning-Morton, J. (2014). *Exploring Well-Being in the Early Years*. Open University Press.
McTavish, A. (2007). *Feelings and Behaviour. A Creative Approach*. The British Association for Early Education.
Porges, S. W. (2017). *The Pocket Guide to the Polyvagal Theory*. Norton.
Rosenberg, S. (2017). *Accessing the Healing Power of the Vagus Nerve*. North Atlantic Books.
Tufnell, M., & Greenland, P., et al. (2000). *What Dancers Do That Other Health Workers Don't*. Jabado.

4f

COMING TOGETHER

Roundtable discussion on language beyond meaning

Ruth Churchill Dower, Abigail Hackett, Andrea Lee, and David Ben Shannon

This roundtable discussion brought together authors of some of the case study chapters in this section (Ruth, Andrea, David) with some of the book editors (Abi, Ruth, David) to share our learnings and responses across the stories, ideas, and practices in this book section. We framed the discussion around the following prompt questions (which are offered to readers in Chapter 1 in relation to this theme).

- How can we plan for the unpredictable?
- How can we make space for things we have not yet imagined?
- How can we value opacity and resist demanding fixed meanings and clear logics?

Finally, we reflect on key messages and recommendations for action we hope readers might take away from this section of this book.

Reflecting on the chapter abstracts – what resonated in relation to your own work? What differed from your own work?

Andrea: The quote that I picked out, from Ruth's chapter, was that language, as well as representing things, includes all the 'tears, sneers and sighs' and that it's not just the words – it includes everything that the person's doing. Therefore, it might be more productive to pay attention not to what the language means, but what it does. That just really resonated with what I was trying to get across in my chapter.

Ruth: I also picked out something similar from Andrea's chapter, around the bias in educational, clinical, and social practices towards normative or typical communication styles and behaviours. That is something that has really challenged me in my research, because it's so deeply embedded into our cultures. It's almost hard to stop ourselves expecting that kind of normative series of behaviours. I was touched by something Karen Watson, Zsuzsa Millei, and Eva Bendix Petersen (2020) wrote: "perhaps we could stop creating difference as problematic and something that needs to be silenced, changed or fixed. We could interrupt our incessant speaking of 'otherness', and instead challenge 'sameness', and with that become curious, and open to the uncertainty". I loved that because something that I find so challenging is, how do we stop becoming complicit in othering practices in the ways that we are trying to write about and work with non-normative ways of being? How do we stop putting non-normative ways into this box marked 'Other' in order to be able to work with them legitimately as part of the mainstream?

Abi: This idea of valuing and celebrating all of the ways in which young children language is something that ripples through our book. We use those words a lot, I think. It can feel hard to make that case in the face of the dominance of existing frameworks. It is interesting to see, in this book section, the power of the practice and still feel a sense of grappling for the explanatory language for why this approach is important to consider.

Andrea: Those existing frameworks are so embedded in the way that we think – both the schools and the academic side of it, but also in parents' expectations. That side of it can be quite tricky.

David: Perhaps the question comes from the wrong perspective. "Why is this as important as language?" sounds like we're trying to build an equivalency. Instead, we could say – the more-than-representational aspects of language are there anyway, whether you ignore them or attend to them.

Ruth: If there's a space made for language to be perceived otherwise, and for children's bodies to express otherwise, that space provides opportunities to see different types of potentials, to see what a body can do rather than constantly measuring the body against what it can't do. Thinking back to your chapter, David, there's a need for joy as well. There's a need for something that leaves frissons of wonderful sensations in your body, that leaves those marks of potential, because it gives a way for the deficit narratives to be contested, for us to see what children can do. When that becomes a narrative which doesn't reduce children into a particular identity, it gives us hope to reimagine children's intra-actions with the world in a more meaningful way. How do we give space for those different ways of being to become a narrative?

David: I think joy is important for the reasons that you said, but also something that came out of writing the chapter with Jess and Willow was how it made behaviour better and more conducive to learning. Thinking about joy with Spinoza and Liselott Olsson, as we do in this chapter, is about giving children more capacities, more ways to express themselves, more ways to enjoy freedom of movement. Having more capacities isn't the same thing as poor behaviour, quite the opposite actually; joy in the café space, for instance, as we describe in our chapter, seemed to improve behaviour in ways that are really valuable.

Andrea: We can also look at that through the perspective of teacher morale. Those shared senses of joy that you define, David, I found interesting. Is a calm day or a day with no big issues – is that a joyful day? For some children and some staff, it might be – it is interesting to ask, how are we defining joy?

How can we plan for the unpredictable? How can we make space for things we have not yet imagined?

Ruth: So much of what we're doing with children seems to involve denying our sensations in the world. For very young children, we place an increasing emphasis on teaching self-regulation and resilience. And yet, for many children, these sensations are becoming more and more overwhelming, more and more overpowering. For instance, for some children who might have a diagnosis of selective mutism or autism, there might be a strong focus on masking, in order for them to 'self-regulate', to be able to fit within an environment and function with language. Perhaps there is also an important need for children to deregulate or to unmask; this might involve running into a big wide space and shouting and moving. Children need this balance, just to be able to cope with all that kind of extra-linguistic stuff, that is beyond language. An over-emphasis on self-regulation, and denial of bodily sensation, I think, can be quite damaging. In terms of planning for the unpredictable, there needs to be more space for that and less pressure on regulation through language.

David: With regards to that question, I was thinking about the practicalities of the classroom. How do you run a classroom in such a way that gives that time to those children who need it but also in a safe way that enables teachers to carry on doing their job? It is not always an easy balance, but one of the things in the chapter we try and think about is that sometimes, if you know a young person well, and you can tune into their needs, it gives you an opportunity to do something for them, to meet that need. I can't run them on the playground right now. But I can let them do the hula hoop for five minutes in the corner, where they're not going to knock anybody over.

Andrea: I agree, and there can be an anxiety from teachers and from speech therapists; we are hearing these messages about the need to allow for more unpredictable behaviour, but trying to fit that into ways that we've worked years and years and years, is a real challenge. Finding that balance between this is what we feel comfortable with and how we are able to work, and what we know from this new research and new theories about children's communication. It made me think about the gap between research and academia and practice. How do we bridge that gap between researchers who are finding these new ways to think about childhood and language, and how can we actually translate that into practice? Predictability is a good example of that – if you have many children in your class, you need some things to be predictable and you can't always go with that unpredictability.

David: I think maybe there's also a risk of creating a false dichotomy between a regulated environment and an oppressive environment. Unregulated environments can be very oppressive for some children.

Abi: Going back to Ruth's description of the movement between the regulated and the dis-regulated is helpful here. Rather than thinking of one as preferable, perhaps it is more helpful to think about regulation and dis-regulation as both being necessary, and the way the one balances the other. Two sides of the same coin, that depend on each other. That balance might look different for different children, or in different settings, and not everyone working with children will have identical practice. Where is that rhythm?

How can we value opacity, and resist demanding fixed meanings and clear logics?

David: I'm thinking about how neurodivergence is sometimes framed as the absence of the ability to understand the why-ness of other people's behaviours: for instance, some of the arguments around executive functioning and theory of mind in autism and ADHD diagnoses. Yet, as we learn from Glissant, trying to understand why anyone is doing something is always an impossible and colonial endeavour anyway. In contrast, Eunjung Kim writes that we need to get away from measuring people against humanist properties, no matter how well-meaning. Maybe it is the same here for the question of why? – rather than trying to argue that neurodivergent children are neurodivergent because they don't understand the "why" of other people's behaviour, maybe we should take that as a prompt for all of us to stop asking "why?" (since we can never know anyway).

Ruth: I totally agree. It links really nicely with Sylvia Kind's (2020) work in experimenting with arts-based methods. She tries to resist asking what a child means by what they're doing, and asks instead how she can participate in their ideas. It's really hard to do this when everything in early education at the moment seems to be focused on trying to explain why something is happening, in order to fix it or change it or progress it. Mazzei and Jackson (2017) talk about thinking about silence as presence rather than absence, so how do we welcome stillness and silence as legitimate spaces for learning and for teaching? – for teachers as well, who feel like they need to be doing all the time. How do we find space for that silence and for that stillness where we, perhaps, don't ask why, we don't look for the meaning. We don't try to interpret and seek, but just wait to see what comes through those spaces. How much more might we be able to sense, how much more attuned might we become to the environment, from this stance? Without trying to understand why.

Andrea: We've had a real shift in practice in our team, especially working with the children with autism where we are very much following their lead and working on trying to get those moments of shared communication with them. It's not about how many words they can produce or whether they can produce a sentence, but rather, are we getting that shared joy in the interaction and the communication with the communication aid?

Ruth: Are you noticing a difference in using this approach?

Andrea: Definitely, but the challenge is measuring it and proving it. Anecdotally, various members of staff are sharing stories about that feeling that you get, where you suddenly connect with somebody.

What key messages and recommendations do we hope others take away from this book section?

David: Carrying on thinking about "why?" questions, perhaps one recommendation could be don't ask "Why do you need this?" but just simply, "What do you need?". Waiting for diagnostic labels, particularly in the face of how overstretched diagnostic services are, before giving children access to provision, is problematic, so I hope that would be a key takeaway.

Andrea: A key takeaway that I would be thinking about is going back to David's point about finding that shared joy in the classroom and what we mean by shared joy in the classroom. So, if shared joy is actually just sitting quietly with that child and that's what that child needs, we need to give value to that as a measure. That involves resisting fixed meanings and the demand to measure. It involves moving away from what is easier for clinicians and teachers to measure, and instead defining what is shared joy for that child and that member of staff, and building that into their setting.

Ruth: Often something doesn't gain validity in early education until it's considered a pedagogy or an 'authorised' way of teaching, and approaches are usually expected to show how they support learning outcomes. Improvisation, the movement and sensory expression within improvisation, can be such an effective and generative force, particularly for neurodivergent bodies. Yet it really struggles to fit into that kind of template of a formulaic pedagogy where learning needs to be measured. Supporting non-lingual ways of being without reducing them to talk, requires an improvised approach. It's about looking for those ways to connect and those sparks of vitality that are emerging between the adult and the child. Improvisation is a way of moving towards those connections with children that are incredibly valuable, that do not rely on language but are full of expression.

David: I'd love it if someone read this book and thought about how they could use these provisions that are supposed to be for the one child, and make them available for all. For instance, that you can do intensive interactions as a model of improvisation with

	anybody, not just the child who's got it on their IEP. It is about opening up who gets to access these tools.
Andrea:	I think there's something about undoing a lot of professional guilt. There's a lot of guilt that people feel if they're sitting quietly with a child, just building that relationship. You feel guilt that you're not doing anything or not achieving a goal or not doing something that is measurable or that is moving that child on. I think there is some unlearning necessary to release people from that guilt of feeling that they should be doing more all the time. I see this a lot with families as well, feeling that it's not okay to just be sitting and enjoying the time. Sometimes they feel that they should be always educating their child. Instead, we need to consider that you can still be learning about the child whilst you're doing that. It's not wasted time. What are you learning about the child in that time?
David:	One final take-home might be that, across the four of us, there are things that we disagree on, and things that are complex. That kind of mess means that sometimes there will not be a clear sense of "what you should do right now", but rather it is always going to be untidy. I think that justification for things being untidy feels like it's not very present right now in schools. There are scripts and processes and an emphasis on 'best practice' in schools right now, but what we have seen from the four of us talking is that different professionals have different ideas about what could happen or what should happen. So we need to make space to acknowledge that kind of mess more.

References

Kind, S. (2020). Wool works, cat's cradle, and the art of paying attention. In C. M. Schulte (Ed.), *Ethics and research with young children: New perspectives* (pp. 49–62). Bloomsbury Academic.

Mazzei, L. A., & Jackson, A. Y. (2017). Voice in the agentic assemblage. *Educational Philosophy and Theory*, 49(11), 1090–1098. https://doi.org/10.1080/00131857.2016.1159176

Watson, K., Millei, Z., & Petersen, E. B. (2020). Silence and its mechanisms as the discursive production of the 'normal' in the early childhood classroom. *Journal of Childhood, Education and Society*, 1(2) 103–115. https://doi.org/10.37291/2717638X.20201236

SECTION V
Rights of the Talker

5
THE RIGHTS OF THE TALKER.

A manifesto for chattering, whispering, translanguaging, not-speaking, non-verbalising, screeching, signing, clicking, twirling, stimming, assistive technology-ing, jumping, shouting, grasping, gasping, dancing, drawing, repeating, refusing, gesturing, glancing, smirking, eye-rolling, whistling......

Abigail Hackett, Khawla Badwan, Ruth Churchill Dower, Ester Ehiyazaryan-White, Warda Farah, Rosie Flewitt, Karen Grainger, Rachel Holmes, Christina MacRae, Vishnu KK Nair, and David Ben Shannon

The aspiration of this book is to make space for a different, more capacious view of childhood, language, and what it means to make meaning and connect with others. A generous view of what 'counts' and should be valued in relation to children's language is essential for numerous reasons. As reflected in the title and subtitle of this chapter, we even struggle for a word generous enough to encapsulate everything we love about how children make meaning in their worlds. Instead, we settle for the simplest of words, 'talker', and we add a long and incomplete list of all the modes, forms, actions, and (un)making of meaning that 'talker' should include.

Rights of the Talker?

In 2006, Daniel Pennac wrote a manifesto called '*Rights of the Reader*' which, with the addition of illustrations by Quentin Blake, has been taken up by educators, advocates such as the National Literacy Trust, and those interested in celebrating children's engagement with books. Arguing for a capacious approach to how adults imagine and validate children's reading (such as skipping, dipping in, reading anywhere, and not finishing the book), Pennac writes: "When it comes to reading, we grant ourselves all kinds of rights, starting with the ones we deny the young people we want to initiate into the world of books" (2006, p. 145).

Whilst we would caution against assuming that a child's (or anyone's) viewpoints and feelings are similar to our own, we agree that reflecting on what we as adults might prefer or find challenging when it comes to talk can be a useful starting point. One example of this would be Jones' (2013) powerful description of doing a round-robin reading exercise with her teacher trainee students, in order for them to experience how this kind of exercise can bring back difficult past experiences that manifest as tension in the body. If you would not enjoy performing in this way, it's likely that many children would not either!

For their own good?

We are inspired by how Pennac's notion of Rights of the Reader has captured the imagination. The notion of the talker or reader having *rights* reframes many ways in which adults have policed, evaluated, or intervened into children's language and literacy practices in the past, by asking:

How would this feel?

By pausing to ask how it would feel, we nudge towards the question:

Do children's feelings matter?

These simple questions can easily be lost in a neoliberal education context. They can get lost when children are measured against norms, when their language is assumed to progress in a neat and predictable way through ages and stages of development that are enshrined in education and healthcare provision.

Shaping children's language practices in specific and narrow directions, heavily incentivising certain ways of communicating, and acting quickly and decisively to squash deviance are strategies that are often seen as benignly in the child's interest. This is exemplified in a recently leaked Ofsted briefing document for school inspectors (Ofsted is England's school quality assurance body). It included instructions on how to respond to teachers who might argue that children shouldn't be made to speak in a middle-class way. The response prescribed by Ofsted pivoted on the central idea that "Teaching standard English is a matter of social justice" (see Cushing, 2023). When children are primarily developmental projects, intervening into their language is considered benign and 'for their own good', no matter how bitter the medicine tastes at the time.

With this in mind, we invite you to join us in making a speculative, unfinished list: the Rights of the Talker…………

This is a list concerned with what it might mean to love everything about children's language, and what our role as grown-ups might be in making space for language, place, and body in childhood.

The right to time

Language development has a close but problematic relationship with *time*. Children's talk is often measured against a fixed timeline of 'normal' development. Labels such as 'language delay' or 'disorder' are labels of being 'out of time'. Discourses of 'catching up' with 'lost' time prevail in discussions of (for instance) the summer-born learning gap, summer learning loss, and children from economically disadvantaged backgrounds starting 'behind' other children. These ideas about language and time have intensified since the onset of the COVID-19 pandemic.

As well as being expected to develop in a rapid and predictable fashion, children are often also required to communicate in ways that are efficient and do not take up unnecessary time. Children's speech can be judged as moving too slowly (deficient) or too quickly (cognitive overload). Stammering (or 'dysfluency') is commonly understood as wasting time. All of these understandings and uses of time rely on normative ideas of *when* speech and language should develop. They make assumptions about the purposes of speech and language, namely efficiency, clarity, and productivity of communication. Moreover, this take-up of talk is assumed to be location-independent – it must be reproducible in school (not just *when*, but also *(any)where*).

We affirm that children have the right to take their time when it comes to talking. They might prolong, repeat, trip, tip, stall, or pause in their language-ing. They might speak in different time signatures, with different rhythms, paces, and tempos (fast, slow, regular, irregular, on-beat, off-beat, iambic pentameter, triplets, quintuplets, or swung). Children's talk can develop in ways that are erratic, unpredictable, and contrary to adult expectations of development, progress, and growth. And finally, we affirm that

FIGURE 5.1 The right to time

when is not separable from *where* – as the case studies in this book have amply demonstrated, children will language differently according to context, according to how their bodies feel and move in places. Children have the right to take time differently in different places.

The right to silence

Frequently, children who do not respond to grown-ups' questions or speak on cue are assumed to be incapable, 'too shy', unable to speak, or lacking enough knowledge of words. A child who does not answer is deemed

FIGURE 5.2   The right to silence

not to have the capacity to answer. Bilingual children in particular are frequently deemed 'silent' in classroom settings. In their study of young children in classrooms, MacLure et al. (2010) describe children's refusal to speak as a site where questions, emotions, and ideas proliferate, while adults "rage for explanation" (p. 494). When a child does not speak, an adult can be left confused, vulnerable, or embarrassed.

Valuing and respecting the silences of children can be how we listen. It is important not to misread silences or jump to conclusions. Silences can emerge as a way of changing the direction of an interaction. They can be a resistance to answering questions or complying with agendas set out by others. Using words can sometimes be confusing. The right word for a feeling may not exist; this is where silence can be important. Silence can be a meditative, contemplative practice. It can create connection and community. Silence can make space for meaning-making through other modes, such as bodily movement. Or it can be a way for children to soak up an experience, to feel their body in a place, to listen fully to human or nonhuman others. Whilst there are many ways that silence is more than disobedience or lack, it is also important to respect and make space for silences even when they do not seem to have a rational purpose.

Children have the right to silence, as either an action or a non-action. There can be a kind of benign violence in compelling children to speak according to adult agendas or questions. This kind of compulsion should not be confused with 'listening to children' or 'giving children a voice'. Silence is laced with power dynamics; it can be (but is not always) an act of resistance or a way to reassert/regain some control. Grown-ups almost always hold power over children, and that is why asserting children's right to silence is important.

The right to be listened to

When adults demand children's transparent, easily understood talk, it is often framed benignly as a desire to listen to children. We agree that children should have the right to be listened to, but we argue that for this to be truly enacted, listening cannot operate within narrow parameters of what adults are prepared to hear or are able to understand.

How might we listen to a child's silence?
To a language with which we are not familiar?
To their body, their mood, and their energy?
How do we listen without judging?

We agree with Yoon and Templeton (2019) who describe "the complexities of listening to children within politically constrained spaces of classrooms

FIGURE 5.3   The right to be listened to

and research contexts" (p. 57). In school spaces, but also in nursery classrooms, playgroups, family centres, museums, and green spaces, certain kinds of responses are anticipated, valued, and validated, to a greater or lesser extent, above others. In particular, adults often want to understand the child through their language; this leap to interpret too quickly, to render the child rational and understandable (and so to align them with normative ways of being), can get in the way of listening to children. Certain aspects of what children have to say are seen as more worthy of being listened to than others.

When we make judgements about which aspects of language are most useful, relevant, or understandable (and certainly when we assess language according to these characteristics), we are determining what language is. Children have a right for adults to *keep* listening, even when it is challenging, confusing, inconvenient, or seemingly uninterpretable for the adult. As Yoon and Templeton put it, the challenge when listening to children is in "hearing children out" (2019, p. 55) – that is, it is not necessarily about understanding everything straight away, but about continuing to listen without judgement or closing things down.

The right to choose how

A dominant discourse in educational policy is that there is a right and a wrong way to use language. 'Standard' English is prescribed, and specific forms of talk are demanded for specific purposes. This marginalises many

FIGURE 5.4 The right to choose how

children and families, including those from plurilingual households and households who use non-standard forms of English. Children might be quiet or silent because they find themselves in an unfamiliar environment and they may need the time and the space to acculturate, perhaps engaging only through their actions and not through words. Neurodivergent children may have ways of communicating that are often not regarded as 'appropriate'. As we described above, silence or hesitancy to speak is often regarded with suspicion.

Across each of these evaluations of children's language sits a hierarchy of preferred ways for *how* children should talk. Medium volume is preferred to silence, whispering, or shouting too loud. Clear enunciation is appreciated. Predictable or logical responses that answer questions or seem to have a rational basis are preferred to unexpected or seemingly unconnected comments, or to playful babbling and invented words. Sentences and phrases should occur in the correct time and place. Clear pronunciation and 'full sentences' are required by Ofsted.

As grown-ups, we need to make spaces where children can choose *how* to communicate. Children have the right to choose how to communicate. This is the only way to enable children to access the full repertoire of languages and varieties that are available to them. Insisting on limiting children's communication choices erases their existing knowledge and diverse cultural identities, affecting their confidence and sense of belonging to their community.

The right to move(ment) and gaze

Bodies jiggle and spin, arms and hands stretch and sweep, breath must be thrust through throats and vocal cords in order for vocalisations of any sort to emerge. Lips and tongues move and flex to make words that might be understood by adults. The connection between children's moving bodies and talking, vocalising, creating, and communicating is well evidenced by both research and practice.

Often words or vocalisations are about more than the meaning they want to convey. They are wrapped up in joy, excitement, and how sounds feel on the lips and in bodies. A gesture, a vocalisation, a word, a nod, a full-body-run across the space are all modes of meaning-making where children use their bodies and their voices. All these modes involve children's bodies sounding and moving in places. Looking at what kinds of sounds and movements a place seems to encourage or invite, and how

FIGURE 5.5 The right to move(ment) and gaze

children respond to that invitation, is a way to think about how environments might enable talkers.

We affirm children's right to movement and right to direct their own gaze. In education and clinical practice, often bodies are forced to be still in order to tame the mind. In schools, children do 'active listening' with crossed legs and straight backs so they can 'pay attention' (and if they're fiddling with their shoes, or blu tack, or somebody's hair, or not looking at the teacher, then they are deemed not to be listening). In clinical practice, such as speech and language therapy, children are taught to regulate their stimming, flapping, and shuffling and to maintain (or fake) 'appropriate' eye contact.

Movement (of many different kinds) is essential to language. It can be easy to forget that language starts in the body, with movement and sound. Because of this, it is important to pay attention to movements and vocalisations that have a meaning, as well as to those times when meanings are difficult to identify, yet movements are filled with energy and connection.

The right to (not) express oneself

Something we frequently read in early years literature is that children need language in order to express themselves. In this context, 'express themselves' often has a specific meaning – it imagines children telling grown-ups their practical or emotional needs, in a way that is legible and makes instant sense to the grown-ups.

We invite the reader to think about expression in a broader way. If expression is about communicating feelings and ideas, these feelings and ideas can be more or less easy for another person to grasp. Expression can occur through all sorts of bodily, (non)linguistic, or artistic modes. It often emerges during encounters with specific materials, movements, animals, or environments that amplify the sensations happening in the body. Within this broader definition, expression does not always need to make sense or have a single meaning!

Children might become engaged with things and stuff. They have the right to express this engagement without being asked what it means, or 'why' they are making sounds, moving, gesturing, or verbalising in this way. Children may invite you to play alongside, or to join in. Grown-ups might respond to this invitation by listening to bodily expressions taking place and responding in similar ways. This approach to expression and connection is much more fun than asking neat questions and receiving predictable responses.

As Glissant's (1997) writing teaches us, no one is fully 'transparent' to another – there is always another layer of complexity. In affirming children's rights *not* to express themselves we are affirming that children, like all of us, are complex beings. Sometimes, like us, they do not know what they think or mean, or they are still working things out. Sometimes, like us, they mean more than one thing at once. Sometimes, like us, they do not want to put the thing they think or feel out into the world at this moment.

FIGURE 5.6   The right to (not) express oneself

FIGURE 5.7   Language is world-making

Concluding comments: language is world-making

In our manifesto, we clamour for the most capacious, generous, inclusive, experimental, caring, and respectful definition of 'being a talker......' that we can imagine.

The challenge is not for children to 'rein it in' or conform to 'appropriate' modes of expression but for grown-ups to:

- create space for worldly encounters to be expressed in all different kinds of ways (including stillness)
- to become comfortable with the unexpected or incoherent
- to let go of trying to interpret or make sense of what a child expresses *before* we value it.

Communication is not only about the exchange of information: it is about establishing, reinforcing, and remaking relations. When we let go of narrow expectations or hierarchical lists of preferred ways for how children communicate, it makes space to ask the question

What kind of relations?

Children's language
whatever the temporal
rhythm
silent or loud
when we listen to it
in all and every one of its forms
entwined with movement and gaze
and (not) expressing as much as it does
is absolutely, always, already valid for each child in each moment, whether we grown-ups understand it or not.

References

Cushing, I. (2023). "Miss, can you speak English?": Raciolinguistic ideologies and language oppression in initial teacher education. *British Journal of Sociology of Education, 44*(5), 898–911. https://doi.org/10.1080/01425692.2023.2206006

Glissant, E. (1997). *Poetics of Relation*. University of Michigan Press.

Jones, S. (2013). Literacies in the body. *Journal of Adolescent and Adult Literacy, 56*(7), 525–529. https://doi.org/10.1002/JAAL.182

MacLure, M., Holmes, R., Jones, L., & MacRae, C. (2010). Silence as resistance to analysis: Or, on not opening one's mouth properly. *Qualitative Inquiry, 16*(6), 492–500. https://doi.org/10.1177/1077800410364349

Pennac, D. (2006). *The Rights of the Reader*. Walker Books.

Yoon, H. S., & Templeton, T. N. (2019). The practice of listening to children: the challenges of hearing children out in an adult-regulated world. *Harvard Educational Review, 89*(1), 55–84. https://doi.org/10.17763/1943-5045-89.1.55

INDEX

Note: *Italic* page numbers refer to figures and page numbers followed by "n" denote endnotes.

ableism 22, 105, 131, 198, 206–207
adults 3, 5, 8, 11–14, 45–47, 51, 53, 54, 61, 64–66, 71, 74, 83–86, 90, 97, 151, 154, 168–169, 171, 183, 188, 190, 193, 194, 204, 206, 219, 232, 238, 239; 'adult-controlled space' 61, 66; anxiety 124; improvisational skills 25; language of 57; listening to children 12, 74–76, 113; practices of body-listening 181–183; "rage for explanation" 242; role of 7; struggles and problematics of 163; working with young children 48
African American Language 109, 113
American Sign Language (ASL) 144, 146, 148
anti-racist 7, 33, 99, 105, 176
Arculus, C. 11, 23, 108, 162
art 46, 47, 53, 182–184, *183*, 187, 212
ASL *see* American Sign Language (ASL)
atmosphere 5, 8–10, 13, 78, 86, 96, 123, 128, 129, 150–152, 184–187
audio-recording 6, 98, 122–124
Augmentative and Alternative Communication (AAC) 163–165, 198–200, 203–209

Badwan, K. 95, 160, 193
Bhabha, H. 111, 172
bilingual/bilingualism 6, 13, 109, 111, 147, 148, 242
Björk-Willén, P. 110–111, 151
Black African Caribbean children 33
body/bodily: and brain 219; expression 161; languages 11, 181–195; listening 25, 181–195, 211–225; mind/body dualism 20, 21, 23, 218; movement 4, 23, 59–68, 85, 108, 206; normative assumptions 22; whole-body communication 71–72; witnessing 220
body languages 11, 74, 181–195, 198
body movement 4, 23, 59–68, 85, 108, 206
brain: and body 219; and consciousness 218; triune model of 218
British Sign Language 3–4

'carrier bag' theory 45–46, 53
Cartesian 20, 22, 26
children's language 3–4, 10, 12, 13, 48, 61, 95, 106–110, 129, 150–152, 155, 160, 161; abilities 22; and communication 101; development 9, 97, 105, 106, 120; evaluations

of 244; KS1 74; learning 100; and literacy practices 203, 238; as 'more-than-human' 5, 12, 13; and places 95, 96, 104, 107–110, 112, 114; practices in context 6, 105; quality of assessment of 106; of research 5–7; skills 65
Churchill Dower, R. 8, 25, 162, 165, 195
Clarke, J. 42n2, 162
classrooms 3, 21, 22, 24, 66, 67, 74–76, 81, 82, 86, 89, 96, 98–100, 106, 109–110, 137, 153, 168, 171, 172, 176–178, 200, 230, 232, 242, 243; anti-Blackness in 41; autistic children in 174; of children 71, 174; in England 98; homes and 194; language and meaning-making in 168–179; learning spaces 108; and places 26, 114; polycontextual 109; silence of 25; spaces 6; straitening effects of 26; unruliness, in special education *see* unruliness, in special education classroom
co-constructive methods 199, 200
consciousness 40, 99, 138, 197, 218
continuing professional development (CPD) 218
control and systemic restrictions 201–205
COVID-19 pandemic 42n1, 239; afterlives of 31–33, 96, 129; on early childhood 125; language and place in afterlives of 119–120; lockdown 62, 97, 100, 182; negative impacts on child development 133; in 2020 184
CPD *see* continuing professional development (CPD)
Crip Linguistics theory 163, 198, 205–206
curriculum 4, 12, 13, 20, 24, 26, 41, 72, 87, 89, 112, 120, 127, 148, 172, 178, 190, 203, 206; Eurocentric curriculum 133, 135; EYFS curriculum in England 46; 'knowledge-rich' 74; National Curriculum 34, 190; vocabulary 202, *202*

dance 162, 165, 182, 184, 189, 191, 192, 211, 212, 216–219, 221, 223, 224
deaf schools, as sanctuary 147–149

"Deep Listening" activity 113–114
Developmental Language Disorder (DLD) 134
developmental psychology 5, 95, 104, 106, 151, 186
dialect 6, 204–205
digital technology 111
disability/ableism 33, 100, 103, 113, 133, 141, 163, 169–170, 198, 201, 205–207
DLD *see* Developmental Language Disorder (DLD)
'double consciousness' 40, 99
Du Bois, W. E. B. 40, 99

early childhood: classroom, language and meaning-making in 168–179; communication in 59; community space 46; COVID-19 pandemic impact on 125; 'edu-care' in 23; education 20, 21, 48, 50, 108, 110, 164; language in 23–24, 85–88, 114, 127; practice in 12, 56
early language 7, 20, 104; children 150; and communication practices 36; development 24; learners 60; spaces for 127–129
Early Years Foundation Stage (EYFS) 36, 46, 100, 169, 172, 178
'edu-care,' in early childhood 23
Education, Health and Care Plan (EHCP) 35, 42n1
England: children in 98, 168; classrooms in 98; COVID-19 pandemic in 120; educational policy in 169; narrowing of neurotypicality in schools 32–36; schools in 31–36, 168; Speech Bubbles 70
'English as an Additional Language' 98–99, 169
entanglement 32, 105; of children's language 112, 114; of language and place 6, 96, 104–106, 150; of signed language 99
environment 5, 6, 8, 64, 66, 68, 70, 71, 74, 82–84, 89, 125, 135, 143, 168, 169, 200, 203, 211, 218, 244, 246; bodies and 60; for communication 77; formal 11, 59; learning 106; and physical movements 63; and place 105–106; school 149
ethics 46, 57, 161, 166, 193
Eurocentric curriculum 133, 135

expressive language, through body movement 59–68
EYFS *see* Early Years Foundation Stage (EYFS)

'familect' 164, 204–205
Farah, W. 77, 99, 101, 105
Flewitt, R. 107–108, 111, 113
Foucault, M. 22
'funds of knowledge' 175–177

games 22, 57, 63–65, 73, 123, 186
gaze 65, 99, 108, 113, 122, 132, 161, 162, 166, 219–221, 224, 245–246
Glissant, É. 11, 38, 231, 246; 'right to opacity' 177; theory of opacity 164

Hackett, A. 23, 24, 38, 48, 96, 97, 101, 108, 200
'helicopter' technique (Paley) 71, 77
Henner, J. 138, 163, 205
hierarchies of language, in educational settings 165–166
HLE *see* Home Learning Environment (HLE)
HMP *see* Humber Museums Partnership (HMP)
Holcomb, L. 99
home 3–4, 77, 96, 107–110, 149, 171, 176, 182, 194, 206, 211, 223, 224; dialect 6; language 6, 98, 99, 112, 144–146, 170; language access at 145–146; language barriers at 144–145; of minoritised families 97; as mobile sanctuary 146–147; practices and behaviours 9
Home Learning Environment (HLE) 9, 96–98, 102n1, 106
Humber Museums Partnership (HMP) 119, 121–122

improvisation 11, 13, 25, 46, 49–51, 53, 56, 80, 109, 161–162, 184, 191, 203, 211, 212, 215, 216, 232
Intensive Interactions 38–39, 88, 211, 212, 232

Kay Rowe Nursery School and Children's Centre 214, *216*
Kim, E. 174–175, 231
Klarnett, L. 162, 165
'knowledge-rich' curriculum 74; *see also* curriculum

language, as bodily and material 7–8, 19–27
language, beyond meaning 159–161, 227–233; expression and improvisation 161–162; hierarchies of language, in educational settings 165–166; opacity 164–165; worlding 163–164
Language Environment Analysis (LENA) 98
Lee, A. 163, 165
Leela, M. 22–23, 25
Le Guin, U. K.: 'carrier bag' theory 45, 53
LENA *see* Language Environment Analysis (LENA)
Leuven Well-Being scale 72
listening 45, 47, 48, 74, 88, 89, 91, 122, 124, 137, 162, 194; 'active listening' 246; and attunement 24–25; body 25, 211–213; to children 75–76, 96, 112–114, 242–243; and "echolalic speech" 134; expense of 52; and sensing 50; speaking and 121

MacRae, C. 11, 108, 162
Magic Acorns 25, 45–51, 53, 55, 57, 89
Magpie Project 211–212, 214, *215*, 218, 219, 224
Makaton sign 3, 4, 113, 199
meaning, language beyond 227–233; expression and improvisation 161–162; hierarchies of language, in educational settings 165–166; opacity 164–165; worlding 163–164
mind/body dualism 20, 21
mirroring games 73
modernity 22
more-than-human 5, 7–9, 12–13, 19, 23, 49, 105, 121, 122, 200
'more-than-words' 25, 48, 57
movement: body movement, expressive language through *see* body movement; children 188; games 72; neurodiversity, growth of 208; nonlingual movement research 182–184, *183*, *194*; spontaneous and surprising movements 183; "unceasing movement" 20
multilingual 96–99, 111, 135, 151, 171, 172, 208

multimodal communication 147, 198, 200
multimodality 4, 9, 147, 182, 193, 198, 200
multisensory 24, 26, 31, 32, 36, 81, 193
museums 128, 129, 151, 152, 154, 243; Humber Museums Partnership 119–122; North Lincolnshire Museum 123, 127; Wilberforce House Museum 124–125

Nair, V. K. 99, 101, 138
name games 73
National Curriculum 34, 190
neoliberal: accountability 48; capitalist context 26; early childhood education 21; education context 238; education system 13, 160; logic 166
neurodiversity movement, growth of 208
neurotypical 24, 26, 32–37, 39–41, 174–175, 201
non-English language 99, 109
nonlingual expressions 182, 183, *194*
nonlingual movement research 182–184, *183*, *194*
non-verbal children 61, 87
normativism 198, 206
Nxumalo, F. 32, 41, 81; "Disrupting Anti-Blackness in Early Childhood Qualitative Inquiry" 31

Olsson, L. M. 168, 185, 186, 188, 193, 195, 229; "bodily logic" 11
opacity 12, 38, 164–165, 231
outdoors 22, 63, 108–110, 114, 119, 121, 122, 124, 151, 152, 175; learning 108, 176, 214

PACE model 67, 74, 76, 85, 90, 100, 125, 127
Paley, V. G.: 'helicopter' technique 71, 77
PECS *see* picture exchange communication system (PECS)
Pennac, D.: 'Rights of the Reader' 238
personalisation 201–202
Pert, C. 218–219
Phonics Screening Check 34, 100
physical development 190, 212

picture exchange communication system (PECS) 4, 112, 113
place 95; in afterlives of COVID-19 119–120; entanglement of 96; environment and 105–106; and language 9–10, 104–105, 150–156; political-ness of 9; re-make 110–112; time and 100–101
play 6, 51, *55*–57, 59, 64, 65, 85, 109–111, 128, 129, 159, 163, 164, 191, 193, 202, 203, 212, 215, 223, 246; children engaged in 9, 11, 23, 73, 172; language in 10, 101, 126; precarity and improvisation in 53
plurilingual 6, 98, 99, 109, 110, 112, 244
polyvagal theory (Porges) 162, 216, 219
Porges, S.: polyvagal theory 162, 216, 219
Power-Annand, A. 25
Preece, J. 163, 201, 209

raciolinguistic ideologies 96, 99
rights: 'rights of the reader' 238; 'rights of the talker' 12; right to choose how 243–244, *244*; right to (not) express oneself 246–247, *247*; right to move(ment) and gaze *245*, 245–246; right to silence *241*, 241–242; right to time 239–240, *240*
Robinson, O. 138, 163, 205
Ronald Openshaw Nursery Education Centre (RONEC) 215, *217*

SALTMusic action research project 108
school readiness 13, 21, 68; resisting narratives on 47–49
'scores' 22, 63, 215–218
SEN *see* special educational needs (SEN)
SEND *see* special educational needs and disabilities (SEND)
sender-receiver model, of communication 199–200
sense 4, 6, 11, 13, 23, 47, 49, 50, 54–57, 64, 71, 78, 82–84, 86, 88, 97, 106, 114, 153, 155, 161, 163, 165, 169, 176, 181, 182, 187, 191–193, 229, 233, 246, 248; of belonging 129, 149, 204, 205, 244; of entalgement 104; of familiarity and comfort 63; of identity 8, 9,

164; of safety 127, 214, 219; of shared creative community 72; of uncertainty 90; working with 188–190
sensory attunements 182, 184, 190–193
Shannon, D. B. 24, 26, 38, 40, 113, 162, 173
signed language 147–149; deaf children, language development of 145; deaf identity and 144; entanglement of 99; interconnectedness of 143
silence 26, 75, 112, 231, 244; children 109; of classrooms 25; practice of 25; right to *241*, 241–242
singing 4, 40, 60, 64, 85, 87, 89, 108, 126–128, 181
sociolect 204–205
spaces 90–91; 'adult-controlled space' 61, 66; classrooms 6; collective space 137–138; creation of 76; early childhood community 46; for early language 127–129; for feeling comfortable 74; monolingual ideologies and 98, 99; museum-based groups and 128; 'Spaces of Reprieve' 131–133, 138–141; Speech Bubbles approach 76; time and 47, 129; unstructured 'natural' outdoor learning 108
special educational needs (SEN) 35
special educational needs and disabilities (SEND) 214, 215
special education classroom, unruliness in 31–32, 41–42; as antecedent to learning 39–41; as communicative 36–37; neurotypicality in schools, England 32–36; shared experience 38–39
speech and language therapy 60–61, 112, 135–136, 153, 198, 209, 246; community 134; interventions and methodologies 132; profession 133–134
Speech Bubbles approach 70–78
Spencer, W. 162, 164, 165, 229
spoken language 4, 45, 60, 112, 143, 145, 146, 155, 164, 173, 185, 192; *see also* "White Mainstream English"
"Standard English" 6, 77, 239, 243

stimming 61, 162, 165, 173–175, 202, 208, 246
storytelling 25, 71, 77, 78
Stratford Circus Arts Centre *213*, *222*
symbol-based AAC strategies 201, 202
symbol communication 198, 199, 201, 203

'talk' 4–5; children 6, 7, 10, 97, 151, 239–240; and movement 61; problem with 185–187; quality 13, 209; rights of the talker 238–239; "talk pedometer" 98; 'tyranny of talk' 60, 61
Tatham-Fashanu, C. 109, 111–112
teaching assistant (TA) 83, 86–87
Templeton, T. N. 13, 242, 243
time 3, 7, 8, 11, 50, 52, 54–55, 57, 67, 71, 74, 75, 78, 120, 126, 145, 149, 173, 185, 188, 200, 201, 214, 220, 225, 230; 'lining-up time' 109; to move 85–88; of pandemic 218; and place 96, 100–101; right to 239–240; and space 47, 129; for unruliness, in special education classroom *see* unruliness, in special education classroom
Tobin, J. 21, 22
translanguaging 6, 98–99, 109

unruliness, in special education classroom 31–42
US Centre for Disease Control (CDC) 133–134

Viruru, R. 11, 46, 164, 166, 189
vocabulary: curriculum 202, *202*; 'lack' of 8; Speech Bubbles approach 76–77; valuing different vocabulary 203–204
vocalisations 3–5, 7, 9, 10, 13, 23, 31, 121–125, 127–129, 155, 160, 178, 198, 245, 246

Western education systems 10, 159
"White Mainstream English" 113
Williams, Y. 24, 26, 173
'word gap' 8; problematic notion of 160; resisting narratives on 47–49; theory of 77
"wordism" 24, 160
worlding 163–164

For Product Safety Concerns and Information please contact our
EU representative GPSR@taylorandfrancis.com Taylor & Francis
Verlag GmbH, Kaufingerstraße 24, 80331 München, Germany